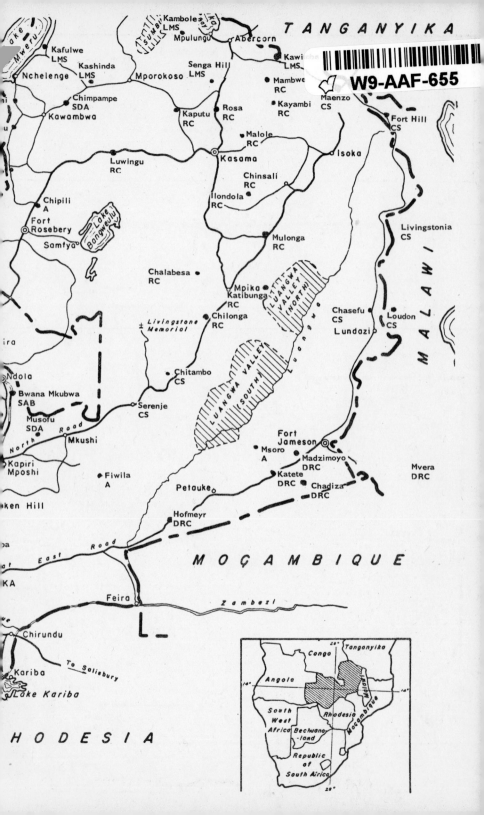

Profile for Victory in Zambia

PROFILE FOR VICTORY

ew Proposals for Missions in Zambia

Max Ward Randall

William Carey Library
CHRISTIAN MISSION BOOKS
South Pasadena, California

PROFILE FOR VICTORY

NEW PROPOSALS FOR MISSIONS IN ZAMBIA

Library of Congress Catalog Card Number: 79-126077
International Standard Book Number: 0-87808-403-7

Published by the William Carey Library
533 Hermosa Street
South Pasadena, Calif. 91030
Telephone: 213-682-2047

PRINTED IN THE UNITED STATES OF AMERICA

To Leroy, my firstborn son, a faithful minister of Jesus Christ and missionary to the peoples of Africa who, with the help of many others, is discipling the tribes of the once dark continent and planting numerous churches, to the glory of God.

Contents

PART IV: The Necessity of a New Approach

Figures

Preface

Interest in Africa has reached new heights during the past decade. The rapid rush of underdeveloped nations into the twentieth-century world has given rise to universal attention. The continent of Africa, with its forty-two different nations, has become an ideological battlefield. All ideas with a missionary motivation, both Christian and non-Christian, are seeking a committment of allegiance from the people of Africa.

As a result of the new and increased concern for Africa, the disciples of Christ need to examine and reevaluate their plan of penetration. No longer is Christianity the favored faith. Disciples of Communism, Islam, and Nationalism are all actively seeking to influence the mind and future of Africa. Gone are the days when personal development through education was dependent on the white missionary's presence. Education is now the responsibility of the National Government. "Christian Missionary" has ceased to be a title of privilege.

These statements should not be interpreted to mean that the people of Africa are indifferent to the Gospel. Not at all. Neither do they infer that the Gospel has lost its effectiveness. Across this vast and great continent ministers of the "Good News" are privileged to witness a response far greater than any ever seen before. The people of Africa are anxious to hear and ready to respond to God's love. They are also ready to assume strategic places of leadership within the framework of the Christian Church.

The developing structure of the Christian fellowship in Africa will be quite different from the traditional structure known in Western nations. Founded on Christ and identifying with the people the emerging African Church will not be as organizationally dependent as its western counterpart. Realizing that this is developing now, the cause of Christ is in great need of redefining its presence and purpose in mission lands.

Max Ward Randall seeks to make this reevaluation in the chapters of this book. For more than twenty years Africa has been his life. His devotion to Christ and his love for the people of Africa are evident in these pages.

The plan he presents here has the potential of sweeping through the villages of Africa with the fire of God and resulting in a full and bountiful harvest. Seeking to take full advantage of existing social structures in African society, this plan takes advantage of African leadership. It sets forth a program that allows to work His good work with His African children.

Even though it is written in an African setting, I am confident that missionaries, and Christian workers around the world who work with tribal peoples, will be helped through a study of this book. It comes as a most welcome addition to the field of missionary methods.

MILTON E. CUNNINGHAM
Baptist Radio-Television
Representative for Africa
Nairobi, Kenya

Introduction

The author began his missionary experience in 1950, serving for ten years in South Africa as Superintendent of the Church of Christ Mission, finding time each year for new-field surveys in both Northern and Southern Rhodesia. These surveys provided the opening for extensive evangelistic, educational and medical missions in Southern Rhodesia, and for evangelistic and educational missions in Northern Rhodesia.

In 1961, the author, with his family, moved to what was still Northern Rhodesia, one of the three colonies making up the short-lived Central African Federation, and he lived under the Federal Government through the concluding days of its history. He saw the new nation of Zambia come into existence and, since October 1964, until his return to the United States in 1967, he lived under the government of Zambia.

Much has happened in Africa since 1950. In 1950, most of the continent was ruled by colonial powers. Colonialism is now almost gone. Newly created independent African governments have taken its place, changing the political, economic, racial, and missions face of these former possessions of European nations.

Through all his missionary experience, the author shared not only in evangelism and church building but also in a fast-growing and popular, multi-pronged, institutional-missions emphasis as well. The first new-field surveys of the Christian Church in both Northern and Southern Rhodesia were carried out by him. In a dozen widely separated areas, he promised both government and local African peoples to provide schools and medical services. Those commitments were fulfilled.

Many observations in this volume come through the author's experiences. He has been intimately associated with a fast-expanding program of missions tightly bound to colonialism. Colonial governments are now gone, but much of mission, in ever so many ways, still functions through the now obsolete colonially-orientated mission pattern.

For this reason, PROFILE FOR VICTORY----New Proposals for Missions in Zambia, has been chosen as the title of this book. It is the author's conviction that a new mode of mission must be developed at once for Zambia and for many of the newly independent countries of Africa as well.

The author spent nine months at the School of World Mission at Fuller Theological Seminary in Pasadena, California in 1966-1967. His studies under Donald A. McGavran confirmed the conviction that much thought must be given to numerous popular methods of mission---ofttimes held sacred---which have seldom been effective means of winning souls and planting sound indigenous churches.

During July and August of 1967, the author did research among the Sala tribe in the Mumbwa district of Zambia, which consisted of in-depth surveys in thirty-seven villages in the area where he had begun work in the early nineteen sixties. This study at the village level revealed significant factors underscoring the failure of missions during the past half century. Obvious were numerous danger signals warning against doggedly proceeding in the future with foreign mission programs perpetually supervised and underwritten by white men.

The village surveys which the author did, with the help of his missionary co-workers, had a number of important objectives. At Fuller Theological Seminary in early 1967, the author had the help of Dr. Alan Tippett in designing the instrument of research to be used in the village surveys, and the sixteen categories for investigation were selected.

This original instrument of investigation may be seen in Appendix A.

In view of the tribal tensions in the church-school community, it was necessary to examine tribal groupings, village relationships, intertribal marriages, and any efforts at intertribal cooperation. With the Church confined to the small Shona-Sindebele foreign community and with its years of failure to win even a few Sala, it became imperative for the missionaries to know the village and family structure of the area.

Hundreds of young Africans had become Christian through school-churches, but there were few signs of actual church growth. An investigation of family and village decision-making patterns could reveal the cause of slow growth through the school-cum-church approach. Examining this problem proved to be a most fruitful area of study.

Polygamy was also investigated. It had provided the greatest of many roadblocks faced by African missions, but its impact in the Sala area was unknown. Knowledge of its extent revealed a major cause for lack of church growth and also defined the need for fearless thinking and pioneer action in an effort to meet the problem through the Gospel and the Church.

It was anticipated that numerous examples of diffusion would be found. A part of the survey therefore was concerned with village wealth, labor patterns, tribal crafts, festivals, and worship. Evidences of diffusion and change in these areas have pertinent bearing on acceptance or rejection of the Gospel.

The health of the people, their diet, and the amount of beer drinking and drunkenness among them would give direction to the planting of churches, and these too were considerations demanding investigation.

For four years the Christian Church had maintained schools in the Sala district, and for more than a half century the Methodist Church had also maintained schools on a much larger scale throughout the area. The Methodists made the same claim as the Christian Church—that the schools were necessary and effective keys for opening the doors to evangelism among the Sala. Two primary objectives of the survey were to determine the number of professing Christians in each village and the part missions-sponsored education played in the planting of churches. The lessons learned have much to say to contemporary mission strategy. Conclusions, believed by the author to be pertinent to the winning of many souls and the planting and nuturing of numerous churches among the Sala, provide the foundation for this volume. These conclusions may be found at the end of Chapter 9.

This book begins with a summarized history of the people of Zambia. Attention is given to the beginning of missions followed shortly thereafter by colonial occupation by Britain, and to the sympathetic role missions played in the colonial era.

A short sketch of the social structure of Zambian peoples is given. The place of marriage, the function of the family, the significance of kin relationships, the nature of social groupings, how they make their living, and how their environment influences their way of life, are all important. Their political structure, their system of law and law enforcement, and their tribal societies must be understood. Knowledge of their world view, of their religion, of the relationship between the living and the dead, and of their concept of the high God is necessary. The author believes this study to be vitally important. So far in Central and South Africa little effort has been made to encourage people movements or to apply church-growth principles to mission, both of which must be based upon a thorough knowledge of the social structure of a society.

This volume offers a number of proposals which the author believes will give new and proper direction to future mission strategy acceptable in the contemporary Zambian context. These suggestions came out of twenty years of observations made concerning the main missions approaches of the past, not only in Zambia, but in other countries of southern Africa as well.

A study of the educational and medical missions approaches, so popular in many missions, is a necessary exercise. The value of the institutional approach, as it relates to mission in the future, must be dispassionately analyzed.

Changes must be made. Indeed, changes will be made, if not by wise and humble, prayer-motivated, Spirit-guided missionaries who read the message of the times, then by African churchmen who will dismiss the missionaries and manage their own churches. The author believes there are still numerous contributions mission can make to the younger churches of Africa. He is aware that many African Christian leaders believe this too. This book offers a few suggestions that may give guidance to those who want to share.

A word of appreciation must be made here for the work of the older missions. Much of the work of the Christian Church which came late in the mission program in Central Africa is, of necessity, built on foundations long since laid by the older missionary societies. Like the Christian Church, they have made their mistakes, but the Church would not be in Central Africa today except for their long and faithful witness.

I must express particular gratitude to Dr. Donald A. McGavran, Dean of the School of World Mission and Institute of Church Growth of the Fuller Theological Seminary, Pasadena, California, for the constant encouragement given as this volume was being written. My thanks, too, to Dr. Alan R. Tippett, Dr. J. Edwin Orr, and Dr. Ralph D. Winter, associates of Dr. McGavran, for many valuable insights and lessons given in the classroom which led to the formulation of the proposals which I have outlined and discussed in this book. Already these concepts have been tried and tested, and they give reason to believe that large numbers of the Sala and other Zambian tribes will soon be solidly won to the Lord.

Appreciation must also be expressed to the Rev. Jack Shepherd and to Dr. James DeForest Murch for reading the manuscript, to the Rev. George Smoker for much hard work in editing, to Dr. Ralph Winter for the many time-consuming tasks associated with the publishing of the book, and to Mrs. J. Edwin Orr for a skillful job in preparing the copy for publication.

GRAPH OF GROWTH, ZAMBIA CHRISTIAN CHURCHES
Sala Area
June 1, 1963 through June 30, 1967

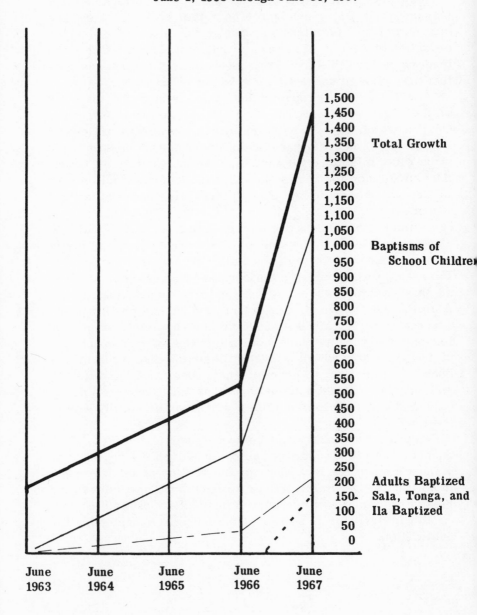

I

The Historical
and Cultural Backdrop

1

The Land and its People

The Republic of Zambia occupies a very interesting land, every bit as fascinating as its peoples.

Geography

Zambia is a big land. Its highlands are a part of the world's greatest plateau. Most of its two hundred ninety thousand square miles undulate at a level above three thousand five hundred feet. This landlocked country is bordered by Rhodesia to the south, Mozambique and Malawi to the east, and Congo and Tanzania to the north and northeast, and by Angola, South-West Africa and Botswana to the west and southwest.

It is a beautiful land. It contains fine forests, great lakes and rivers, greater game-watching and hunting areas. The incomparable Victoria Falls, "The Smoke That Thunders," is the greatest spectacle of them all. Four rivers----the Zambezi, the Kafue, and the Luangwa---which drain to the southeast and flow into the Indian Ocean, and the Luapula, which empties into Lake Mweru and ultimately reaches the River Congo and the Atlantic, do much to determine the natural character of Zambia.

Most of Zambia's wealth comes from the fabulous Copperbelt, bordering on the southern boundaries of the Congo,

1

making Zambia the second-largest producer of copper in the world. Much of the land is comparatively unfertile, but agriculture is being rapidly expanded in new areas with noteworthy success.

The rainy season begins in late October and ends in early April. June and July are the cool months when the weather is sunny and dry and the nights crisp and cold.

The Sociological Structure

Zambia holds some 3,494,000 people of all races and beliefs. Over seventy different tribes live and work together in surroundings varying from modern towns to bush-country villages. The last pre-European tribal migration into the area took place about the year 1835, when the Ngoni in the east and the Kololo in Barotseland in the west crossed the Zambesi River. They came northward from South Africa, driven by the pressures of the Zulu wars. (See Figure 1)

The other tribes of Zambia were already reasonably well settled where one finds them today. According to "Zambia Today," a bulletin put out by the government, the largest of the tribes of Zambia are

the Bemba, Ngoni, Chewa and Bisa in the northeastern districts, the Lozi, Tonga, Luvale, Lenje and Ila in the western and southern districts, and the Senga, Lala and Lunda, sections of which live in both the eastern and western areas of the country.

There are some thirty different dialects in use, but many of them vary so slightly that a knowledge of six of the main languages and English would enable one to converse with every Zambian.

One may find villages of one tribe completely encircled by villages of another tribe. Tribal differences are strong but are now being replaced by a sense of national unity. Often border tribes extend into neighboring countries with the paramount chief living outside Zambia.

With the exception of a flow of immigrants from Portuguese East and West Africa and from Rhodesia and South Africa, the noteworthy movement of Africans today is from the tribal areas to the cities.

ZAMBIA, F.A. Praeger Inc., Pub. New York. p. 12.

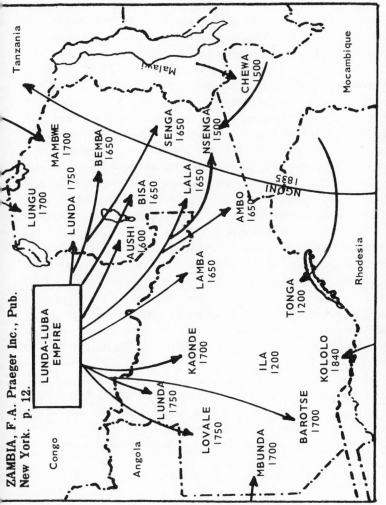

Routes by which Zambia's principal tribes reached their present homes, with tentative migration dates

Figure 1

The economy of the peoples of Zambia has depended primarily upon swidden (slash and burn) agriculture. The principle food is maize, but eleusine, millet, and sorghum are popular, and food crops such as peas, groundnuts, yams and green vegetables are grown. Rice is produced in some swamp areas. Most tribes possess cattle and belong to the milking complex. A considerable number of goats, sheep, dogs, chickens, and some pigs are kept. Among some tribes fish and wild game provide part of the diet, along with wild roots and plants. Men are responsible for hunting and fishing, clearing the land, and caring for the cattle and they share somewhat in agricultural work. It is primarily the responsibility of the women to plant, cultivate, and gather the crops.

Of the two main groups with which we are most interested, the Lozi maintain two villages—one on an artificial mound in the Zambezi flood plain and the other at the edge of the plain into which they move during the long Zambezi flood season (Brelsford 1960:366). In the Tonga area, which includes the tribespeople known as the Tonga, We, Totela, Lenje, and Ila with its Sala subgroup, each village is an independent unit separated from other villages by bush and forests or fields. Some are compact, with huts arranged in two rows in a slightly curved line. Others are clusters of huts along the slope of a hill. Many are composed of widely scattered hamlets, well removed from the central core of the village. The average village might contain 100 to 150 men, women, and children.

The prevailing shelter among most of the tribes is a cylindrical hut with walls made of woven mats or wattle or poles, daubed with mud and convered with a conical roof of thatch. A few tribes, however, live in hemispherical mat huts, and others construct small rectangular-shaped houses.

Marriage and Kinship Patterns

Marriage contributes to the well-being of the community, the extension of the family, and the perpetuation of the tribe, and African society invests it with formality and ceremony. The basic unit in the tribe if the family, consisting of the husband, his wife or wives, and children. To every adult in the family unit parenthood is one of the supreme delights, and a barren woman or sterile man is almost a social outcast (Brelsford 1960:162). The prime purpose of marriage is to insure the preservation of family and tribe. In order to stabilize marriage, the tribes have required the presentation of things of value or service rendered by the young man to the family of the bride, thereby making the marriage legitimate and compensating the bride's parents for the loss of their daughter. This system has also guaranteed that the husband would fulfill his obligations. If tendered in tangible assets it was technically called the bride-price, though this did not mean that the husband then "owned" the wife, or that she had lost her own rights. If rendered in services it would be called bride-service (Murdock 1959:25).

The basic kinship unit in much of Zambia is the matrilineal group that commonly supposes descent through a female line from a common ancestress. Members within the group have obligations in common, such as visiting each other when ill, mourning the deaths of members of families, helping provide bride-wealth, assisting in paying of fines and damages, assisting in purifying the wives of those who die, and finding people to inherit the positions and "mizimu" of their dead. They should assist each other with food and gifts in time of need; they should also share in the bride-wealth given for the women of the group; and they share in the estates of their deceased members (Colson, in Lessa and Vogt 1965: 441). One of the men in the oldest living generation in the village who could trace his kinship back to this founding ancestress would usually be the leader of such a group.

In kinship societies, proper terminology in speaking of one's kin is most important. Such terms speak of the proper relationship of kinsmen and of the appropriate behavior required towards them. President Kaunda of Zambia has described this relationship:

> I do not restrict the title "father" to my male parent.
> I also address my father's brothers as "father." And
> I call my mother's sisters "mother" also. Only my
> father's sisters would I address as "aunt" and my
> mother's brothers as "uncle." My "brothers" would
> include not only the male children of my father but

also certain cousins and even members of the same
clan who have no blood relationship at all... These
are not just courtesy titles. With the title "father,"
for example, goes all the responsibility of parenthood and in return all my "fathers" receive my filial
devotion. Hence, no child in a traditional society is
likely to be orphaned. Should his literal parents die
then others automatically assume the responsibility
for his upbringing. By the same token, no old person
is likely to end his days outside a family circle. If
his own offspring cannot care for him then other
"children" will accept the duty and privilege (Morris &
Kaunda 1968:27).

Every African knows his clan, and regardless of how
emancipated he may be, he knows that it is wrong to marry
within the clan. Clan membership affects his daily life and
emotions far more than his relationship to his tribe. Among
the Tonga

the clans alone are thought to be eternal. Most Tonga
take them as a part of the natural order of things left
to them by their ancestors from long long ago... This
division into clans is considered to be an invariable
human institution. The Tonga find it practically impossible to conceive of any society in which people are
not divided into clans (Colson 1962:68-69).

The Zambian's attitude is that God gave the clans so that
they could marry properly.

If this is the role of the clan, it is still performing
it efficiently despite the changes in other parts of
... (the) culture (Colson & Gluckman 1961:132).

Groupings by Residence

However important kinship relationships may be, they are
not the only important social structure. In Zambia, the
local community represents a universal kind of social
organization. The families which compose the local group-
ing live in villages. Murdock's conclusion, however, that
"very widely in Africa the village . . . is itself a genuine
kin group (1959:30) does not necessarily hold true in Zambia.

Colson has observed that

> to maintain the ties of kinship, it is not necessary
> for all, or even the major portion of a group, to re-
> main in close proximity with one another. The Tonga
> have never believed that kinsmen should live together
> in a single village, or even within a single neighbor-
> hood (1958:20).

Because the place of a family's residence is a matter of
personal choice, each village is composed of a diverse mixture of kinship associations of related people with perhaps
a few strangers without any ties at all. There were few hin-
drances in the past to keep a man from moving from one
village to another. There was little pressure on the land, and
he could always find a field. His material possessions were
few and such as would tie him down to one spot. If he chose
to change villages he could do so.

In many parts of Zambia today, however, there are evidences of stabilization in the population of the villages. A
few progressive agriculturalists are making improvements
of permanent value, and lands are carefully stumped, properly rotated, and sometimes fertilized. By careful handling,
these lands are increasing in productivity. Some have also
planted orchards, dug wells, and built permanent houses.
Such developments tend to stabilize the population.

Normally from four to eight villages make up a neighborhood. A man may move as freely from one neighborhood to
another as from one village to another. No kinship ties are
needed. As soon as he has built his hut and cultivated his
field, he is accepted as a member of the neighborhood.

There are significant aspects to neighborhood life. All
land not occupied is open for the entire neighborhood. All
may gather the wild produce; every man's cattle may pasture
there; all may hunt in the area; and firewood, timber, potting
clay, reeds, and thatching grass are equally available to all.
Neighborhood obligations are met through cooperative work
patterns. Whenever numbers of men are needed for community improvement, neighbors are called to share in the task.
Most beer parties are neighborhood affairs with those in
attendance coming only a short walking distance from their
own homes.

Identification with the neighborhood is emphasized in a number of rituals kept at particular times by the community. All are to be present at the funeral of anyone who dies in the neighborhood. Mourning is an obligation accepted by all. Furthermore, a person ought to die at the place of his kraal. To die away from his own neighborhood is an offense against the land. Also, all are expected to participate in the rituals at the local shrines. These include sharing in the rain ceremonies at the time of planting and in the harvest festivals at the time of reaping.

Colson says:

Today an increasing number refuse to participate in what they dismiss as pagan rituals. Absence is usually passed over in silence or accepted with grumbling by others in the neighborhood who find in this an explanation if the rituals fail of their purpose. But in conservative areas those who aggravate their offence by working in the fields on ritual days may still be threatened with a fine (1958:30).

The Political Structure

Murdock calls "the first and simplest, as well as the most wide-spread type of political system . . . a primitive democracy" (1959:33). This system defines the decision-making structure in the Zambian village. Leadership and prestige is vested in the headman and council of elders, who can advise and persuade, but decisions are only reached after an informal consensus is obtained. Neither the headman nor any other leader has the power to enforce authority. Discipline is applied only thorugh informal mechanisms and social control.

The real leader of the village, however, is likely to be the headman. The residents refer to themselves as his people, and he is said to be the owner of the village cattle kraals. The Tonga, Ila, and Sala are politically organized into small districts lacking any form of corporation more complicated than Murdock's "primitive democracy." Each community is locally autonomous and under the nominal leadership of a local headman.

Zambia also has a number of tribes with political structures differing radically from those described above. Two
examples are the Bemba and Lozi who have centralized forms
of government under a hereditary Paramount Chief. The
Paramount Chief of the Bemba is called the Citimukulu, who
is believed to have descended from the original ancestress
and to have inherited the guardian spirits of chiefs. Richards
says that the chieftanship is

> the dominant institution among the Bemba because the
> belief in his power, both political and religious, is the
> main source of tribal cohesion throughout this scarce-
> ly populated area. The worship of the dead chief's
> spirits is the essential element of Bemba religion:
> war under his leadership was formerly the dominant
> ambition of each individual: and, in a community
> without any storable form of wealth such as cattle,
> rank and social status were determined, not by the
> number of a man's possessions, but by his kinship
> with the chief or by the services he had been able to
> do for him (Colson and Gluckman 1961:168).

Also, according to Richards, the duties of the chief are:

> (a) to carry out religious ceremonies both at the relic
> shrines and the spirit centers throughout his district:
> (b) to exercise political powers in the appointment of
> sub-chiefs, officials, and headmen of villages; (c) to
> administer justice; (d) to initiate economic enter-
> prises, such as the firing of the fields preparatory to
> sowing, or the organization of elephant hunts; (e) to
> lead in the case of war (the last two functions being
> no longer performed); (f) to provide food for his
> followers, and often to arrange for their marriages,
> and to support his villagers in times of famine
> (Colson and Gluckman 1961:170).

The Citimukulu is the ruler over the center of the country
which is his district. His territorial chiefs are members of
his immediate family. Over them he acts as overlord. This
kinship gives the chiefs firm control. Subchiefs, also members of the royal clan, are responsible to the territorial
chiefs. Sisters and uterine nieces of the chief rule over
villages as chieftainesses, and Candamukulu, the chief's

mother, is responsible for a territory of her own. Being a relative of the chief establishes positive rank among the Bemba. Thirty or forty hereditary officials, each responsible for a particular and secret ritual duty, make up the tribal council. Many of these are also of the royal clan. Their responsibilities are both religious and political.

Foremost among the chief's responsibilities is the task of maintaining peace. There is little actual law, and the duty of the chief is not so much to dispense justice as to maintain peace and harmony. Arbitration begins first at the family or village level. Domestic differences are generally settled by an older kinsman or a disinterested person. Even differences between persons from two neighborhoods might be settled by a village elder or headman. Most serious differences are dealt with as civil cases in court. Mitchell said

> murder was essentially a civil case in which one party
> sued for compensation against the murderer's kins-
> men . . and . . adultery . . as a civil case . . was looked
> upon as a kind of theft or trespass of rights held by
> the husband (Brelsford 1960:144).

Some offenses are criminal cases. Stopping rain through the use of magic is a serious crime, as is shedding blood in the presence of the chief. In such cases it is the chief who is injured and compensation is payable to him. The courts administer justice and serve as means by which behavior is defined and controlled.

The Religious Structure

In Zambia you will find little external evidence of religion. There are no temples----nothing more than a miniature thatched hut or two---and yet religion is everywhere:

> not as an organized cult separable from the rest of
> their life, but as part and parcel of it, all-pervasive,
> motivating, controlling, guiding, strengthening (Edwin
> Smith 1946:101).

Myths provide the African with a satisfactory explanation of the creation of man, of all mysterious phenomena, of animal and plant life, of the fall of man and the presence of evil in the world, and of death and life beyond the grave.

Tippett, writing of the Solomon Islands, says:
Myths conceptualize a high god responsible for the
work of creation. The myths vary in each island but . .
the Great Spirit(s) were remarkably similar. They
supposedly produced their respective islands out of
chaos, gave them form and order, created the original human beings and classified them into their
present social groups (1967:3).

Malinowski, also writing from a Melanesian context, has
suggested that
Myth as it exists in a savage community, that is, in
its living primitive form, is not merely a story told
but a reality lived . . . This myth is to the savage
what, to a fully believing Christian, is the Biblical
story of Creation, of the Fall, of the Redemption by
Christ's Sacrifice on the Cross. As our sacred story
lives in our ritual, in our morality, as it governs our
faith and controls our conduct, even so does his myth
for the savage (1954:100).

What Tippett and Malinowski have said about myths in the
South Pacific is applicable to myths and their significance
in South Central Africa. Speaking of Africa, Parrinder has
said that
nearly all Africans, "untutored" though some may be,
do conceive of God. For most of them God was the
creator of all things, but he was withdrawn to that
remoteness which is part of his greatness (1962:42).
The Africans' myths provide them with a satisfying explanation of sun, moon, stars, sky, wind, rains, seasons, life and
death, the world, and all that it contains. They have an explanation for everything about them. This is their world
view.

The concept of God as Creator is common. From this
come titles such as Moulder, Creator of souls, Giver of
breath, and God of destinies. The African believes that God
brings the seasons, the rain, the sunshine, the bow in the
heavens, the thunder and the fire. His omnipotence and om-
niscience are also well-defined in names such as
He who gives and rots, The ancient of days, The limit-
less, The One from the first, The irresistible, The

wise one, He who bends down even majesties, He who
roars so that all nations are struck with terror, He
who is of himself, and The One you meet everywhere
(Parrinder 1962:39-40).
Other titles speak of the providence of God. He is the
Father of little babies, Father of the placenta, The
great Mother, Father-mother God, the kindly disposed, Greatest of friends, Master of the forest, The
providence who watches over all like the sun, God
full of pity, God of comfort, The One on whom men
lean and do not fall (Parrinder 1962:40).
Life to the African is a gift from God. To him the existence
of God is an actuality.

"Leza" is the most common name for God in Zambia. At
least eight translations of Scripture common to Central
Africa use the name Leza.

Whatever exists owes its existence to Leza, and whatever happens is due to his activity, even though it may
often baffle one to discover any other reason why a
thing should take place (Smith 1950:62).

The Ancestral Cult

Though the Zambian believes in Leza, he is more concerned about the spirits of his recently departed ancestors
who, he believes, are most interested in his daily life. The
"mizimu," or "spirits of departed ancestors," are believed to
have considerable power over both good and evil. All kinds
of misfortunes are attributed to the influence of an offended
spirit, and when troubles come it is essential that sacrificial
offerings be made.

Beyond all other forces is Leza, and existence and increase
are gifts from Him. But, after Leza come the first fathers---
the clan founders. They establish the link between Leza and
man, but these incorporators are no longer considered human.
Next to the founders are the so-called "dead" of the clan and
they are the streams through which the vital forces flow to
the living generation. Within the physical membership of the
clan are the living who, according to their age and rank, also
form a hierarchy. The link between the ancestors and their

descendents is the oldest in the clan. Finally, the chief, because he has been installed in harmony with the traditions of the clan, undergirds the life of the people.

The term "mizimu," generally speaking, refers to all the spirits of the ancestors of both the father and mother and may include all the spirits of former members of any kinship group. Guardian "mizimu" are associated with names given to children shortly after birth. Social responsibility is assumed with the naming of a child, and names are identified with "mizimu." From these "mizimu" a person is believed to derive personality, and in a special way they serve as his guardians throughout his lifetime. Each household will have house "mizimu," who are installed as guardians of the household by its owner as spirits of that house. Many persons will have inherited "mizimu"---by being given, as a part of the funeral ritual, the name of a person who has recently died. A person's own "muzimu" will come into existence only at his death, No living person has a "muzimu" of his own ("muzimu"---singular, "mizimu"---plural).

Colson says that besides the "mizimu" and Leza, the Tonga distinguish three other types of spirits.

These are the "basangu," which are effective in affairs of general community interest and which make their demands known through people whom they possess; the "masabe," which are described as the spirits of animals or of foreigners and which cause illness to those whom they possess until these learn the dances appropriate to the possessing spirit; the "zelo" ("celo" in the singular), which we may call the ghosts of dead people (Ottenberg 1964:374-375).

The "mizimu" most concerned about a person during his lifetime and about whom that person is most concerned are the spirits of former members of the matrimonial kinship groups of his mother and father. The two guardian "mizimu" whose names a person bears---the first given from his father's matrilineal group, and the second from his mother's---have special significance. He is identified with them. They determine his character and interests. Thus a man's accomplishments and failures belong also to those who supplied him with his guardian "mizimu."

However, when a man establishes his own household, he acquires a new social position. His household is now one of the units of the community, and he takes his place at its head. Joined with his own maternal and paternal matrilineal kinship groups are the matrilineal groups of his wife. When his new position is ritually recognized, he can himself make offerings to the "mizimu," and his house "mizimu" are properly installed to hold a dominant position in all that concerns him with the well-being of his house. This new position is recognized in that now, if he should die, he himself will become a "muzimu." Every matrilineal group insists it is united in relationship to its "mizimu." The binding tie is said to result from the fact that all in the group are affected by the same "mizimu."

A number of offerings are given, whether there are misfortunes or not. The people know there are occasions when offerings are to be made. When the household moves, the "mizimu" must be told before leaving the old dwellings and again soon after entering the new. When a new household is established, the "mizimu" must be informed. They must know of the building of a new cattle kraal, of the purchase of some special piece of equipment, the launching of some new activity, and the beginning of a journey---all these call for offerings to the "mizimu." Finally, the household should make special offerings to the "mizimu" to inform them that all is well and that their continued help is both needed and appreciated.

Another group of spirits which affect the Zambians are the "basangu." If rains come too early, or too late, are too heavy, or too light, or if they continue too long or stop too soon, the economy of the neighborhood can be severly altered. Pestilences and major disasters can beset a whole community. Many clan groups in Zambia believe there are spirits, called "basangu," capable of relieving them from the threat of such catastrophies. These spirits are invoked annually at the beginning of the rains at shrines constructed for that purpose. The shrine might be a hollow tree, or a hilltop, or the spot where a hut shrine once stood. Or it might be a man-made structure called a "kaanda" which simply means a "small hut." Invariably two black pots are found at each shrine, one for beer and one for the food for the communion feast which

is an essential part of the ritual. Often the shrine is built
at the grave of the "ulanyika," the first resident of the neighborhood, and this is done because during his lifetime he led
the community. The "ulanyika's" spirit is invoked as a "basangu" at the shrine and everyone in the community is expected to share in the rituals. After all the people have
gathered at the shrine and the communion meal has been
eaten, the leader addresses the spirit:

> Send us rain and good crops and health. We have done
> all the things you told us to do. We are still living in
> the way you showed us. We have not forgotten what
> you told us. We have not forgotten you. Send us rain.
> Help us (Colson 1962:95).

Some shrines are in the hands of "rainmakers" who become
possessed with "basangu" and who may, during their lifetime,
become famous over a wide area. Most shrines, however,
have only local appeal. Once each year every person in the
community is expected to cooperate in the common rituals
at the rain shrine. Only in this way can they be certain of
securing the necessary rains for pastures and fields.

The "cilyango" or "spirit gate" is also a significant shrine.
This shrine, however. may be the "cilyango" of the homestead as well as the shrine of the village. The man of the
homestead generally makes the offering at the prompting of
a particular "muzimu," but he will try to propitiate all that
have a concern for him. These include his house "muzimu,"
his guardian "muzimu," which he may have inherited, those
that have given him special skills, the "mizimu" of his
parents, and very likely that of a famous hunter, or a wealthy man whose attributes he desires. He may also name
others about whom he has heard his elders speak, and he
will ask these to bring with them other "mizimu" of their
line whose names he may have forgotten or never heard of.
This latter is not important. They are "mizimu," and there
are favors which they can bestow.

Dynamism and the Manipulation of Power

The Ila word for dynamism is "bwanga." The abstract
root of the term is also found in the name for doctor, "mu-

nganga." Many things to the African are inexplicable. As he labors with his fields and cattle, as he observes the seasons and weather, and as he beholds the sky he is filled with awe at the mystery of life. He becomes aware of powers that excite, bewilder, and perplex him. Some events are traceable to his "mizimu," and he practises the rituals that conciliate them, but other events are not traceable to his "mizimu." How to deal with the impersonal powers that bring about those events is a matter of great concern.

It is possible, he believes, for those with ability to put to work the impersonal power as well. Surely the witch doctor can manipulate the power for other uses, but it is dangerous. Within itself the power is neither good nor bad. It can be used beneficially by a good "munganga." It can bring illness and death when manipulated by men and women of wicked intent. There are different grades of "munganga." The specialist with the medicinal qualities of plants and other materials is simply a herbalist. A very fine line distinguishes the witch doctor from the sorcerer. Both can manipulate the impersonal power. Sorcerers, however, are persons able to use medicines and magic to bring evil to those toward whom they direct their evil intent. Thus the sorcerers are feared and hated. On the other hand, the witch doctor has the approval of society for he is believed capable of ridding the community of the evils of witches and sorcerers.

The "munganga" may also be a diviner. He is believed able to determine the cause of death, misfortune, and disease. His bag of "medicines" will contain many amazing items. Concerning the diviner, Mitchell says that

in each case the client will consult him in order to discover the cause of some misfortune that has befallen him. The diviner usually finds the cause in a breach of some taboo or hallowed custom, or the anger of some spirit who has been neglected, or very frequently the evil designs of either a witch or a sorcerer. On the basis of his finding, the client is able to take appropriate action whether it be to remedy his behavior in respect to custom, to make a sacrifice to his ancestors or to make counter-magic against the sorcerer (Brelsford 1960:171).

The Christian Attitude Towards African Religion

Is there anything in the religion of the African that prepares him for Christian faith? Is there any indication that the Spirit of God has been preparing the way for Christ among the African people? Early missionaries gave a resounding "No" to the above question. Because they saw little external evidences of religion, they concluded that the African had no religion at all. But with the African, religion is intermingled with all of his life, with his homestead, his family, cattle, fields, planting and harvest, joyous and sad occasions. It motivates, controls, guides, strengthens, and pervades the whole of his life. He lives with the conviction that death is not the end. He is part of a community of members in the flesh and members out of the fleshly body . . . all living together as one community, and all mutually interdependent.

The strongest bond molding African society together is the belief that the spirit of man survives beyond the grave. The African's strongest emotions rest upon the conviction that the land is the abiding place of his ancestors, whose bodies were buried in it and whose spirits hover over it. Tribal customs still maintain a firm hold upon the African's loyalty and allegiance to his ancestors. Belief in the ancestors is still very real, in the lives of the pagans and in the lives of the emancipated as well. I have known second-generation Christians who in times of trouble found strength in the knowledge that concerned ancestors from beyond the grave were anxious to help.

Some point out that there are points of contact between Christianity and the pagan religion of Zambia. The African's hope, the concept of fear, reverence, and affection, the concept of prayer and sacrifice, of placation and appeasement, of communion with the other world, the idea of belonging, the concept of community, of good and evil, of mediation, and the concept of deity, are suggested as legitimate places for the sowing of the Gospel seed.

That these are points of contact, Hendrick Kraemer would answer with a "discerning 'No'!" And yet he gives a dialectical "Yes":

At the same time, however, this revealing light (the
points of contact enumerated above, M.W.R.) means
a dialectical "yes," a comprehension of religion and
the various religions that is deeper and more adequate
than their understanding of themselves, because it
uncovers the groping and persistent human aspiration
and need for "the glory of the children of God" in the
misdirected expressions of religious life (1947:136-
137).

I would agree with Edwin Smith, who holds

Whatever view we take, we cannot deny, I think, that
"ancestor worship" comprises values that should be
conserved; and it becomes a question of how the
Church can retain those values---that sense of continuity with the past, that reverence for established
things, that intense awareness of the immediacy of the
spiritual world, that sense of dependence upon unseen
powers (1946:109).

Social structure is now rapidly changing. Evidences of
the old conservative society are still present, but changes
are fast modifying the old system. Many younger Africans
are throwing off the old ways.

Contemporary mission cannot ignore the patterns of the
past nor should present-day missionaries encourage the dis-
carding of those aspects of tribal culture still adhered to by
the African. There are customs in his society that he should
not lose---that the missionary should encourage him to
retain and beautify with the Christian faith.

Obviously there are practices in the old culture that must
go as the African embraces the Christian Way, but functional
substitutes must be introduced to fill the gap made by the re-
moval of the unacceptable old customs. No place can be given
to the shrines, the libations and offerings, the bwanga or
taboo, and the witch doctor, but rejecting them is not enough.
Functional substitutes are necessary.

What could better replace the shrines where sacrifices
were offered to appease angry ancestors than humble village
churches---built by village Christians as the shrines were
built by village ancestor worshipers---where tithes and offerings in basket and store are given to a compassionate,

loving Heavenly Father and where prayers can be offered to Him for healing, good rains, a good harvest, and for protection from the powers of the evil one? There is no place for the witch doctor, but what could better replace him than a village pastor and other church leaders praying for the sick that God will heal them. Little place has been given by the missionary for prayers for the sick in the African Church.

I do not mean to imply that the missionary doctor is unimportant, but it is possible for the pagan to assume that the medical doctor is simply a white "munganga" with more "bwanga" or power than his own African "munganga." I suggest that the white medical doctor does not serve as a functional substitute for the witch doctor. Only one of their own race and culture who knows their problems, suffering and needs can lead them, through prayer, to the Great Physician in whose power and love they must put their trust for healing, provision, and forgiveness of sins. None but the African pastor can fill that office.

No effort is made to catalogue all the other unacceptable practices that have to be replaced. The above are suggested only to stress the necessity for knowing the structure, decision-making patterns, worship and rituals of the Zambian people, and to emphasize that the Gospel must be proclaimed to satisfy every longing and need of the animistic ancestor-worshiping African.

2

Prelude to Missions Advance and its Expansion 1855 - 1914

Most Europeans in the late 1700s were virtually unaware of the slave trade. Though the slave ships sailed to and from British and European ports, they carried only human cargo from Africa to America.

The Problem of Slavery

When the question was discussed, it was never considered from a moral point of view but as a commercial enterprise. However, the arguments defending the slave trade could not prevail in Britain, once her people were convinced it was immoral, and it was in Britain that opposition first arose. Initial resistance in 1765 was small, but it grew. The horror of the slave trade was revealed to the nation by a small group of prominent men such as Granville Sharp, Thomas Clarkson, and William Wilberforce, who demanded its abolition.

Fage points out three political results that came because of their organized campaign:

First, in 1772 the Lord Chief Justice of England, Lord Mansfield, was brought to declare that the state of slavery was not allowed by the law of England . . . Secondly, in 1807 an Act of Parliament made it illegal for British subjects to engage in the African slave trade. Finally, in 1833 another act was passed which abolished slavery throughout the British Empire (1962:100).

In Denmark, the slave trade became illegal in the year 1804; in the United States of America, in 1808; in Sweden, in the year 1813; and in the Netherlands, in 1814. France made it illegal in 1818, while Brazil outlawed the trade in 1825. Portugal, in 1815, and Spain in 1817, were persuaded to restrict their traders to the southern hemisphere. It soon became apparent, however, that other nations either lacked the determination or the facilities to enforce the laws. Only Britain placed a naval contingent in African waters for halting the traffic, and with no cooperation from other countries, African export actually increased. From the west coast between 1810 and 1830, the volume grew from 85,000 to 115,000 slaves a year.

Britain's next move was directed against those countries whose subjects still participated in the slave trade. From about 1817 Britain, Portugal, and Spain each had the right to stop and search ships sailing under the others' flags; and from 1831 France approved a similar treaty. Still the export increased. British patrols, however, made slave-running increasingly hazardous. At least 1,287 ships were captured and 13,000 slaves released between 1825 and 1865, but during the same period it is estimated that 1,800,000 slaves were taken from the west shores of Africa.

The difficulties were as great in the Indian Ocean as they were in the Atlantic. Slaves had been exported to India for hundreds of years and also to the island of Mauritius. Both were now under British control. In 1822 a treaty between the British Government and Seyyid Said, Sultan of Zanzibar, forbade traders to ship to either of the two areas. The bulk of the Zanzibar trade was, however, with the Oman. The Moresby treaty of 1822 did not interfere with this trade. A further treaty was made with the Sultan of Zanzibar in 1845. It had little effect.

Wilberforce and his associates insisted that the British anti-slavery movement follow a two-pronged policy. It should devote its military resources towards stopping the transport of slaves to world markets, but it should also develop a positive policy summed up in three words: Christianity, commerce, and colonization.

Out of this desire came a number of interdenominational missionary societies. The Baptist Missionary Society was founded in 1792. The London Missionary Society followed in 1798. In 1799 came the Church Missionary Society, and in 1803 the British and Foreign Bible Society.

The African colony of Sierra Leone was established by this same committee, and the "Association for Promoting the Discovery of the Interior Parts of Africa"---founded in 1788---was later absorbed by the Royal Geographical Society---founded in 1830 to organize the exploration of the continent.

David Livingstone

The greatest explorer of Africa was David Livingstone, who arrived at the Cape in South Africa in March, 1841. By latter July he was at Kuruman. Within his first year he had traveled 350 miles north to the Bamangwato people and laid the foundations of the Faith among them. In 1843 he established the mission at Mabotsa. In 1845 he married Mary, eldest daughter of Robert Moffat. The mission at Kolobeng was founded in 1847. He crossed the Kalahari Desert and discovered Lake Ngami in 1849, and in 1851 first saw the Zambezi River. In 1852 Livingstone was back at the Cape with his wife and children. His family returned to England, and the great years were just before him.

In November, 1853, Livingstone left Linyanti for the Atlantic coast to the west, arriving at Loanda, Angola, more than six months later without the loss of a man. The return was begun in September, 1854, and

the whole party reached Linyanti again safe and sound on September 11, 1855 (Groves Vol. 2, 1964:166).

Livingstone observed that the greatest obstacle for missionary advance was malaria, but he found a large African population with chiefs anxious to welcome European missionaries.

He was soon preparing for the journey to the east coast which began in early November, 1855, and on the 15th he became the first white man to see the famous falls on the Zambezi River which he named for his queen. On May 20,

1856, he reached Quilimane on the east coast.

Groves says of the transcontinental journey:

It was an achievement that marks a watershed in the history of the continent, and which, together with Livingstone's total contribution, has meant more for the expansion of Christian missions in Africa than any other single exploit (Vol. 2, 1964:169).

Livingstone wrote on March 2, 1856:

I am not so elated in having performed what has not, to my knowledge, been done before in traversing the continent, because the end of the geographical feat is but the beginning of the missionary enterprise. May God grant me life to do some more good to this poor Africa (Schapera 1961:303).

In December, Livingstone was back in England----as a national hero, having placed Africa squarely on the maps of the world.

In May, 1858, he was back at the mouth of the Zambezi, leader of an official government expedition to explore the Zambezi basin, to establish white settlements on the highlands surrounding it, and to sail his ship up the Zambezi, "God's highway into the interior" as he called it. He failed in his main objects (Northcott 1957:20).

Defeated by the Zambezi, Livingstone turned into the Shire River and opened the way into Nyasaland, now called Malawi. In 1861 he explored Lake Nyasa, and in early 1863 determined that the highlands were suitable for European habitation. He returned to England in July, 1864.

By January, 1866, he was back in Africa and by August had trekked from Zanzibar to Lake Nyasa. The following April he was at the southern end of Lake Tanganyika. He discovered Lake Mweru in November, 1867, and Lake Bangweolo in July, 1868, reaching Ujiji on Lake Tanganyika in March, 1869. In mid-July he began the exploration of the Manyuema country in the Congo. He returned to Ujiji in July, 1871, and was met by H. M. Stanley in November. With Stanley he set out for Tabora, Tanganyika late in December, and returned alone to Lake Tanganyika in August, 1872. He was at Lake Bangweolo in what was later to become Northern

Rhodesia, now Zambia, in January, 1873, and here at Chitambo's village, Ilala, he died on May 1, 1873.

As early as March, 1852, Livingstone had expressed the
hope that he might be

able to solve some interesting problems in relation
to the slave trade, my full conviction being that this
nefarious traffic will be abolished by the influence of
Christian Missions (Schapera 1961:194).

He entertained, as early as 1851, the idea of legitimate
commerce as a means of overcoming the slave trade:

That Christian merchants who may have enterprise
enough to commence a trade in these parts would be
no losers in the end may be inferred from what has
taken place on this river . . . I feel assured, if our
merchants could establish a legitimate commerce on
the Zambezi they would soon drive the slave dealer
from the market, and be besides great gainers in the
end (Schapera 1961:183-184).

As Livingstone's years grew in number, so the motive to
end the slave trade became more powerful. The Central
African trade centered in Zanzibar, controlled by Arab merchants who dealt in both ivory and slaves. Northern Rhodesia,
Nyasaland, and Tanganyika, now Tanzania, were wide open
for their traffic.

Powdermaker says:

Burton, a British explorer, estimated that in order to
capture fifty-five women, whom he observed in one
caravan, at least ten villages had been destroyed, each
having a population of between one and two hundred
(1962:28).

By the middle of the nineteenth century

about 15,000 slaves a year passed through the squalid,
sandy square of the Zanzibar slave market . . . For
every five captured in the interior, only one reached
his or her destination (Marsh and Kingsnorth 1966:37).

In a letter written to John Kirk dated March 25, 1871,
Livingstone wrote describing an episode witnessed by him:

Coming back they demanded ivory for the 25 rings
and began to shoot the men in cold blood, and capture
women and children and grass, cloth, goats, and

fowls. They continued their murdering for three days
in a densely peopled district and carried off an immense number of women and children (Foskett 1964:
146).

Livingstone's battle with the slave traffic was a one-man
affair. He was the enemy of the Arab slavers. While he was
alive their trade was doomed, and yet it was his death that
killed the slave trade:

His revelations and the enquiries which followed, and
then the news of his death, all combined finally to con-
demn the trade (Northcott 1957:66).

The Mission Advance

Two missions were planned for the interior of Africa as a
result of Livingstone's 1857-58 visit to England. He suggested a mission north of the Zambezi between that river and
the Kafue. The London Missionry Society approved the plan.
Holloway Helmore, with seventeen years in Bechuanaland, was
appointed leader. With him were his wife and four children
and two recruits, Roger Price and John Mackenzie, and their
wives. The party arrived in Cape Town in July, 1858. One
year later from Kuruman, they began the last leg of the
journey to determine the beginnings of their first missions
efforts. The Mackenzies remained at Kuruman.

In mid-February 1860, they arrived at Linyanti. By April
21, the adult Helmores with two of their children and the
Price infant were dead from virulent fever. Mrs. Price died
as she and her husband with the two remaining Helmore
children were returning to Kuruman. Of the original nine,
only three came back in February, 1961. Thus concluded the
first effort to establish a mission in what is today Zambia.

The second mission was inaugurated by the Universities'
Mission to Central Africa. Its initial thrust was into East
Central Africa, now known as Malawi. The Oxford and Cam-
bridge Mission to Central Africa was formed in 1858. By
July, 1861, Bishop Mackenzie, heading the pioneer party,
was in the highlands south of Lake Nyasa. Misfortune
plagued the party, and in late January, 1862, Mackenzie died.
For two years the mission hung on, but the situation did not

improve. With the slave trade, famine, pestilence, and war; without supplies and with their ranks decimated by sickness and death, it became evident that, for the time being, Central Africa was closed to them. On the decision of Bishop Tozier, Mackenzie's successor, and with the approval of the Bishop of Cape Town, headquarters were moved to Zanzibar in 1864. Not until the year 1870 did the Universities' Mission enter Northeastern Rhodesia, a part of modern Zambia.

The first missionary to labor in what is now Zambia was Frederick Stanley Arnot, born in Glasgow in 1859. In 1881 Arnot came to Africa, commended by the Glasgow Assembly of Brethren. The Zambezi was his goal. He reached Lealui in Barotseland (see frontispiece map) on December 19, 1882, to receive a warm welcome from Lewanika, Paramount Chief of the Barotse. Arnot was resident in Barotseland until May, 1884. From Lealui he made his way to Garenganze in the southern Congo, where he met the powerful chief, Msidi, in January, 1886. There he began the work of the Plymouth Brethren, now under the aegis of Christian Missions in Many Lands.

Shortly after Arnot had moved northward, Francois Coillard of the Societe des Missions Evangeliques, or the Paris Evangelical Missionary Society, arrived in Barotseland. Coillard had already served in Basutoland for twenty years. He and his wife first attempted a mission among the Banyai---a section of the Shona peoples of Rhodesia---in 1876, but were turned back by the Boer authorities. One year later they made a second attempt, without difficulty crossing the Transvaal to Mashonaland. There they were taken captive by Lobengula, Paramount Chief of the Ndebele people, and after four months were deported. They made their way to Bechuanaland and met the Christian Kama, Chief of the Bechuana, who encouraged them to go to the Barotse. With their Basuto companions they set out again, and, reaching Sesheke, Barotse outpost on the Zambezi, sent word to Lewanika telling him of their purpose and desire to meet him. The rains arrived before the meeting could be secured, but Lewanika gave them permission to return. Not until January, 1885, was Coillard back in Barotseland. Twenty-four months later they were settled on their first station, and on March 4, 1887, the first mission school was opened.

The Primitive Methodists reached the Zambezi in August 1889, but were detained for four years before obtaining permission to go to the Ba-ila or Mashukulumbwe people to the east. Not until December 6, 1893, did the Methodists reach the Nkala River where their first mission was opened.

The Livingstonia Mission, The United Free Church of Scotland, entered Nyasaland in 1875:

> Dr. Elmslie and two others joined them and the work gradually extended into what is now North-Eastern Rhodesia, including Chitambo---the place where Dr. Livingstone died and where, in his memory, a station was planted in 1906 by his nephew and his grandson, Malcolm Moffat and R. Hubert Wilson (Mackintosh 1950: 33-34).

In 1887 the London Missionary Society opened its first work in Northeastern Rhodesia at Fwambo.

A short chronology of the early missions cannot tell the story nor portray the sacrifice of the pioneers. Speaking before the Primitive Methodist Missionary Society in 1897, Francois Coillard said,

> We have five stations---five places like light houses amid the darkness . . . We have not only stations, but we have graves. We have taken possession of the country by our graves (Groves Vol. 3, 1964:152).

The Initial Impact of Missions

Before the "Scramble for Africa" in 1885, little was known of the interior. Livingstone had trekked across what was later called Northern Rhodesia and shortly after his death the first missionary penetration into largely unknown territory began.

> By the end of 1881, seven different missions were established within striking distance of what is now Northern Rhodesia . . . by the end of 1890 five of these were actually within the modern borders of the territory (Taylor and Lehmann 1961: 2-3, 5).

Central Africa was occupied by missionaries before the introduction of commerce and government. They paved the

way for other European secular influences and agencies
(Spiro 1963:364). Their immense importance in the expansion of European interests in Central Africa in the latter
Nineteenth Century, when the interior was opened to the
ouside world, cannot be over-emphasized. In this early
period, however, missionaries "were not trying to draw
government into Africa" (Dougall 1963:41). To a degree impossible in other parts of Asia, Africa, and Latin America,
missionaries became administrators of considerable African
populations. Initially the missionaries set up mission compounds to provide Africans with work, safety from slave raiders, and mutual support. Unusual circumstances demanded
the building of large stations. Houses, churches, schools, and
clinics were constructed, gardens were planted, irrigation
schemes laid out, aqueducts built, and stockades raised---
all with African labor. The people, afraid of slavers, moved
into the compounds and looked to the missionaries for
protection.

Rotberg too harshly criticizes the missionaries "who had
become unquestioned rulers of a large part of Northeastern
Rhodesia" (1965:57). He is guilty of exaggeration, but it is
easy for him, standing eighty years this side of their time
to judge them harshly.

Perhaps the missionaries went too far, but the circumstances under which they labored must be recognized. The
slave raiders had so disrupted the social structure of villages and tribes that authority patterns were destroyed.
Under peaceful conditions Africans had effective means of
discipline and control, but under repeated raids discipli-
nary patterns had broken down. Because discipline had been
destroyed, the missionaries also had to protect the people
from themselves. Without fully realizing what they were
doing and unable to foresee the future implications of their
actions, they transformed the immediate necessity for offering protection and exercising discipline into a system of
rigid control. Conflicts between Africams under normal circumstances were settled by the Africans. Now order within
the missions had to be enforced, and the missionaries were
soon making laws and judging, sentencing, and punishing
violators of those laws.

Early Missions Introduced Government

Rotberg's assertion that missionaries "came to govern absolutely" (1965:57), is hardly likely in so large a territory, but they did introduce a government of sorts. Africans living at the mission compounds were required to attend worship and send their children to school. Villages must be kept clean. Guns were not allowed. Violation of these laws was cause for punishment. Serious crimes demanded flogging.

Missions Involvement in Commerce

On December 4, 1858, at Cambridge, David Livingstone concluded his lecture by saying,

> I go back to Africa to make an open path for commerce and Christianity; do you carry out the work which I have begun. I leave it with you (Groves, Vol. 2, 1964: 176).

The first concern of the missionary pioneers was to bring African people to a saving knowledge of Jesus Christ and obedience to Him, but they were also interested in pursuing economic enterprises. There were practical reasons for this. Support from home was slow in coming, and missionaries soon learned that through trading with Africans they could lessen their dependence upon home support. They were also interested in improving their surroundings. Thus they began to engage in commerce, living off the land, and making a modest profit through their trade:

> Many of the original mission sites had been purchased for calico. The first houses had been constructed by Africans whose wages had been calculated in yards rather than shillings or rupees. Porters had been paid from the contents of the loads that they carried. New desires were thereby stimulated, and the missionaries, whether or not they supported Livingstone's theoretical coupling of commerce and Christianity, became intimately involved in the mercantile arrangements of a secular society (Rotberg 1965:96).

The missionaries were industrious. Some developed

gardens, cared for by labor from Africans. One mission
specialized in the production of beeswax and honey. Another
grew livestock. On another was located a furniture factory
in which young Africans were trained. Income was turned
back into the mission. These were not schemes for private
gain.

The commercial activities promoted by early missions
served another purpose as well. They did much to prepare
the people for the commercial role thay would soon play in
the development of their country. Interest in economic
development grew with the Africans as they watched the
missionaries. They learned new skills. They adopted new
customs and dress. They learned the value of work for
material gain.

Also of note was the movement from villages to the city.
This movement would assist in development of the gold and
diamond mines in South Africa and the copper mines to the
north of the Zambezi.

Missions Involvement in Politics

The charter for the British South Africa Company was
granted October 29, 1889. It was said that this company
would be

able peacefully and with the consent of the native
races to open up, develop, and colonize the territories to the north of British Bechuanaland with the
best results both for British trade and commerce
and for the interest of the native races (Hall 1965:58).

Almost from the first, the early missions were involved
with the Company. A representative arrived at the court of
the Paramount Chief of Barotseland in May of 1890. Before
the end of June a treaty had been signed between the Company
and the chief, and the missionaries were identified with the
Company. The missionaries welcomed the treaty. One of
them wrote:

For my part I have no doubt that for the nation this
will prove the one plank of safety. The Barotse are
incapable of governing, and left to themselves, they
would annihilate each other (Mackintosh 1950:18).

The missionaries were white, as were company administrators, and their philosophies were similar. The white
man's judgment was superior. Whatever he wanted was believed to be best for the people and country. That segregation was practised by officials, settlers, and missionaries
was a matter claiming little missionary thought. Administration of the company offered a solution to many problems
of the missionaries, and they welcomed it. Relationships between the missions and company were mutually beneficial.
Though some agents for the government had little sympathy
with the spiritual emphasis of the missionaries, yet they
knew that the more missionaries did the less it would cost
government to keep order. Missionaries felt a sense of security and they placed their dependence concerning matters
large and small in the government. They urged the Company
to introduce taxation---failing to see the implications of their
action with the Africans.

With but few exceptions, the missionaries were happy
with the Company's methods. They believed it was an instrument of benevolent rule, one of its objects being the "uplift
of the natives." Few among them championed the rights of
Africans, and this situation continued into the Twentieth
Century.

Cooperation between Government and Missions

The Order of Council (Constitution) of Northern Rhodesia
was often revised after granting the charter to the British
South African Company in 1889. Through those years the
Order of Council recognized the primacy of the Charter
Company (Franck 1960:23). Relation of missions to govern-
ment was one of fraternal good will. Few objections were
heard concerning any action of government regarding the
African people.

African Reaction

Early missionaries enjoyed only limited success. Real
victory did not come. Children, through mission schools,
entered the churches but adults remained aloof. Zambia's

population still clung to the ways of their ancestors:

> Although the indigenous inhabitants of Northern Rho-
> desia appreciated the sacrifices the missionaries
> claimed to have made. . . . they nonetheless responded
> to the missionaries ambivalently and, in many cases,
> with real animosity (Rotberg 1965:145).

In 1890 only a few Europeans lived north of the Zambezi.
With the coming of settlers, traders, and government officials, their number increased, and the African became increasingly familiar with the white man.

> In 1911 the white population for Northern Rhodesia
> amounted to 1,494 (Census Report 1 Sept. 1911, 3/7,
> Northern Rhodesia Public Records).

No further census was taken till 1921, but immigration from
1911-1914 cannot have exceeded a few hundred (Gann 1958:
175).

To the Africans all Europeans were Christians, and they
could see inconsistencies between preachment and life.
They resented the greater wealth of the Europeans, including
the missionaries, in contrast to their own poverty. Above all,
they resented the physical and mental abuse of the settlers,
traders, government officials, and police---who treated them
as inferiors. Since the missionaries did not dissociate
themselves from the whites, but rather---for the most part---
fell in with the accepted patterns of behavior towards the
blacks, they too appeared to be oppressors---albeit kindly
oppressors!

3

The Birth of a New Nation
1914-1964

The February 4, 1960, publication of *The Cape Argus*
of Cape Town, South Africa, contained the text of British
Prime Minister Harold McMillan's address given before the
South African Houses of Parliament the previous day. The
Prime Minister said:

The wind of change is blowing through the continent.
The most striking of all the impressions I have formed
since I left London a month ago is of the strength of
national consciousness. Whether we like it or not, this
growth is a political fact. We must accept it as a fact.
This means, I would judge, that we must come to terms
with it. I sincerely believe that if we cannot do so, we
may imperil the precarious balance between East and
West on which the peace of the world depends.

A quick review of the history of Northern Rhodesia's
political development indicates rapid change taking place
from the date of the country's formation.

The Creation of Northern Rhodesia

The Charter granted the British South Africa Company in
1889 was revised during the following decade to include the
whole territory. In 1899, the Barotseland-Northwestern
Rhodesia Order in Council established the South Africa

33

Company's rule of the western area on a solid foundation.
One year later came the Northeastern Rhodesia Order in
Council which brought comparable results for that area.

In 1911 the two territories amalgamated. The combined
area was designated Northern Rhodesia. The British South
Africa Company administration continued until 1924. On
April first of that year the first Governor was appointed,
and Northern Rhodesia came under the administration of the
British Government.

Not until 1918 were European settlers given a voice in
the administration of the territory. The first Legislative
Council sat in 1924, but it was 1948 before the first two
African members were appointed to represent their own
people. In 1954 the number of Africans on the Legislative
Council was doubled to four, but they were still appointed.
The Constitution of 1959 was of tremendous significance:

> The intention was that all elected members of the
> Legislative Council were returned by, and became
> responsible to, a multi-racial electorate. The effect
> of this arrangement was that African representation
> in the House was increased to seven members, six
> of whom were elected (Zambia Today 1964:10).

The 1962 Constitution resulted from the report of the
Monckton Commission in October, 1960. The Commission
had been authorized to review the first seven years of the
Federation of Rhodesia and Nyasaland. Demands for a new
Constitution for Northern Rhodesia were the result, but the
document of 1962 brought little satisfaction to any of the
political parties. The election of October, 1962, was, however, of immense significance politically. It was the first
time for a national electoral confrontation between Africans
and Europeans. Northern Rhodesia's first African government and the end of the Central African Federation were the
results. The Constitution was unwieldy, and the election of
1962 failed to meet the constitutional requirement of minimum support from both races. The consequence was a constitutional impasse which led to the formation of a coalition
government by the United National Independence Party (UNIP)
and the African National Congress (ANC) that commanded
more than half the elected members of the Council. The new

government was announced by the Governor on December 15, 1962.

Federation of Rhodesia and Nyasaland

Northern Rhodesia (now Zambia), Southern Rhodesia (now Rhodesia), and Nyasaland (now Malawi) joined together on October 23, 1953, in the Federation of Rhodesia and Nyasaland. It lasted one decade. The attitude of the vast majority of the African people was one of implacable opposition. The growing resistance, especially from Northern Rhodesia and Nyasaland, led to a Federal Review Conference being held in London in December of 1960, which brought about the Victoria Falls Conference in July, 1963. The decision was made there that the Federation should end. The dissolution was completed on December 31, 1963.

Northern Rhodesia Self-Government

Northern Rhodesia first voted under a self-governing constitution in January, 1964. The franchise, also for the first time, was based on universal suffrage. More than 1,400,000 people of all races registered and voted. The United National Independent Party of Dr. Kenneth Kaunda won fifty-five of the sixty-five main roll seats and Dr. Kaunda became the first Prime Minister of Northern Rhodesia.

Political and Economic Acceleration

Few areas of traditional African life have been so affected as the area of personal economy. Until the opening of the copper mines and the recent introduction of industries, few Africans lived in urban areas. As recently as 1963 only 16 per cent of the African population lived in the cities; and the influx of Africans had already been under way, particularly in the mining areas, since the mid-twenties. The move into industry for the African was almost indiscernible at first, but it came because of the vacuum in the areas of unskilled cheap labor which he was able to fill.

For many Europeans, bringing Africans into industry, even at the lowest rung of the ladder, was a threat to their entrenched positions. Income for the European was set to permit him to live on the high standard believed essential to make up for the privations suffered by being away from his home country. In contrast to his income, Gibbs says:

> The African's wages were not wages at all in the sense that they were intended to provide him with a living. He was given meagre rations by his employer, he was provided with the minimum requirements of shelter and in addition he was made an almost negligible cash payment which in theory enabled him to meet his hut tax, and after that he could buy some second-hand rags to cover himself---although even for these most Africans relied on the charity of their employers--- and indulge himself in beer and women as far as his means allowed him (1961:93-94).

There were, therefore, two quite separate categories. One reached £1000 as a minimum in the ten years after the Second World War. The other, in exceptional cases, reached £100 per annum.

Initially, jobs requiring skill were kept for the European--- or to put it honestly, work with the mark of meniality was done by the African. But as the increased skills of Africans brought them into job competition, the differentiation in salary was no longer between skill and lack of skill but hinged on whether one was black or white.

Thinking Africans like Kenneth Kaunda were aware that the affluent lives of Europeans were being subsidized at the sacrifice of the physical, economic and social welfare of the African people. They made available to the European the supply of cheap labor needed to do the menial jobs too low for him to put his hands to. Kaunda pointed out the contradictions in the wage scale between black and white:

> In the printing shops in Lusaka an African who operates a linotype machine gets thirty-five pounds per month, while the European doing the same job gets 110 pounds per month. . . The whole position is iniquitous because there is no qualitative difference between African and European. Africans, given suitable training can do any job at present done by Europeans (Morris and Kaunda, 1960:51-52).

This same anomaly was obvious to the African working alongside Europeans in the factory or the mine in Northern Rhodesian towns:

Before the outbreak of the Second World War the average white mineworker's wage was something over forty pounds per month, though many were receiving up to seventy pounds a month. The average African monthly wage was two pounds fifteen shillings and four pence for underground workers, and two pounds eight shillings and nine pence for surface workers (Taylor and Lehmann 1961:143).

Out of this explosive tension came the development of an African "voice" demanding greater equity, but it did not stop there. Self-assertion was also making its influence felt in industrial relations and politics. Evidence of the strength of the African "voice" became apparent in African Welfare Societies. A number of Zambia's most trusted leaders gained their first experience in the formation and building of these early societies that gave expression to the changes sought by the African people. These societies grew from strength to strength. In 1946 they joined in a Federation of Welfare Societies with a Conference planned annually at Lusaka.

While the Welfare Societies turned more to the political arena, other developments took place in the field of industrial relations. By 1946 a Works Committee was set up at each mine, and in 1949 came the formation of the African Mineworkers' Trade Union.

The Federation of African Welfare Societies in 1948 became the Northern Rhodesia Congress; and this in turn, in 1951, became the Northern Rhodesia National Congress. A splinter group from the Congress in 1959 became the African National Independent Party (later renamed the United National Independent Party). In 1962, there came the first confrontation between Europeans and Africans at the polls. The Africans won the election.

Franck says,

Perhaps the most meaningful social revolution in Africa today is the rapid urbanization of the African population (1960:138).

Accelerating Urbanization

The move began slowly. Initially the administration would not accept that Africans were moving to the urban areas as settled residents. Providing good housing was therefore resisted by municipal officials. As recently as the year 1941

> the government was still insisting that it could not be committed to the policy of establishing a permanent industrialized native population on the Copperbelt (Hall 1965: 129-130).

The rapid growth in numbers of Africans employed in the Copperbelt from 1924 through 1930 gives some idea of the development of the industry, but it also indicates the migration of Africans to the city. In 1924 there were 1,300 Africans employed. In 1925 there were 4,000; in 1926, 10,000; in 1927, 10,946; in 1928, 16,073; in 1929, 22,341; and in 1930 there were 30,000 Africans employed in the copper mines. In 1958 there were 207,866 Africans in the whole of the Copperbelt. There were also 31,448 non-Africans (Taylor and Lehmann 1961:31-32). By latter 1964 there were 409,000 Africans and 46,200 non-Africans, for a total of 455,200 people living in Copperbelt cities (Zambia Today 1965: 18). Since the conclusion of the Second World War, a great new African labor force has emerged. The African has become a recognized and substantive member of the urban community and a political and economic force to be reckoned with.

Colonially Orientated Missions

Most missions, following the First World War, were involved in education. Much time was given to training in skills such as printing, carpentry, and bricklaying. The first employees in industry were trained by the missionaries. The missionaries honestly insisted that their major objective was to convert the African, but they were also concerned about helping the African generally, prohibiting abuses, protesting his land rights and bringing civilization to him. In this, they worked hand in hand with the British civil servants and the district officers. Particularly between the two Great

Wars, the missionaries were in sympathy with the administration in its policy of trusteeship. The benevolent image
of missionsries and the administration is reflected again
and again in government records and missions minutes
throughout the period.

However, after the Second World War Africans were
often disappointed with the missionaries. Increasingly, discrimination was impinging upon Africans' rights. If they
expected missionaries to intercede with the administration
on their behalf, they hoped in vain. Though a few championed
African interests, the voice of the Church was seldom heard.
Kenneth Kaunda said a number of years ago:

> My own view is that the Church as a whole has not,
> ever since the change in our society was accelerated,
> been out-spoken enough in its criticism of what has
> been obviously unjust as far as the African is con-
> cerned (Morris and Kaunda 1960:105).

The African saw that the majority of missionaries were
actually "arms" of the government. They shared in the administration of the school system and cooperated with the
ministries of health and agriculture. They accepted government subsidies.

Ralph Dodge has said:

> It must be admitted that missionaries generally share
> four things with colonial government agents: common
> nationality and culture, common race, administrative
> authority, and a position of privilege (1964:19).

Many missionaries before 1964 were warmly sympathetic
with the Africans, yet they were effectively compromised in
the eyes of the African people. Colin Morris wrote:

> It seems to Africans that the missionary as the voice
> of protest has become more and more softened until
> now with few exceptions, they are viewed as suppor-
> ters of the European position (1961:159).

Northern Rhodesia attained self-government in January,
1964. Dr. Kenneth Kaunda and his strong nationalistic leadership, with the support and respect of the people, made possible this achievement. On May 27, 1964, the day following
his return from London and the independence talks, Dr.
Kaunda told Parliament in Lusaka:

> We are being given a new opportunity to make this a
> country where all our people will be happy to stay; a
> country where people for twenty-four hours in every
> day will not feel afraid to go outside their homes on
> account of their political, religious, and other beliefs
> (Zambia Today 1964:13).

The Problems of Transition

On October 24, 1964---United Nations Day---Northern
Rhodesia became the new independent republic of Zambia
within the British Commonwealth. The principal objectives
in the struggle for freedom were now won.

Political restiveness, however, was soon apparent in
many parts of the country. So long as there was a common
enemy, all energies were directed towards it. Colonialism
was the opponent, and all traditional differences and tribal
friction ceased. Educated men and illiterate farmers, rural
and urban dwellers, and leaders of tribes with differing traditions stood together so that attention might be focused on
the dispossession of the colonial power.

Kaunda and his compatriots were aware of this problem
of transition from colonialism to independence. The new
President said:

> Once the common enemy is removed, the citizens of
> an independent state find themselves on their own
> in a cold, hard world where clear judgement of their
> calibre is not obscured by the presence, inhibiting or
> otherwise, of an alien factor. . . It must be admitted,
> however, that certain elements in their societies
> having been weighed in the balance of achievement
> and found wanting, may cast around for other scape-
> goats to replace colonialism and in so doing revive
> traditional tribal or regional animosities . . . With
> the removal of the common enemy, there is no longer
> a 'they' to take the blame for our failures. We must
> stand or fall without the aid of the colonial crutch
> . . . Inevitably, the overthrow of the common enemy
> takes some of the dynamism out of nationalism. . .
> (Morris and Kaunda 1968: 53-54).

The Problem of Race

Race in Zambia is no longer viewed from the colonially orientated vantage point. It is now determined from a Zambian context. The question is no longer how the European will treat the African, but how will the African treat the European. Until independence, racial and social segregation was a predominant factor in every African's life. His opportunities were limited. His movements were defined. In his own country he was a second-class citizen, ostracized because of his alleged inferiority. The place of residence was determined for him. His children must go to separate schools. He was taken to a separate hospital in a separate ambulance. His earning power was not more than one tenth that of the European. He was a stranger in his own land. All this changed very abruptly when independence was achieved.

Europeans were accustomed to a society structured for their advantage. Any changes must be for the worse. Consequently, after independence, many Europeans suspected the new government of malevolent intent to make it as difficult for them as possible. However, the changes were designed to establish society, and they were directed towards no one. The government was determined to end racial exclusiveness and to bring a greater sharing of the wealth of the land. A large segment of Zambia's people, before independence, were denied those elements of life deemed essential to the European. Education beyond lower primary in all but few cases, health services, reasonable compensation for labor, freedom of speech, and the right to vote were not available to the African people.

Some of the changes do create a disadvantage to the European community. The exclusive and racial advantage of the past is gone. Dr. Kaunda has said:

This is a hard fact of life and Africa is no place for any European who cannot accept it. To come to terms with this truth is the essential condition of a happy, well-adjusted life in Zambia (Morris & Kaunda 1968:68).

Many committed European doctors, nurses, lawyers, engineers, scientists, professors, industrialists, and mis-

sionaries are in Zambia to share in building the nation.
These must not be held to account for the deeds of the white
racists of the past. These Europeans must be accepted by
black Zambians, not merely because they are engineers,
doctors, scientists, or missionaries, but because they are
men of Zambia as Africans are men of Zambia.
Many Europeans want to identify with Africans, but this
can only be done as African men freely share in this identification. There are, fortunately, evidences among the African people of forgiveness and a willingness to accept the
Europeans as Zambians among Zambians.

East versus West

Communism is a growing threat in Zambia. Peter Lessing
says, however, that:
> Until 1958 the Soviet Union not only had no organiza-
> tion working anywhere in Africa south of the Sahara,
> except the small South African Communist Party, but
> the Soviet policy-makers were so ignorant about Af-
> rica that they were incapable of shaping a coherent
> policy (1962:25).

President Kaunda has affirmed that this is true:
> Communism appears to have discovered Africa so
> late in the day that the liberation struggle was almost
> over before the ideological offensive upon the conti-
> nent got under way (Morris and Kaunda 1968:118).

Under colonial rule Britain, France, and Belgium kept a
watchful eye on all attempts of the Communist world to in-
filtrate their territories either with propaganda or personnel.

If the Communists got off to a slow start, they were fast
in catching up. Beginning with Ghana in 1957, there has been
a procession of African countries obtaining independence.
The Communists were quick to use the new governments and
capitals as means of entering the continent with delegations,
ambassadors, and trade missions. Most of the new capitals
have embassies from both Peking and Moscow. Radio pro-
gramming has accelerated. Short-wave transmitters in both
China and Russia beam propaganda broadcasts towards
Africa each day. Moscow and Peking have also been quick

to offer educational advantages to African students. Five
hundred or more students per year travel to these cities to
study. But Russian and Chinese embassies and trade com-
missions in most of the African capitals do not mean that
Africa is rushing into the Communist bloc. However, it must
be accepted that African nations will establish diplomatic
relationships with the Communist as well as with the Western world.

All African leaders are aware of the struggle over Africa
between the East and the West. Both blocs count it a valuable
prize. Both East and West are lavish in long-term loans
provided at low interest. Both beam propaganda to all the
continent in many languages, and both have been generous in
providing highways, railways, hydroelectric and irrigation
schemes.

Zambia is determined not to become a pawn in the struggle
between East and West. She wants to keep the cold war out
of Africa.

As Hughes says:

As they see it, they are not fighting either Communism
or Westernism but their own intensely personal battle
against poverty, backwardness and centuries of in-
dignity (1961:284).

Kaunda has recently said:

We are equally adamant that Africa's destiny is to
remain non-aligned. This non-alignment . . . is not
neutrality . . . Our role in world affairs is not to remain aloof from the basic human issues which have
led to the creation of two power blocs, but to exercise
our influence with both sides in order to cement understanding between them and testify to the universal
desire for peace and fruitful co-existence (Morris and
Kaunda 1968:117-118).

The Church and Nationalism

Church membership and attendance in Zambia are condi-
tioned by numerous factors. There is much denominational
divisiveness, and competition is extreme. Membership,
however, has little of substance or strength.

The churches undertook the conversion of the peoples of Central Africa with numerous advantages. They have received abundant financial assistance from overseas denominations. Most have been given generous grants of land by the government. They have enjoyed almost exclusive control of education and have received generous subsidies. Many have shared in medical services for which they also were subsidized. The churches have enjoyed considerable social and political prestige.

However, in spite of these favorable factors, the relationship between the churches and the Africans remains flimsy. Christianity is rejected, not for what it teaches but for what it practises. In the past many of the churches of Zambia have not practised what they preached. Few Africans were inclined to reject the fundamental doctrines of the Church. Many have accepted faith in God and Christ---but they were dissatisfied when the Church appeared unconcerned with regard to their political, economic, and social aspirations (Taylor and Lehmann 1961:121). African Christians were also aware of the double standard between declared position of the churches regarding great issues and the practice of Christians quite contrary to the pronouncement. In many congregations in Zambia, prior to independence, no Africans were welcome. Christianity has come to be known as a "white man's religion." It must lose this stigma.

The Church in the Future

The government of Zambia is fast taking over the responsibility for all social work, formerly conducted by missions. Education, health, and welfare will soon be the care of the state. Contemporary mission in Zambia faces a dilemma. Many missions, deeply involved in institutionalism, having given little emphasis to evangelism, are confronted with major decision. With the transfer of schools and hospitals to the government, will they voice the naive claim that Zambia is Christian, or will a new emphasis be given to preaching the Gospel, winning the multitudes of pagans and unconverted "church-roll" adherents firmly to Christ, and establishing them in sound rural and city churches?

What of the Church's attitude concerning the great issues facing the new country of Zambia? J. V. Taylor has observed:

> If the Church in Africa (by which is meant the whole Christian community spread throughout Africa, but focused, as it must be, in the congregation of the locally organized church) gives the impression that God is not concerned with man's social and political affairs, then men will not be very much concerned with such a God (1958:9).

With Zambia now a self-governing nation and with feelings of nationalism running high, the relationship of the missionary to the national churches must come under careful review. Melvin Hodges has said that the

> rising tide of nationalism demands that the native church be freed from the domination of foreign missionaries (1953:13).

This being true, the future place of the missionary must be prayerfully evaluated.

Many changes have swept across Zambia in the past decade, and great changes are yet to take place. McGavran has said,

> The most significant and most overlooked fact about rapid changes the world is presently undergoing is that through them often arises an amazing receptivity to the Gospel (1965:12).

If this is true, then there is ground for optimism and expectancy that multitudes from the tribes of Zambia may be won in the coming decade by those men who commit themselves to that supreme objective.

II

The Churches of Zambia

4

When and Where the Churches Began

The death of Livingstone provided the force motivating a number of missionary societies to enter Africa.

Beginnings

The Free Church of Scotland, The Universities' Mission to Central Africa, The London Missionary Society, The White Fathers, The Jesuits, and The Paris Evangelical Mission were within striking distance of what is now Zambia by the end of 1882.

The man who was Livingstone's successor, however, belonged to no missions organization. Frederick Stanley Arnot was a member of the Plymouth Brethren,

whose "Christian Missions in Many Lands" are individually autonomous, while keeping in touch with a central office in Bath (Taylor and Lehmann 1961:3).

Arnot reached the capital of the Barotse in December, 1882, and stayed for almost eighteen months.

Francois Coillard, following Arnot, set up the first station of the Paris Evangelical Mission in 1885. The year 1893 saw the beginning of the work of the Primitive Methodists among the Ila on the Nkala River. The first mission of the Dutch Reformed Church was opened among the Ngoni people in Northeastern Rhodesia in 1889, and 1887 marked the opening of the first work of the London Missionary Society south of Lake Tanganyika. In 1890 the White Fathers opened a station among the Bemba. Fred Arnot returned from Angola and moved among the Lunda in 1886 to open the first work of the Plymouth Brethren. Before the close of 1890, mission stations were located on every side of the territory but the southeast. Five pioneer stations were already within the borders of the country.

Francois Coillard returned to Europe in 1896. In 1898 he was back in Barotseland with twenty-four recruits, including one medical missionary. Eight died and eleven were forced to return to Europe invalided or widowed.

> Up to 1926 the mission cost the lives of twenty-two adult Europeans, besides several children (Smith 1928: 74).

In 1889 the Paris Missionary Society opened a new station at Kazungula. The year 1892 saw the first work in Lealui, and Nangoma was opened in 1894. Senanga was established in 1898; Sefula, rebuilt in 1899; Mabumbu, opened in 1900; and Seoma, in 1902. The first work in the city of Livingstone was started in 1904. Lukona was begun in 1908. Besides its village schools, the Paris Missionary Society operated a teacher-training school at Sefula, and also a Bible School. A boarding school for boys was built at Lunkona in 1926, a similar school for girls at Mabumbu in 1927. The mission also had a printing press and book depot at Sefula. In 1950 the mission entered into discussions with other societies to explore the possibilities of church union. *The World Christian Handbook* shows that the Paris Mission is now one of six participating societies in the United Church of Zambia (1968: 97).

The first convert of the London Missionary Society was baptized in 1891 in Northeastern Rhodesia. Kambole Mission was opened by the L. M. S. in 1894. Mbereshi and Mporokoso were opened in 1900. In 1923 the society built stations at Senga Hill and Kafulwe. Eight schools were opened by the L. M. S. at Kawimbe in 1926. At Kambole in the mid-twenties a large industrial school was opened, and Mbereshi became one of the best girls' schools in Central Africa. A hospital has been built; a boys' boarding school and an industrial

training program have been added. The London Society also
moved into the Copperbelt to share in the evangelistic, educational, and welfare services so much in demand. The
society is now affiliated with the United Church of Zambia.

The White Fathers began their work in Northeastern Rhodesia in 1891; and in 1895, moved to Kayambi. Chilubula and
Chilonga were opened in 1899. The year 1903 marked the
planting of a station on Chilubi Island in Lake Bangweulu, and
in 1904 Kambwiri was opened in the Luangwa Valley. In 1905
the White Fathers opened missions at Kapatu and Lubwe.
The year 1910 marked the beginning of Chibote; and 1914
dated the establishing of Ipusukilo. In 1922, stations were
opened at Malole and Rosa.

The Society of Jesus attempted in 1881 and 1883 to establish their work in Barotseland. Their first successful
opening came in 1905 between the Kafue and the Zambezi
at Chikuni. Kasisi station was established in 1906. In 1910
the Jesuits transferred their work from Miruru in Mozambique to Kapoche and Katondwe in Northern Rhodesia. Chin-
gombe was opened in 1914. In 1922 the Society of Jesus
established its first work in Lusaka, and in 1923 work was
begun at Broken Hill. The Northern Rhodesia Jesuit Mission was separated from the Southern Rhodesia Mission in
1927, and the Prefecture Apostolic of Broken Hill was
instituted. The Livingstone Diocese was given to the Capuchin Fathers in 1936. The Italian Franciscan Fathers were
given oversight of the Copperbelt, Solwezi, and Mwinilungu
in 1938. The name of the Prefecture of Broken Hill was
changed to Lusaka by decree of the Congregation for the
Propagation of the Faith in 1946, and the Prefecture of
Lusaka was raised to the status of a Vicariate, and finally
in 1959, to an Archdiocese. The year 1937 marked the
establishing of the Prefecture of Fort Jameson, which was
raised to the status of a Vicariate in 1953.

The opening of the first station of the Primitive Methodists was near the Nkala River, a tributary of the Kafue, in
1893. The year 1895 dated the beginning of Nanzela Mission.
Sijoba in the Zambezi Valley was opened in 1901. Nambala
was opened in 1905. Mudodoli dates from 1907; Kasenga was
opened in 1909; and the Methodists moved from Mudodoli

and Kanchindu and opened another new station in Kampilu in 1910. Chipembi was planted in 1912. In 1915 the station was opened at Kafue.

The first station of the Wesleyan Methodist Missionary Society in Northern Rhodesia was named Chipembi and was established in 1912. The work soon extended to Broken Hill with outstations in the great Luano valley and as far south as the Zambezi.

In 1932 a Northern Rhodesia synod was created to take charge of the two streams of Methodist mission and to combine them into one unified work. The church has in recent years engaged in evangelistic, medical, and educational work in both the Southern and Central Provinces and is now a part of the United Church of Zambia.

Four stations of the United Free Church of Scotland have been planted in Northern Rhodesia and an extension of the work begun in Nyasaland in 1875. The first work in the territory had its beginning at Mwenzo in 1895. Ten years later David Kaunda, the father of Zambia's first president, established Lubwa Mission. A new station was opened at Serenji in 1907, to be moved to Chitambo in 1909. The year 1922 marked the opening at Chasefu.

In 1898 the Dutch Reformed Church of South Africa chose as its Northern Rhodesia field the East Luangwa district, and in 1899 its first station was opened at Magwero. Madzimoyo was established in 1903, and 1905 marked the opening of Nayanje and Fort Jameson. Nsadzu was opened in 1908. Hofmeyer Mission was begun in 1914. and a church was established at Broken Hill in 1921. Merwe Mission was started in 1922, and Tamanda was opened in 1924.

Frederick Stanley Arnot reached the land of the famous Msidi in 1886, and founded Garenganze Mission of the Plymouth Brethren. From about 1897 the Brethren moved southward and across the borders of Northern Rhodesia, investigating the possibility of a mission at Johnson Falls. The field opened in 1901. Kalene Hill was established in 1906, and in 1909 Kaleba was started. A station was begun at Lufimba in 1912. The year 1914 marked the opening of Chitokoloki on the Upper Zambezi. A station at Chilubula was started in 1915. Mansa, later Fort Rosebery, was

opened in 1919. Mubende was started in 1921. In 1922 the
Brethren returned to Johnson Falls and established a new
station at Chavuma on the upper Zambezi river. Kamapanda
and Kanganga were both started in 1923.

The first work of the South African Baptists had its beginning in the Luangwa district of Northern Rhodesia in
1905. Kafulafuta was opened in 1910, and Ndola became the
center for a church in 1924. A European church was established in Ndola in 1952; another at Kitwe in 1956; and three
European congregations were established in 1959—one at
Lusaka, one at Chingola, and one at Luanshya. The European congregations are now fully integrated.

The Southern Baptist Mission Board from the United
States began its work in Northern Rhodesia in the early
sixties. It has concentrated on mission to the Africans
and has a number of churches in Lusaka and along the
rail line through the Copperbelt. In 1966 a publishing center
was opened in Lusaka, with recording studios for the preparation of broadcasting tapes to be used in Zambia and
throughout Africa. There were twelve regular places of
worship in Zambia in 1968. A ministerial training was
opened near Lusaka in 1967.

The Seventh Day Adventists came into Northern Rhodesia
and planted their first station at Rusanga in 1905. The year
1917 marked the opening of Musofu east of Ndola, and Chim-
pempe near Lake Mweru was started in 1921.

The Brethren in Christ opened the first work at Macha
on the Batoka plateau in 1906. In 1923 a station at Sikalongo
was established. A third station at Nahumba was opened
later. All three stations are located in the Choma district.

The Universities' Mission to Central Africa established
its third diocese in Northern Rhodesia in the year 1909.
It was under the direct authority of the Archbishop of Can-
terbury. This relationship remained until 1955 when it
became a diocese of the Province of Central Africa and
changed again in 1964 to be the diocese of Zambia. Stations
of the Universities' Mission were established at both Livingstone and Fort Jameson in 1910. The year 1911 marked the
beginning of Msoro and Mapanza, and in 1912 stations were
opened at Ng'omba and Shakshina. Chilikwa was started in

1915, and Fiwila was established in 1924. As a result of the 1935 riots on the Copperbelt, the Universities' Mission (Anglican Church) joined with others to form the United Missions to the Copperbelt—to provide necessary welfare services and schools. The Anglican Church now has nine large urban parishes. In the early nineteen sixties a large and beautiful cathedral was built at Lusaka.

The South African General Mission opened its first station at Chisalala in 1910. Subsequently the work was extended to Musonweji. The year 1912 dated the beginning of the mission at Lalafuta, which was moved to Musonweji in 1915. The decision was made in 1927 to concentrate on Mukinge Hill near Kasempa. Agreements were made in 1923 between the South African General Mission and the Paris Evangelical Mission to permit the S. A. G. M. to develop the area between the Kabombo and Zambezi rivers west of Livingstone. Kaba Hill and Luampa were opened in 1923. Since 1964 the name of the South African General Mission has changed to the African Evangelical Fellowship.

The work of the Church of Christ in Northern Rhodesia was started by African evangelists from Southern Rhodesia. In 1923 Sinde Mission was established north of Livingstone. Kabanga, on the Zambezi escarpment south of Kalomo, was opened in 1927; and Namwianga was started in 1932. There are today congregations of the Churches of Christ in Lusaka and in the Copperbelt as well.

The Zambia Christian Mission and the Church of Christ Mission have common beginnings both from America and from Southern Rhodesia, though the Zambia Christian Mission came into Zambia in 1962. The first station was opened at Nangoma Court eighty miles west of Lusaka in mid-1963, in the heart of the Sala tribal area. The work has, since 1967, extended to Livingstone, Lusaka, and the Copperbelt.

The African Methodist Episcopal Church is affiliated with the A. M. E. Church of America which broke away from the Methodist Church in the United States in 1787 in opposition to the color bar practised in the Methodist Church. The work in Northern Rhodesia dates from the year 1930 and first started in the Copperbelt.

The work of the Salvation Army had its beginning at the

old government camp at Ibwemunyama in the Batoka district. Stations were soon opened at Mazabuka and Chikankata.

The Scandinavian Independent Baptist Union, established
in the Lamba-Lima Reserve around Ndola in the Copperbelt,
was begun in 1931.

The work of the Pentecostal Assemblies of Canada was
begun in 1955 in the Fort Jameson area and later extended
to the Copperbelt.

The Full Gospel Church of God began its first work in
Northern Rhodesia in the mid-1950s and now has work in
Lusaka and the Copperbelt.

The work of the Wisconsin Synod of the Lutheran Church
is located in the Lusaka area and west of Lusaka. It too had
its beginnings in the mid-1950s.

A Unique Kind of Mission

The World Christian Handbook named twenty-three Protestant Churches and Missions working in Zambia in 1968.
It also noted the Roman Catholic and Independent Churches.
More than half of these societies and churches began before
1910, and five were in the area before 1900 (see Figure 2).
With few exceptions missions have concentrated on education,
and many on medicine, from the beginning. Attention is directed to Figure 2, which illustrates the slow growth of Zambian Protestant Churches.

In eighty-one years the Paris Evangelical Church (through
1962) claimed only 3,066 baptized believers. The London
Missionary Society in seventy-nine years (through 1966) had
8,066 members. The Methodist Church in sixty-five years
(through 1957) reported 1,458 communicants, and the Church
of Scotland in sixty-two years (through 1957) claimed 2,766.
The Brethren, beginning in 1906, had 1,124 members in
1968. The African Evangelical Fellowship reported 4,635
communicants after fifty-eight years of labor. The Church
of Christ, beginning in 1923, reported 1,300 baptized believers in 1968.

Only three Protestant Churches in Zambia showed evidences of reasonable growth. The Dutch Reformed Church,
begun in 1899, claimed 21,113 communicants in 1968. The

COMPARATIVE STUDY
COMMUNICANT MEMBERSHIP
CHURCHES OF ZAMBIA

CHURCH	BEGUN	1949	1952	1957	1962	1968
Paris Evangelical	1885	667	1160	2510	3066	UC*
London Miss. Soc.	1887		4256	7093	8066	UC
Methodist	1893	1660	1028	1458		UC
Church of Scotland	1895			2766		UC
African Reformed (D.R.C.) . . .	1899	14670	14670g	14670g	18101	20000
Dutch Reformed (Mother Ch.) . .	1899					1113
Chr. Miss. to Many Lands . . .	1901	1500	1500	1500	1500	
Baptist, South Africa	1905	234	555	946	1209	
Seventh Day Adventist	1905	3841	5526	8210	8762	13510
Brethren in Christ	1906	449	531	531	735	1124
Anglican	1909	10514	7582	10042	20000	23000
African Evangelical Fel.	1910	1046	1046	2076	2926	4635
Church of Christ	1923	100	1000	1250	1300	1300
Church of the Nazarene						
Full Gospel Church						
Lambaland Baptist Church . . .						1200
Lutheran Church						60
Afr. Methodist Episc. Ch. . . .	1930					7500
New Apostolic Church						
Pentecostal Assmbls. of Can. .	1955					800
Pilgrim Holiness Church						
Pres. Ch. of So. Africa						
Refrmd. Bapt. Miss. of Can. . .						
Salvation Army						
Scandinavian Ind. Bapt.	1931				550	1000
Zambia Christian Mission . . .	1962				150	1348
Southern Baptist	1962					3000

UC* United Church of Zambia
g   Includes Southern Rhodesia

	1968	
Roman Catholic (Community)	1968	449,955
Independent Churches of Zambia (Community)	1968	100,000

Figures from WORLD CHRISTIAN HANDBOOK

Figure 2

Adventists, beginning in 1905, reported 13,510 believers in 1968, and the Anglican Church claimed 23,000 members from 1909 through 1967.

It should be noted here that on up through 1967 an unusual kind of church growth had taken place. The records show that the missions and churches, with but few exceptions, came offering schools---and sometimes clinics or hospitals--- in advance of churches. The oft-stated object of the missionaries was to lift and civilize their converts won through a school-cum-church program to an educated and well-developed Christian status.

Until 1960, for all but a very few Africans, the only way to obtain an education was through the mission school. Few other educational institutions existed. There as they learned to read and write, they were taught the Bible; and many professed the faith and became members of the mission church.

By 1968 the twenty-three Protestant churches listed in the *World Christian Handbook*   (p. 97) reported 104,000 communicant members in 2,000 congregations throughout Zambia, most of them worshiping in school houses and led by teachers in the schools. Only in the cities and at the mission centers were there larger congregations worshiping in church buildings most often built and paid for by the missions.

This kind of school-church approach did not encourage people movements, and few such movements---sometimes called revivals---have taken place in what is now Zambia. One exception occurred shortly after 1926 at Chipili when the Universities' Mission (Anglican) Bishop reported:

Our people are increasing with alarming rapidity. For nearly ten years after we began work at Chipili we deliberately restricted the flow of converts within the narrowest limits possible: circumstances eventually arose which compelled us to relax our restrictions, and the result has been that the stream has burst its banks and well nigh threatens to overwhelm us. (Smith 1928:94).

This type of movement, however, so common during the periods of revival in other parts of the world, was not the rule in Central Africa, and the school-church pattern produced its own unique kind of converts and its own unique kind of growth.

The arguments used by institutionally oriented missionaries for this school-church emphasis will help to explain how this very limited growth was theologically justified.

(1) The pioneers, because of the filth, murder, thievery, immorality, drunkenness, and laziness---which they witnessed---concluded that adult Africans were so pagan and vile as to be beyond salvation. (2) Polygamy, which the early missionaries viewed as adultery, was believed to be so firmly anchored that it was impossible for the majority of adults to accept the Christian Way. (3) The tribes were so evil that it was necessary to break them up and establish a new Christian nontribal society. (4) The only means of solving these problems was by educating the boys and girls through years of schooling. In the schools it was hoped that considerable numbers would become Christian before they married and would remain faithful in spite of old tribal attractions, thus eliminating the curse of polygamy, drunkenness, murder, theft, and other grievous sins. With the gradual dying off of the old pagan generations, the new Christian community, having come through the schools, would rise up to take its place. (5) The obvious responsibility of missions, therefore, was to establish schools, dispensaries, clinics, hospitals. agricultural stations, and social centers and through their combined Christian influences to raise up a new, civilized Christian generation. (6) The only safe growth was controlled steady growth. Great ingatherings must not be allowed. To do so meant unacceptable surrender of Christian convictions, which dare not be permitted. (7) Therefore, slow steady growth was argued to be the best possible kind of growth, and with a new generation of detribalized Christians at the top, the Christian pattern would filter downward through pagan African society until the whole population became enveloped by it.

With missions heavily committed to institutional programs, the above arguments are still used, but the low return in souls added to the household of faith cannot be hidden. The picture can and must be changed.

5

The Growth of Independent Churches

Compared with South Africa, Zambia has few examples of Independent Church movements. The Watchtower Society and the Lumpa Church are the best examples of separatist movements in Central Africa.

The Watchtower Society

The Watchtower movement, or Jehovah's Witnesses, has been a disturbing factor throughout Northern Rhodesia. The movement originated in the United States and is known by such names as Russellites, the International Bible Students' Association, Jehovah's Witnesses, and Watchtower. It teaches that both Roman Catholics and Protestant churches have been rejected by God, and that worldwide chaos will soon bring the Resurrection and Last Judgment. It also emphasizes the imminence of the final celestial conflict with immediate inference that millions now alive will never die.

In 1900, a young Nyasaland Tonga, Kamwana, associated himself with Joseph Booth, affiliated with Jehovah's Witnesses. Booth baptized Kamwana and gave him the name of Elliot. In 1908 Elliot returned to Nyasaland and began preaching. He soon baptized 10,000 people and greatly disturbed the Scottish Presbyterian Mission. By 1910, the government considered Kamwana's teaching that all human governments were doomed dangerous enough to warrant his arrest. He was not, however, considered guilty of subversion and was permitted to return to South Africa.

In recent years the name of Elliot Kamwana has appeared again. The Bamulonda, or People of the Watchman, hail Kamwana as their prophet and founder. They have little influence, but are found in Copperbelt towns and in the Luapula valley. They are now little more than a relic of early prophet movements.

During the First World War Jehovah's Witnesses were proscribed, driving the movement underground. From that time, teaching was propagated entirely by African preachers. Through the 1920s large numbers were won, but the CID found no direct political significance in it, and the government wisely exercised toleration.

In latter 1925, Tom Nyirenda appeared in the Mkushi district as a prophet and witch-finder. He had knowledge of Watchtower doctrines---calling himself "Mwanalesa," God's child. He adapted the rite of immersion to the ancient craft of witch-finding and became an instrument of Chief Shaiwila to get rid of enemies of the chief. In a short period thirty or more were found to be witches and killed. Mwanalesa also declared that leaders of all organized churches and all Europeans were snakes.

Taylor and Lehmann reveal that

> The Native Affairs Department stated at the time that the Watchtower movement cannot be charged with direct responsibility for these murders, but it does appear to have provided the first germ of Mwanalesa's idea and then the prepared soil in which it grew (1961: 26-27).

Likely, after the 1935 disturbances on the Copperbelt, the government laid too much responsibility at the door of the Watchtower Movement.

Groves says that

> The commission appointed to inquire into the disturbances in the Copperbelt in 1935 recorded their conclusion: "The Commission find that the teachings and literature of the Watchtower bring civil and spiritual

authority, especially native authority, into contempt;
that it is a dangerous and subversive movement; and
that it is an important predisposing cause of the recent
disturbances" (1964, Vol. 4:230).

All Witness literature was banned. In some districts chiefs
carried on a campaign of suppression and many meeting
places were destroyed.

The contemporary picture in Zambia is somewhat brighter.
Taylor and Lehmann record that:

In 1959 the Public Relations Officer of the Watchtower
Society wrote that the number of active preaching
members had risen from 15,000 in 1952 to 18,000 in
1959, and that there are now 79,500 Africans and 5,000
European adherents of the Watchtower society in
Northern Rhodesia. A few days later the same news-
paper published a report on the four-day assembly
in Ndola in April, 1959, where 30,800 had gathered
and 400 had been baptized by immersion in a nearby
stream (1961:227).

There is considerable contrast between the prophetic
announcements of 1918 and 1919, when Watchtower prophets
foretold that Europeans would become slaves of Africans,
to the mild refusals of present day Witnesses to take part in
trade union and political activities.

The Lumpa Church

The Lumpa Church dates from September, 1954, when
Alice Lenshina Lubusha of Chinsali is said to have come
back from the dead. During the week after Lenshina had
recovered from a faint, numerous people heard that she had
returned from the dead, that angels brought her books from
heaven, and that Jesus came to speak to her.

In April of 1955 an African minister who knew Lenshina
said:

At that time Alice started to proclaim the Good News
with all her power, and telling people about Jesus
Christ. She said that the people should stop adultery
and hatred and cursing and stealing and lies and
swearing (Taylor and Lehmann 1961:249).

At first she was zealous in bringing people to the church. Because of her great faith people believed her.

In the 1954 planting season, she gave people seeds to mix with their own seeds; and she began pronouncing blessings on their seeds. At the same time she began baptizing, though leaders of the church tried to stop her. She next started admonishing people to bring their magic charms to her, for only then would they be saved.

In a short time people from all the northern districts, Protestants and Catholics, were coming to her. Her fame spread beyond her tribe, into Southern Rhodesia, Tanzania, and the Congo. Soon many came to be baptized, and returning to their homes built small churches in which they held services as often as three times a week.

Worship consisted of simple hymns Alice had taught them and listening to self-appointed preachers whom Lenshina granted permission to proclaim her message.

There was fear on the part of the government that Lenshina's movements were a repetition of early witch-finding movements in Nyasaland in 1934, but she did not need to point out those who used witchcraft. Masses flocked to her voluntarily to rid themselves of all their objects of magic.

A pupil of a nearby Catholic School reported to the White Fathers after a holiday that he had seen a whole hut full of magic implements, including rosaries and crucifixes, which the converts had given Lenshina before their baptism (Taylor and Lehmann 1961:251).

Older missions tried to keep their numbers in orthodox ways, but Lenshina's promise of salvation to all who brought their objects of magic for her to destroy proved more attractive than the efforts of missions churches. Shortly, those who refused to make the pilgrimage were accused of unwillingness to give up their witchcraft, and a number of African priests were threatened. When the matter was brought to trial a near riot ensued.

By 1958 the schism was complete, and the government had to recognize the new "church" as a fact. Now the name "Lumpa Church" appeared, and the government became aware of the moral and doctrinal views of Lenshina and the Lumpa Church. The movement was often charged with deception, and its leaders were accused of extortion. It is doubtful that the charges were true. In the late 1950s Lenshina was accused of being a tool of radical politicians. This charge, too, was unfounded.

Zambia's first Prime Minister, Kenneth Kaunda, came into office January 23, 1964. Within months his government was engaged in violent military clashes with the followers of Alice Lenshina. Tension had been mounting---causes of which are somewhat obscure---but almost certainly they had to do with local officials of the United National Independent Party trying to force Lumpa church members to join the party. In 1963 attempts were made by Kaunda himself to smooth out the dissension, but outbreaks continued. During the first half of 1964, followers of the Lumpa church began harassing neighboring areas. As a result, government forces were dispatched to the district.

By this time 5,000 hard-core members of the sect had gathered at Sione. On July 30, the security forces surrounded the village and after being attacked fought their way into the church.

Hall says:

. . . 74 people died and 40 were wounded. As a reprisal, the Lumpa followers attacked Lundazi township, over-running it, capturing the police station and killing 150 persons before fleeing at dawn. Senga tribesmen wiped out the Lumpa village of Paishuko; there were 46 victims. Although Alice Lenshina herself surrendered on August 11, and was placed in indefinite detention in Mumbwa prison near Lusaka, elements of the sect continued to hide in the Luangwa valley until the end of 1964. Some fled as far as the Congo. In all, the Lenshina troubles cost at least 700 lives; this official estimate is conservative. (1965:229-230).

With Lenshina in detention the sect has created no further trouble since 1964.

Other Small Schisms

Breakaway from European-sponsored missions was evident through the 1950s. The objection was that the European

missionaries were agents of the government. So in the cities
of Mufilira and Chingola divisions came from the Plymouth
Brethren's Christian Mission in Many Lands. Similar pro-
tests were apparent with the Children of the Sacred Heart,
a breakaway from the Roman Catholics. Objection to European domination is voiced in the claim that Europeans have
lost their place as successors to the promises of God and
Africans now have a stronger inclination towards spiritual
things than do the white man.

When Jesus was persecuted by the European Herod,
God sent him into Africa; By this we know that Afri-
cans have naturally a true spirit of Christianity
(Taylor and Lehmann 1961:267).

The Problem of Syncretism

Studies like Sundkler's *Bantu Prophets in South Africa*,
or Welbourn's *East African Rebels*, or Barrett's *Schism
and Renewal in Africa*, underscore the urgency for consideration of the independent churches.

Evidences of syncretism among these churches are easy
to find. Examples may be given.

Among the people of the Watchtower, Elliot Kamwana,
prophet and founder, is believed to be the seventh "angel"
in the history of the Christian church. In worship, dancing,
and drumming---"as in old times"---are used. Michael is
Jesus Christ. They do not believe in shaking hands nor in
European medicine. They keep the food laws of the Old Testament and practise polygamy. Tom Nyirenda, who appeared
as a prophet in 1925 in the Mkushi district adapted baptismal
immersion to the craft of witch-finding. The "return from
death" with a message for those still alive is common among
many independent groups. Alice Lenshina is the best example,
but there are others.

In the Lumpa church only Lenshina baptizes, and baptism
takes on a purifying concept. Through baptism those who
have used magic or charms are purified, and Lenshina is a
glorified witch doctor exorcising witches and evil spirits.
It seems obvious that Lenshina is linked with "ngulu"-
possession. Ngulu refer to

Secondary divinities whose abode is supposed to be in
waterfalls, large trees, pythons, and is also used as
a name for a person possessed by such a divinity, a
"chief of spirits,"---("mfumu ya mipashi").

Taylor and Lehmann, in linking Ngulu with Lenshina say:
These "Ngulu" prophesy and heal, that is, they have
the power to find out under whose authority is the
spirit who troubles the sick person. When this is established, the sick person is initiated, and on joining
the society of the "ngulu"---"it is a kind of church"
. . . his sickness will stop. "Sometimes when a man
becomes an "ngulu," he will find that he has the power
of healing and he knows how to give people medicines
which can cure them." One of the best known "ngulu"
is Mulenga. This name, however, is very common
among Bemba people, and it is therefore possible
that Lenshina's use of it has no connection with former
spirit possession or initiation. It is difficult to assess
whether, in many people's minds, this name still
evokes the idea of a supernatural being, whose concern is with healing. A hospital orderly who is one
of the best respected church elders in the Northern
Province said that the "ngulu" represent the main
belief and practice which challenge the Church. It is
perhaps not just coincidence that of her four names,
Alice Lenshina Mulenga Lubusha, the prophetess has
chosen as the important ones, with which she signs
her letters, the two middle ones, the names of two
powerful "spirits," one of the new and one of the old
religions of her country (Taylor and Lehmann, 1961:
267).

Missionaries Contributing to the Problem

Kraemer declares that the missionary takes too much for
granted when he presents the message of the Gospel. The
missionary is under obligation
to strive for the presentation of the Christian truth
in terms and modes of expression that make its challenge intelligible and related to the peculiar quality
of reality in which they (the peoples among whom he

labors) live (1947:303).

The Gospel must be related to all problems of life. Missions have often registered alarm to the splintering off of nativistic sects, never realizing that a share of the fault may lie with the missions themselves. Perhaps their message did not relate to the problems of family and tribal life in a way that African people could comprehend. Africans see religion as all-inclusive. Their civilization and structure of society are rooted in religion, and introducing Christianity should affect every aspect of their lives.

To suggest that missionaries are guilty of contributing to syncretistic nativism through failure to make the message relevant is disturbing. It is also disconcerting that we have contributed to the evil through proclamation of our own accretions which, as Jack Shepherd says,

> get mixed up with the essential core of truth and even confuse and conceal the message. Such a blending or combination, though it is not deliberate and may be well intentioned, is actually syncretism (quoted in Lindsell, 1966:91).

The Essential Core of the Gospel

The danger for evangelical missionaries is not that they will be compromised by an eclectic or ecumenical syncretism. So far from allowing themselves to be drawn to that common denominator that rejects the corn of the Gospel for the sake of peace and union, they have insisted on protecting the truth of the Gospel with considerable husk and they have proclaimed the husk as being an indispensable part of the truth. In the encounter with non-Christians, however, missionaries must get to the essential Gospel. This requires the peeling away of layers of accretion which the missionaries, and their supporting denominations, have attached to the central message.

The missionary's Western way of life has no sanction in Scripture, though often he has equated it with the Christian Way. It is one of the layers that must be peeled away. There are standards that have special significance to the Western missionary. To go counter to those standards within his

own culture might be offensive, but they are not part of the
basic message, and they must be removed. Ecclesiastical
traditions must go. These, to African Christians seeking to
be acceptable children of the Father, are viewed as an af-
front.

On January 4, 1967, the President of Zambia said in part:
There may be many good reasons why the Christian
Gospel came to us in the form of the "denominations"
of the West, but I cannot see any good reason for those
same denominations continuing in these days. We become more and more confused as new sects from the
West spring up in our towns. How can I believe in the
sincerity of Christians who, in Lusaka alone hold
seventeen separate denominational services for Europeans every Sunday. This denominational idiocy is a
terrible condemnation of Christianity, and is a con-
fusion to my people and to myself. (Copy of an address given before the Synod of the United Church of
Zambia, in possession of the author).

We are called to reveal the central truths of the Gospel
and then allow the Spirit of God to work through the hearts
of those who have heard and accepted the message. The
binding of externals onto the heart of the Gospel and making
them of equal value with the Gospel may so obscure the message that it is misunderstood or rejected.

The missionary must also allow for creative expression
in the witness and worship of the young church. The new
formulation of Christian life cannot possibly duplicate his
experience of salvation or his expression of faith.

Visser 't Hooft has said:
Is there no place for any form of dialogue between
Christians and non-Christians? Our answer would
have to be affirmative, if dialogue left no room for
witness. But that is not the case... The presupposi-
tion of genuine dialogue is not that the partners agree
beforehand to relativize their own convictions, but
that they accept each other as persons . . .I do not
impose my personality on him but put myself at his
disposal with all that I am. As a Christian I cannot
do this without reporting to him what I have come to

know about Jesus Christ. I shall make clear that I consider my faith not as an achievement but as a gift of grace, a gift that excludes all pride, but which obliges me to speak gratefully of this Lord to all who will hear it (1963:117).

Visser 't Hooft is right in suggesting that the missionary must recognize those to whom he witnesses as persons, and he must reveal the saving power of Jesus Christ. But the missionary must exercise care. It is possible for him to impose his own personality upon his hearers, and his faith as an achievement of which he is very proud. Nonetheless it is true that the missionary must feel a community of fellowship with those to whom he is witnessing. He must know himself to be one with them. Bavinck says it very well:

As long as I laugh at his foolish superstition, I look down upon him; I have not yet found the key to his soul. As soon as I understand that what he does in a noticeably naive and childish manner, I also do and continue to do again and again, although in a different form; as soon as I actually stand next to him, I can, in the name of Christ stand in opposition to him and convince him of sin, as Christ did with me and still does each day (1964:242-243).

And Kraemer has said:

The real Christian contention is not: "We have the revelation and not you," but pointing gratefully and humbly to Christ: "It has pleased God to reveal himself fully and decisively in Christ; repent, believe, and adore" (1947:119).

The missionary himself is the point of contact. It is "by the foolishness of preaching," as frightening as the responsibility is, that men of any tribe or race or country or continent are saved.

A Growing Theology

Missionaries in Africa have not always appreciated the place of the Old Testament in their witnessing. Kraemer has pointed out that

people who adhere to tribal religions, and the masses
in the great cultural religions that practically belong
to the sphere of so-called primitive religion, are
more impressed by the Old than by the New Testament. The Old Testament is in the real sense of the
word to them the door to Christ (1947:331n).

Traditional African thinking was mythical. Before introduction of the Christian Way, traditional religion was bound
up with the beginning of things. It had a world view that
gave explanation of the creation-primeval age. The story of
the first man and the development of mankind was fundamental to this conception of life. Though their myths were different, yet each tribe claimed its own "original revelation"
around which it enacted annually recurrent festivals. These
myths spanned the whole of existence---from heaven to the
individual heart.

With this world view so near with relation to their Chris-
tial walk, it is natural that they see the parallel between
their primitive world view and the Biblical revelation of the
beginning. They see in the creation story their own beginnings as the people of God. History is a remembrance of
that which was in the beginning. Recognizing this, it is not
difficult to see why the Old Testament is central to the theological conception of African pastors.

Sundkler has seen this:

The Old Testment in the African setting is not just a
book of reference. It becomes a source of remembrance. The African preacher feels that Genesis belongs to him and his church, or rather vice versa---
that he and his African church belong to those things
which were in the beginning (1962:104).

For this reason they take such an interest in Abraham and
Moses. These figures are recognized as archetypes and are
reproduced in rich and tangible terms. The pastor becomes
leader of the flock, bringing his people from bondage to the
promised land.

One other focus of the theological encounter relates to
the situation in Zambia. This has to do with the corporate
life of the clan . . . the link between the living on earth and
the generations of "living dead" ancestors gone from their

earthly existence but still very present and alive. The clan system keeps before its members the facts of life: the importance of the fertility of the individual, the place of the family, the significance of marriage and procreation, the continuity of birth, life, and death.

More clearly than the missionary, the African has seen the demands the clan puts before the Church. Concern for the life of the extended family on the one hand and for death and the ancestors on the other presents the Church with one of its most persistent challenges.

The lives of Lenshina, Mulolani, Kamwana, and Nyirenda of Zambian Independent churches reveal the close relationship between the leader and clan. The linking of ngulu with Lenshina is an expression of the loyalty of Lenshina to the clan and ancestors---to the things of the past, just as surely as teaching about Jesus Christ link her and her followers to the Christian Way. One can see the ambivalence of her clan relationship. The traditional clan fellowship is loaded with pagan values, and she has bent to them. The independent, separatist churches of Zambia carry the dangers of prophet movements of other parts of Africa. Fortunately Zambia is not plagued with many such movements.

One can hope in Zambia that young churches will become a witness before the world to Christian unity rather than turning to a separatistic nativism similar to that of South Africa.

III

The Main Mission
Approaches of the Past

6

The Educational Missions Approach

The pioneer missionaries were faced with the problem of persuading the Africans to attend school. The African people had little desire for Western education. They could see no reason for learning to read and write, and the early missionaries found that gathering the Africans for instruction was an all but helpless effort (Rotberg 1965:43). All sorts of enticements were used. Some used coercion. Others offered gifts.

The Obvious Need for Education

By 1901, only small success had been realized, and for another twenty-five years missionaries continued to have difficulty in bringing students into their schools and in holding them. They faced constant competition. Lands had to be cleared. Grain had to be planted. Fields had to be protected. Fish were running in the rivers. Game asked to be hunted. These long-established chores could not be easily changed, and attendance in school suffered.

Rotberg recounts (1965:38) that Frederick Stanley Arnot described vividly the "awful heathenism" by which he was surrounded. Francois Coillard declared that the Lozi were without exception "utter heathen." Missionaries of the London Missionary Society were eloquent in their condemnation of the "cowardly, lazy, thieving and depraved Mambwe." The Primitive Methodists wrote of the "purely heathen" Mashuku-lumbwe. It was said of the Ila that they were beer-drinking, fornicating polygamists.

It is not easy in 1970 for national leaders of Zambia or for missionaries to understand the difficulties facing the pioneers. Some have accused the missionaries of unpardonable severity in their criticism, but they lived in the midst of a rough, cruel and heartless social order dedicated to a way of life which enabled survival in a crude and savage age. They moved into Central Africa shortly after the Zulu wars that took millions of lives and created an upheaval in Africa south of the equator that is still felt today. It must also be remembered that slave raiders were still preying on the tribes with kidnapping, plundering, and thieving as their stock in trade, and great areas were left desolate.

Arnot gave a vivid description of the practices he witnessed in 1882:

> Nothing of importance can be sanctified without human sacrifice---in most cases a child . . . A common occurrence is tying the victim hand and foot, and laying him near a nest of black ants, which in a few days pick his bones clean. The details of scenes which I have been forced to witness are too horrible to put on paper (Mackintosh 1950:10).

Two factors stand out in this period. The first is that the missionaries would continue to live and work in the midst of such horror. The experiences of the Coillards at Sesheke in 1885 were shared by others:

> The very first night they crossed the river, some fugitive women rushed into their camp and implored Madame Coillard, who was alone at the moment, to save them, as the king's people had arrived to execute their menfolk (as rebels) and they expected to be killed too . . . There were no means of protecting the poor creatures, who, before dawn, had all been massacred (Mackintosh 1950:13).

The second factor is that a change for the better was soon apparent. Introduction of law through the chartered company did much, but the influence of the missionaries, living in close proximity with these tribes meant even more in eliminating those tragedies of eighty years ago.

The decision to concentrate on educating the children was sound. If they could not plant churches because of the sinfulness of the adults, they would build schools in anticipation of churches yet to come through children converted in them. It was not long until missionaries gave pride of place to provision of schools with religious and secular emphases, and the educational missions approach became the most important of all their preoccupations.

Thus a distinctive kind of mission came into being. The educational missions approach with the school coming in advance of the Church is peculiar to Central Africa. There are few tribal societies where it is possible for children of animistic parents to become Christian without going counter to family and tribal authority patterns. This could not happen in Latin America or India or in the South Pacific where children would not dare make a decision that might drastically affect the future of the tribe.

This unique missions approach made obvious the need for concentration on education. If through the schools many could be made Christian, then the missions would concentrate on education.

The Growing Demand for Schools

This picture of the early twentieth century changed rapidly after 1924. The early resistance against education soon became a demand for education, and missions soon found themselves with a task of accelerating proportions. Now instead of the missionaries coercing Africans to attend school, African communities were begging the missions to provide them. From the missions' point of view there was unquestioned need and an opportunity they dare not ignore. They had come to lead the people to know Christ, but how could these pagans understand the Gospel if they could not read? Furthermore, it was argued that education itself was an investment that would result in better citizens and, ultimately, better Christians. In 1925 the government took over African education, facing the task of establishing a unified curriculum, raising the standards of teaching, and providing means of paying grants to mission societies who, by meeting government standards, would still operate and manage schools (Hall 1965:135).

Up to that time the objective of missions was to produce teacher-evangelists, and most were hardly literate. Establishing a higher standard forced larger missions to create teacher-training centers. This demanded recruitment of qualified educationists from overseas. The Department of Education examined candidates, granted teacher's certificates to those qualified and began paying small subsidies to provide salaries and texts and other needs.

By 1936, the demand for schools was greater than missions could supply, even with the help of the government. Numerous unaided "bush schools," without any facilities and with unqualified teachers, were springing up in many parts of the territory. These bush schools had enrolled 83,000 children, almost four times the enrollment of approved government-aided institutions (Hall 1965:136). Admittedly they were very nearly worthless, but they demonstrated that the African peoples were now clamoring for education. This cry will probably continue till every child is in school.

The first schools provided by missions were usually situated at the village of the chief. Initially children came from neighboring committees, but shortly the central school could not cope with the numbers wanting to attend. Outlying schools were soon provided. The central school would then advance to upper primary and, in a number of instances, to secondary level. As interest grew, committees of capable, highly respected headmen, elders, and chiefs were formed. They were allowed to collect tuition fees to be used for textbooks and for other equipment. The value of these committees grew, and out of them came district advisory-committees.

There was a constantly growing clamor for education. At first the plea was for lower primary schools, but lower schools expanded into upper, and upper into secondary, and secondary schools are now expanding into the University of Zambia.

The School-Key Opened the Door for Missions

Missions were quick to see the advantage of schools in anticipation of churches. The African peoples were eager to accept the schools, willing that missions should propagate their doctrines if only schools were there. In less fortunate areas within the past decade, African communities vied with each other to attract mission societies, ostensibly inviting them to bring them the Gospel, but with the condition that schools come first. If schools would be provided, assurances were made that the people would gladly join the church (and thus have the advantage of schools).

One should not be critical of the African's equating of church and school or of his attempt to bargain with missionaries in offering his membership to one to get the other. He had observed the missionary practices very well. After all, they had agreed to provide schools on condition that the adults and children go to church each Sunday. There was little distance between missionary policy of the recent past and the Africans' own contemporary policy.

This polite game of offering schools for churches and churches for schools has also been popular with the Department of Education in the government.

To illustrate, I recall my first contact with government officials in Northern Rhodesia in August, 1955. When I revealed the purpose of my 2,000 mile flight from Cape Town to Livingstone, I was taken to the Provincial Educational Officer. It was assumed that if our mission proposed to open a field in the Gwembe Valley it would begin through provision of schools. The We people of the valley needed them. All missions of Northern Rhodesia were in the education business, and thus our mission must share it too. No objection was expected by the Provincial Education Officer, nor was any offered. I was anxious that our mission get into Northern Rhodesia at this time in her history. The provision of schools was the key. Committments were made so that the Christian Church might enter the country, not to major in education, but to give first place to evangelism. The educational commitments would serve as a means to an end, but the end in view was evangelism.

Missionaries of our fellowship in Africa in the mid-fifties were anxious to use the educational key to open new fields in both Northern and Southern Rhodesia. Every encouragement was given by our supporting American churches to use this means of getting into these new lands. At least a dozen new areas have been opened with schools being the key that unlocked the doors.

Not only did we have to convince the Department of Education that we would provide schools. Chief Shakumbila and Sala tribal heads plainly stated that schools were the condition of their wanting the mission to come. I gladly committed ourselves to an educational program that brought approval from the chief and his advisers, for I was convinced that schools were effective avenues through which souls could be won for Christ.

The pioneer missionary, Edwin W. Smith, was convinced of the value of education as a means of evangelizing:

The Missions, with hardly an exception, have always given education a prominent place in their programme. If they were asked the reason, they might reply that the schools have been their best evangelistic agency. Probably ninety per cent of the Christians have come into the Church by way of the school (1928:153).

The Christian Church was concerned about the spiritual welfare of the people. If through teaching African children, numbers of them could be won to the Lord, then the educational key would be used.

The Educational Approach
Popular with the Missionary

In June of 1963, I flew into the Zambezi Valley of Southern Rhodesia to survey the area with the possibility of opening a new mission field among the Tonga people. This was the first of many surveys, and the impression influenced my thinking for years to come. After watching the hundreds of excited Tonga dancing and singing around my airplane, the crowd opened to make way for Chief Binga. This was our first meeting, and, presenting him with a lovely gift, I introduced myself to him.

"Ndiya Umfundisi uRandall." (I am missionary-teacher Randall.)

This pagan, polygamous, spirit-worshiping chief responded, "Umfundisi, iskolo, ihospitaal."

There was no mistaking the fervent prayer of this pagan chief. He was saying, "Please, missionary, bring my people schools and a hospital." Nothing more was needed to persuade me of the value of education and medicine as the legitimate tool of mission.

Numerous arguments in favor of schools have been given to supporting churches back home. Some are very plausible. All have been given within an evangelistic context with strong affirmation that schools are the tools of the Church, that education is a means to an end, and that through Christian educational emphasis has come the most fruitful means of evangelizing the African.

Through schools the evangelistic thrust is directed to the young people, and the strongest arguments for the educational approach are that it will convert and Christianize the oncoming generation. We have used this argument, and have quoted astounding figures to prove the point. No other method has produced comparable results.

Missions educational emphasis has been popular with the Department of Education, and those sharing in the program have been favored by the government. The future of every mission depends on its relationship with the government, and missionaries are aware of this.

Missions offering education are popular with the people themselves, but subtle arguments underscoring the popularity of the school-centered approach with the missionaries suggest other motivations as well. The school emphasis is popular because of the material, visible, and numerical results produced. One's soul would be cold if it were unaffected by 100 baptisms in the jungle stream. But it is impossible to assess the real spiritual impact upon newly converted young people soon to be scattered over the countryside. It is difficult and perhaps impossible, to follow, nurture, and guide them into mature Christian growth. To report such labor is apt to sound unrewarding and perhaps to imply waste of missions money.

The popularity of the school program comes because it produces tangible results. It requires schools made of brick and steel, and easily photographed construction in which the missionary is participant. It provides a roll call of thousands of children walking miles each day to the school. These children, hungrily seeking knowledge, are very concrete. Like the buildings and the books, they can be seen. Praise God for this work, but it is often popular only because its apparent goodness covers up the lack of spiritual emphasis and the scarcity of churches that are churches in their own right.

It is also popular because it attracts large sums of money from overseas. The physical and visible, the classrooms filled with children, serve as continuous propaganda for attracting a steady flow of finance. Subsidies granted to a mission sponsoring schools with a hundred teachers and thousands of students amounts to many thousands of dollars annually. The larger the overseas income and the greater the subsidies, the more rapidly the program will expand, attracting more overseas money and more subsidies for more expansion.

It is agreed that all of this is a means towards the evangelization of Africa, but a study of progress reports reveal little said about evangelism or building of churches and efforts to save the lost. William Read points out that

Institutions tend to become ends in themselves. The school aims to become an excellent educational instrument. Finances often determine policies and in the end it becomes an efficient school, but the main purpose for which it was founded, that is, serving the work of evangelization of the National Church has been pushed so far into the background that it is practically forgotten. . . This evolution can take place in hospitals or any other institution (1965:89).

The Education Approach
Popular with Supporting Churches

Congregations of children with a smattering of adults worshiping in clean, well-lighted rooms of the brick school buildings are more impressive than a congregation worshiping in a mud-walled, thatch-roofed hut with a cow-dung floor.

The visible property makes the educational approach popular with home churches. American congregations, involved as they have been in the building of new edifices, have come to judge the growth of the church by the size and cost of the building in which it worships. The transition from America to the mission field setting is not difficult, and a description of a hundred schools with three hundred classrooms offering facilities for thousands of students is exciting, especially when it is stated that this is the tool effectively pointing young Africa to Christ.

The American congregation is inclined to compare the annual growth on the field with the annual growth of that one single congregation. Assuming that the home church has added 100 to its membership during the year, a thousand from the field sounds like tremendous growth. There is little comprehension of the fact that the mission field encompasses many congregations with extensive investment and outreach across the entire nation.

Missions sponsored by the Christian Churches in southern Africa have been as fruitful as any they have underwritten across the world. The resulting arguments sound conclusive. African missions have stressed education. African missions have consistently reported large numbers of souls won annually. This great growth, it is concluded, has come because African missions have majored in the educational approach. Perhaps other fields should do the same.

The Schools as Tools of Evangelism

The large ingathering of young men and women into the African churches is proof that schools are effective instruments through which the Gospel can be taught. In our schools in Zambia, one of the rules was that children must attend Sunday School each Sunday. At least ninety per cent of our enrollment was in Sunday School. Our mission was in good company. Other missions had made the same stipulation. Rotberg, writing of the early twentieth century, says that the missionaries compelled the school children "to attend morning services and Sunday meetings" (1965:iii).

After missions began accepting subsidies, the above rule could not be arbitrarily enforced. However, since our mission was paying its own way we were able to enforce regular attendance as missionaries from other missions advised us to do, though the rule did not need enforcement. For every child in school there were two or three out of school because there was no place for them. African parents, with their children in school, reasoned that it was expedient for them to attend religious services — rule or no rule. Attendance might be that additional factor necessary to keep their children in the classroom, or to make way for younger brothers and sisters to come.

During the school week the children took the government-prescribed Bible study, shaped to the theology of the sponsoring mission, and on the Lord's Day, either by rule, or out of expediency, the children attended services. They afforded a captive congregation that the missionaries could depend upon.

That students in our mission schols are taught by qualified Christian teachers has been an argument needing constant qualification. No mission has been able to employ only teachers of its own faith, nor has it been able to maintain a Christian standard. Roman Catholics employ Protestants. Protestants employ Roman Catholics and those of other faiths or no faith. Many missionaries have complained about the disregard of their teachers for the Church, and I have known godly men to weep because of the moral decay in their schools that got its start through the teaching staff. There are many notable exceptions, but too often the influence of the teachers in Kingdom building is little more than a myth.

The problem as defined by Basil Mathews in India in the early twentieth century is a perfect description of the educational dilemma of missions in Central Africa:

> Because of the dearth of educated Christians to cope with the multitude of students, the missionaries had to fall back on Hindu and Muslim professors of science or law . . . But this intensive effort led relatively few educated Indians to give their lives as disciples of Christ (1960:151).

I determined that our educational program would not accept government subsidies. We paid our own way, surpassing government standards as to buildings, texts, curriculum, teachers' qualifications, salaries, and in every other requirement. We set the standards. We wanted desperately to maintain a high Christian level. Our teachers knew that we could dismiss them for any serious misdemeanor, but out of the first eleven men employed, all commended for Christian moral integrity, we had to release five because of adultery. Had we accepted subsidies, we could not have removed those men even for so serious a charge as immorality. Immediately a mission accepted government subsidy it lost control almost entirely of its teachers.

Once a mission assumes the responsibility of schools, that responsibility must be maintained. Schools have to function. Buildings have to be provided. Teachers have to be employed. Salaries have to be paid. Supplies have to be kept in stock. Books have to be kept up-to-date. Correspondence has to be handled. Community-school differences have to be solved. There is no end to the problems, and they do not diminish. When the school year begins, teachers have to be in the classrooms. Dedicated men of high moral caliber of any faith are difficult to find. It is next to impossible to staff the schools with teachers from the church of that mission only. I know of none who are doing it.

The stultifying truth is that regardless of the lack of qualifications of the staff, the schools have to go on. African people have only a minor concern about the morality of the teachers, and government has only a secondary concern. Mission involved in educational responsibilities finds itself in a constant state of tension. It has a high Christian standard to maintain, but it is faced with the sober truth that it is not and will not be able to do it. And yet the schools must go on. The mission is committed. Subsidies from the government demand it. Its relationship to the communities decree it. (The tie that binds the community and the mission is always the school in a missions-school context, regardless of what the church emphasis may be. The church is a minor consideration.) If the mission loses its right to the schools, it will lose its right to the communities because the government.

will turn the educational program over to another agency. African people will accept the change because the schools have first place over the church. Their reasoning is logical. In their relationships with the mission, the mission gave first consideration to the schools. Why should they not do it too?

One of the affirmations of missions involved in education is that Christian teaching is prescribed in the curriculum by the Department of Education. We have rejoiced in the courses in religious instruction. Forty-five minutes a day for every class is given to Bible study, and at the end of each year children are examined as they are on geography or arithmetic. There are weaknesses, however, that are seldom mentioned. The impact of religious instruction can be measured by the caliber of the teachers. The spiritual vacuum of the teaching staff can be multiplied by the students receiving instruction from the unspiritual teachers. Ideally, Scripture study is a marvelous blessing. Beginning each day with prayer is a strong argument for continued participation in secular teaching. The argument has, however, forced a theological opinion in the minds of the African people, and often in the minds of the missionaries, that these studies and prayers are as important as the establishment of congregations. They may be even more important because they teach more Bible and teach it better. The American churches are persuaded of the same thing. This is excellent mission work. Exposing so many young people to the Gospel is ideal mission, whether souls are saved or churches are planted or not.

But schools are not the body of Christ. They do not baptize. They do not celebrate the Lord's Supper. They are increasingly run by the government. The school is no substitute for the church.

Missions involved in education have used the numerical factor to justify the unbalance of educational emphasis. During the 1966 school year the Zambia Christian Mission reported 830 baptisms. In spite of the fact that the first breakthrough in village evangelism came during that year, the majority of the converts came through the school program.

Till 1966 no in-depth study had been made by any mission in Zambia or Rhodesia to determine how many of these children developed into sound adult Christians. Many lost through lack of shepherding could be salvaged. Seldom is this done. The reason is that personnel involved in the school program have little time for this essential ministry. Schools created to be the servants of mission have become exacting task-masters.

Why are young Africans apparently so easily persuaded to reject their tribal ways in favor of Christianity? Why do their still-pagan parents allow them to move counter to the accepted decision-making patterns? It is not that the pagan African looks lightly upon his animistic religion. It is inseparably bound to the whole of his life, his fields, crops, cattle, the seasons, the fertility of his wife, the unexpected and unknown, sickness and health, and life and death. He is not apt to do anything that will anger his ancestors and bring evil upon himself, his family, his village, or his tribe. To allow his children to reject the ancestors for the Christian faith could bring catastrophe.

It is safe to assume that pagan Africans have recognized the tensions created by the demands of mission-oriented education. They have developed a sort of theological accommodation all their own that says it is permissable with the ancestors for the children to profess Christianity because of advantages that outward allegiance to mission offers them. That the ancestors do not disapprove is seen in the fact that no curses have come, and in any case it is general knowledge in the adult community that many of the children revert to the old ways after they have finished school. John B. Grimley suggests that this is so (1966:202).

The African knows the results being sought by missions. He has observed the pattern of carelessness that gives emphasis to ingatherings and little concern for those who drop out of the Church. He sees the stress given to special days, to baptismal services at the stream, to the suggestion oft-repeated that children in the schools should become Christians (or, to the African, members of the mission church). His mathematical limitations may not permit him to count beyond the number of his fingers and toes, but he can see the hundreds being brought into the church, though year following year that congregation never grows. He concludes that the missionaries are only concerned about bringing in large numbers of school children and that the continued faithfulness of those brought in is of little consequence.

It is easy to allow children to "join the mission church." This makes it less difficult for them to receive the blessing of the mission, and there are always younger brothers and sisters coming along, and it will be easier for them.

School-Orientated Evangelism a Means to Offset Polygamy

The greatest single problem missionaries of Zambia have had to face is the problem of polygamy. The missionary Arnot had to come to grips with the practice immediately he began to work among the Lozi in 1882. It is said that he "urged the Chief (Lewanika) to eliminate witchcraft and trials by ordeal, to eschew sacrifices to idols, and to forbid adultery and polygyny" (Rotberg 1965: 15). So frustrating has the problem been that missionaries concluded that it was impossible for adults of a polygamous household to become Christian. The only way to overcome this problem must be through schools. Getting the children while they were small and keeping them in the classrooms and persuading them to become Christians before marriage would bring an end to polygamy. There are fewer polygamous households in Zambia today than forty years ago, but it is doubtful whether this can be attributed as much to missions as to the changing economic structure. Polygamy is still of significance to mission. Radical changes must be made in the approach to the problem.

Losses When Children Leave School

In July and August of 1967, I shared in village surveys in Zambia. With other missionaries of the Christian Churches I visited thirty-seven villages among the Sala tribespeople. The Methodist Church had carried on schools in this area for more than sixty years. We had been in a part of the district for four years and had baptized hundreds of young people through our school-centered program.

The field research proved to be of crucial importance.
Here it is sufficient to say that the missions-school approach
has left few lasting converts. I have discussed this problem
with missionaries from other backgrounds. The reports
differ little, irrespective of the mission. The children who
remain with the church after completing their studies are
from Christian homes. Children from non-Christian homes
revert to the ancestor worship of their tribal patterns.

The Problem of Immobility

Roland Allen said, "We must treat the external as the
servant, not the master" (1964:109). Often schools built to be
the servants of mission become the taskmasters. If there is
a shortage of funds and a decision is made between evangelism and schools, evangelism suffers, for schools have to be
maintained. If there is a shortage of personnel, or time, it
is not schools that suffer. The future of the mission with its
relationship to the government and the community is dependent on the educational program. If anything must give, it is
evangelism, village preaching, and church-building. Missionaries, now slaves of the system they helped to create,
have lost their freedom and mobility to preach. All their
time is required by the schools.

Schools also circumscribe the missionary geographically.
Once the schools have been built and are functioning, the mission is chained to the area. Perhaps the church does not
grow. It makes little difference. The missions' investment
in time and resources, and the institution it has created,
binds it to this limited geographical spot whether churches
result or not.

In school-centered communities where people are responsive and churches are planted, the picture still is not bright.
The assumption that schools are effective tools of evangelism
that plants a church in every hamlet and village and city ward
is without foundation. The outreach of the mission is not
more than five miles beyond its outlying schools. The evangelistic outreach is defined by the outreach of its schools. In
a few years the field is saturated with the Gospel. Reachable
families have been reached. From that time the only in-

gathering comes through children of the schools. It is not difficult to understand why ninety per cent of all converts come through the educational approach. This is the only real source. Nor is it difficult to understand why there are great losses once the school-convert has finished his education--- particularly with the un-Christian example he gets through many of his teachers. Though the area has been Gospel-saturated, yet the missionaries must stay. They are tied to the school system. They have lost their mobility. Let the neighboring tribe a hundred miles away become receptive. The missionaries are committed to a static institution and a static area, and unless other help can be found, the neighboring tribe must go unevangelized.

Melvin Hodges has said:

The missionary must be a man of dedication who will consider himself expendable. He must be willing to keep himself mobile and sufficiently flexible so that his program and plans can be guided by the Spirit of God (McGavran, Guy, Hodges, and Nida 1965:34).

The institution demanding oversight of the missionary to satisfy the government denies the expendability of the missionary. He cannot leave. His first responsibility is no longer to the people, nor to his Lord, but to the government. Schools destroy his mobility. They destroy his flexibility. They deny his freedom to develop a program which can be guided by the Spirit of God.

Nida has written:

Elaborate institutions demanding heavy financial commitments, rigid systems of priority in personnel (which tend to prejudge the movement of the Spirit of God for years to come) and the vested interests which many times grow up around missionaries' own pet projects or which reflect arbitrary regional divisions of responsibility, have resulted in startling lack of mobility in the missionary enterprise. In the present stage of unprecedented historical and cultural fluidity and change, such immobility may result in the complete ossification of a dying institution, spelling doom to the present system of Christian missions (1954:258).

J. W. Dougall has given added force to the same argument:

Looking to the fulfillment of the missionary motive, with the greatest flexibility and freedom, we need to examine the programme of work for which missionary bodies have made themselves responsible. It has been a matter of deep concern to many that the greater part of the personnel and funds made available for mission is exhausted in the ongoing life of the Younger Churches so that there is no room for manoeuvre, no resources for advance, no mobility in the character of the mission. It is bogged down in the support of the Church . . . much of the effort and expenditure goes to pay for work which goes far beyond the needs of the Christian community in schools, hospitals and welfare services (1963:102-103).

Mounting Costs and Diminishing Returns

As the number of schools grow, as new classes are added requiring new teachers, additional texts, athletic equipment, and numerous other items, costs of the schools become greater and greater. Admittedly government subsidizes the salaries and costs of study materials, but it does not pay for the buildings, nor does it meet other costs that the mission must carry. It is true that local people, anxious to have a school of their own, will often provide the classroom block and teachers' homes. Still the mission is burdened with ever-present expenses that never cease. As the school program expands, the expense account grows with it.

Argument for the educational approach says that the schools are economic tools for evangelism. Mounting costs in contrast to low returns declare this untrue. As expenditure increases, so numbers of souls and numbers of churches ought to increase correspondingly. But even in a responsive community this cannot happen. After the adult community has been evangelized, the only growth for the future must come from the children. Children becoming Christians do so in their mid-teens, and their number annually may be expected to remain reasonably constant. Expenditures for operation of the schools, however, do not remain constant, and schools as tools for evangelism become more and more costly.

The Problem of Westernization

In Zambia a certain prestige attaches to missionaries because they are European, and in the late sixties because they are American.

Thus in their work,
The mission is identified with all the benefits that civilization brings. The young people flock to the schools. They do not come because they want our religion. They come because they want the good things civilization seems to offer (Smith 1946:16-17).

It was easy for early missionaries to believe that Western civilization and Christian faith were synonomous and that they were agents of that civilization as well as of Christianity. It was easy for Africans to make the same equation. It was not long until tribespeople developed a desire for the things of the white missionary and his civilization,and as these things could come only through education, mission schools became increasingly popular.

Schools were established as a means for evangelizing the African. His acceptance of Western ways was believed proof that tribespeople were becoming Christians, a belief that soon brought disillusionment. Blandishments of the Western way of life have been offered through schools as advantages to those accepting the Way of Christ. African people, caring little for the Faith, have made a profession for the sake of the advantages of the Western Way.

Language and Literature

The first missionaries found seventy tribes and perhaps thirty distinctive language groups in what is now Zambia, but no written language. It was evident that they must give first place to language study, reducing the language to writing, and translating Scripture, hymns, and other materials into the vernacular. Pioneers were committed to years of language study and translation. Their efforts contributed much to Christian witness and Western knowledge, and they gradually produced fine dictionaries, grammars, and secular and sacred translations.

There was no common language. Only the Lozi of the west who spoke a derivation of Sesuto and the Ngoni of the east, whose tongue was related to Zulu, had languages similar to those for which grammars and dictionaries had been prepared. Rotberg suggests that it might have been wise for the pioneers to have introduced a lingua franca for the country (1965:47). One of the Commissioners of British Central Africa in 1888 proposed introduction of Swahili, but the missionaries rejected this suggestion. Their reason was that "Swahili, language of the Muslim slave traders of East Africa . . . was infected with Islam and was to them unsuitable as a language for Christian instruction" (Rotberg 1965:47). The objections may have been well-founded. In East Africa, Islamic faith is possibly strongest today where Swahili is most used. English too, was a possible common language, but missionaries were fearful that teaching it in schools would encourage their students to go off to the towns.

Thus the missionaries were drawn into the task of reducing major languages to writing and into the work of translation. In due course thousands of Africans were learning to read and write in their own tongue. It is foolish, however, to teach people to read and to fail to supply them with adequate materials for reading. Edwin W. Smith's observation is true:

No one could claim, I think, that up to the present the provision of vernacular literature has kept pace with the provision of schools. The virtue of printer's ink has never yet been fully recognized in the African mission field. Missionary Societies have sent out trained medical men and women, trained nurses, trained teachers, trained agriculturalists and artisans; but how many have selected men and women with literary gifts, given them special training, and sent them out to write books and edit newspapers? Such scanty literature as exists has been produced mainly by enthusiasts in such moments as they could snatch from other exacting duties (1946:183).

The vacuum, however, is being filled. Tons of the cheapest secular literature are flooding the market at prices the African pay. Nor is this all. China and Russia are flooding Africa with attractive, English-medium materials expounding the superiority of the communistic philosophy and atheism. Nothing from the West is more beautifully done. Such materials are subsidized by the communist nations, but the appeal of the books, magazines, and technical articles is irresistible.

There is much wrong with a missions' philosophy which has taught millions to read but which has provided them with so little. The solution must be in flooding the peoples of Zambia with proper materials that will satisfy their hunger and provide them with entertaining, educational, and spiritually uplifting literature.

School Administration

One of the most difficult problems in mission-school relationships has been administration. The manager of schools is responsible for providing classrooms, ordering textbooks, writing materials, athletic equipment, and other supplies, and for getting them into the hands of the proper teachers. He must keep buildings in repair, provide teachers' homes, make provision for water, watch sanitation, and give oversight to gardens. Each month he must acquire sufficient money to pay all salaries. He must act as moderator when troubles arise between teachers, and between teachers and parents. His books have to be kept in order. His reports have to be in at headquarters on time. He is the government official at school level, and it is his responsibility to pass on all government decisions affecting schools. He must meet with the chief and headman and with school committees. It is his task to transport cement, steel, and roofing for school construction. He has to enforce discipline, push his workmen, and sometimes dismiss them. He must give rides to town; provide delivery, day or night, to the clinic eight miles away or to the hospital ninety miles away, provide stamps and writing materials; loan tools, sell gasoline---all these are expected of the school administrator. It takes all of his time and resources. The sad conclusion is that the missionary involved in school administration is often nothing more than a school administrator. He is seldom a missionary. The burden of his responsibility denies him the time, money, and mobility to preach and teach the Gospel.

Ram Desai's views of the contribution of missionaries across Africa are often distorted, but his comments regarding the employer-employee relationship of the missionary to his school personnel are valid:

> The large number of Africans with whom I have had discussions raised many objections against the missionaries and their activities in education. They declared that discrimination against African staff members in housing and pay is quite common and that most missionaries were authoritarian. Furthermore they made no attempt to understand the modern African who is becoming critical of authority, and a large number of them were neither professionally trained nor equipped with knowledge of African life (1962:28).

Most missionaries freely admit the above objections as voiced by numerous Africans. They would not agree with their critics that discrimination is premeditated or that authoritarianism is desirable. While they would deny the allegation that no attempt is made to understand the modern African, they would admit that they are ill-equipped in knowledge of African life. Regardless of their different perspectives, however, in general Africans regard missionaries as being guilty of exercising discrimination in housing and pay, as being authoritarian, and as seriously lacking in understanding of the African situation.

Coming from the colonial past, the whole system placed the missionary in an impossible position. His was the responsibility for hiring teachers, but so often his teachers noted that he lived in the big, modern home. At best they lived in tiny houses or huts with cow-dung floors. He paid their salaries, but they knew his was many times as great. He drove a car. They walked or peddled a bicycle. He exercised authority. Discipline had to be exercised, and teachers were subject to the missionary's authority as their students were to theirs, and the analogy was difficult to accept. They were not children but men. The missionary's relationship to his teachers was but one part of the picture. The community expected the missionary to keep his teachers in check because they were teaching the children of the community.

The missionary's relationship to his staff of laborers from the community was a different matter. His tools, cement, nails, roofing and lumber were disappearing before his eyes. Only his crew could be pilfering the hard-to-get materials. Gasoline by the drum would mysteriously drain away; diesel fuel would leak away; and engine oil would vanish. An eight-hour day often was a five or six-hour day; absenteeism was highest when the missionary was away; and the only good workdays came just before payday. The first two days after payday were nearly worthless with several of the crew coming to their jobs drunk. Inevitably the missionary in his employer role would have to fire one or more of his crew. Immediately the community would become angry with him because the man laid off had numerous relatives that extended through the clan, and without explanation a dozen villages would become cool and unfriendly. The above anomalies must go, and the time is short.

Paternalism

The problem of paternalism continues to be a very sore spot with the Africans. Basil Matthews' reference to it is almost as true in 1970 as it was in 1900:

The first weakness was the "grandfatherliness" of the missionary, who was every where at the top in the church, the school, college, hospital, and social work. At the end of the nineteenth century, most missionaries were sure that if left to themselves, the younger churches would go disastrously astray (1960: 175-176).

In that peculiar kind of mission in Central Africa where educational and medical emphases have preceded the Church, it has been with reluctance that missionaries have stepped down from their places of authority in favor of the African. If reasons were requested, it was pointed out that schools, clinics, and hospitals were provided at tremendous expenditure from overseas. These monies required responsibility not found in the African. Maintenance of properties required judgment found only in mature missionaries. American congregations and brethren could never entrust large sums with assurance if oversight of the institutions was placed in the hands of the "natives."

Both educational and medical institutions, demanding continuous capital, have fostered this paternalistic attitude:

> They all depend upon money for their existence. It is inconceivable that they could continue without large funds of money. This is true, not only of those activities which are concerned with the material and physical welfare of the people at large, such as public education, or public hospitals, and the like; but it is true also of those activities which are more immediately concerned with the expansion and establishment of the Church, such as training schools for evangelists, or pastors or teachers. It has invaded the very organization and life of the Church itself (Allen 1965: 101-102).

As continued foreign capital has given argument for perpetual oversight of institutions, so steady flow of funds said to be essential for preaching the Gospel has justified continued oversight of the Church. Many missionaries and their supporting societies can only think of the mission church in terms of a ministry paid by funds from overseas and supervised by missionaries. Church architecture must be Western; only missionaries have the know-how for building such structures. The African church would be lax in the exercise of discipline; missionaries must handle the problem. African Christians might develop a syncretism of Christianity and paganism; doctrines dare not be trusted to the young church. The missionary must stay on to preserve its purity. He has experience that fits him for the job better than his African co-workers.

This paternalistic superiority of missionaries is turning many away from the Church. In this connection, Taylor and Lehmann, with reference to Christians in the missionary churches at Nchanga Mine in the Copperbelt, have observed:

> . . . We found that in missionary churches on Nchanga Mine, with the possible exception of the Roman Catholic Church, the African congregations and their elders did not seem able to see a missionary in relation to

their church in any other way than that of the White
"boss" to his gang underground. It is not surprising
that African Clergy are still called "slave," "Mission stooge," or "the white man's dog." Something
startling is required to shift this pattern which is
stamped so firmly on people's minds. That might be
done if the Church proceeded to make its African
clergy the exact equivalents of their European coun-
terparts in respect to the scope and the autonomy of
their ministry (1961:172).

Isolation of the Missionary

The demanding oversight of schools isolates missionaries
from the people they have come to serve. The school mana-
gers are a hangover from the recent colonial era. They were
a part of the colonial order most irritating to African people.
Because of their managerial position in which missionaries
hired and fired, exercised discipline, and in all matters
agreed with the judgment of the white rulers, it is no wonder
that new African governments are anxious to control their
own schools.

The white manager is constantly in danger of being accused of racism. With the contemporary spirit of nationalism, this is understandable, but it is dangerous to missionaries and the work for which they are called. The office of administrator forces missionaries into the baaskap
("top boss") figure abhorent to the African, making it difficult to work with African Christians in planting churches.
It is an isolation from which missionaries must free themselves and soon.

Lack of Adult Response to the Gospel

One's reaction towards congregations made up of young
people is that of approval, especially if a number of older
Christians lend maturity to the service. That these older
persons may be teachers and employees who come well
dressed and clean---they can afford good clothes---only en-
hances the picture. The few ragged, dirty, sin-marked old

men and women who take back seats, and the small number
of younger husbands and wives, smelling of cowdung, and
with swarms of flies about them, are tolerated. This being
the situation, it is not difficult for the missionary to con-
clude that his ministry must be with the young. They are
eager and cooperative. They attend services scrubbed and
dressed in school uniforms. They come on time---a big
thing with the time-conscious missionary---and they are
disciplined. They listen and sing and memorize and quote
Scripture. With little effort they are persuaded to make the
good confession and are baptized.

None dare decry the genuine conversion of many teen-
agers, though under the peculiar mission-school relationship in Central Africa one is justified in questioning mo-
tives by which many profess Christianity. But the difficulty
on every field where the educational approach is favored, is
that few adults are won.

James Sunda writes of this difficulty among the Kapaukus
in Indonesia:

> The majority of those responsive to the Gospel mes-
> age during this period were of the younger generation.
> Many young people attended the village schools con-
> ducted by the Indonesian workers. Some then trained
> in the Bible School, which had been established at
> Enarotali, to take the Gospel to their own people.
> Their ministry found little response among the adult
> Kapaukus, until 1957. This was due to the fact that
> being young men, they were not respected as leaders
> amongst their tribesmen, and in many cases were
> resented. The older Kapaukus considered them rebels
> (1963:9-10).

The situation among the Kapaukus is comparable to that
in Central Africa. Youth come into the church with tacit
approval of the non-Christian community because adults
want their children to obtain an education. Joining the church
is the key, but this does not imply that the pagan community
rejects its ancestor worship in favor of the Christian Way.
Those few remaining faithful to their Christian profession
instead of reverting to paganism when they leave school are
resented by tribal elders and considered rebels.

School-churches worshiping in the school are not congregations of a reasonable number of adults. Donald McGavran declares in "Church Growth and Group Conversion,"

It is the adults who must be taught. At no place does the central station tradition (with its schools, M. W. R.) mislead more effectively than in its assumption that the chief task is teaching children ... Teaching children who go back to a community of untaught and unchanged adults is largely a waste of effort. The unconscious life of the adult group is a very effective school in any village. When this adult life is at variance with the conscious program of the mission school, the latter always suffers and too often is largely neutralized (1962:113-114).

I have witnessed the baptism of hundreds of young men and women in Zambia. All of them have come through the schools. Others have recounted the same pattern, and churches have been predominantly congregations of children. Regardless of where one goes in Central Africa this is the picture. The adult community, largely unresponsive to Christ because of the missions educational approach, has been greatly ignored.

Low Estimate of Evangelism and Conversion

The school-cum-church has no self-image. The church is a by-product of schools which have always had predominance of emphasis. The pagan community and members of the church have seen this. Little churches emphasized the image of the big schools. Like agricultural shows, inter-school track meets, and community health demonstrations, the churches were part of the school and were so considered. Schools have never given the church an image that would contribute to the growth of the church.

McGavran has spoken to this particular point:

A self image conductive to growth is desirable. Churches multiply which think of themselves as indwelt by the Savior and commanded of the Lord who wants His banquet hall filled. Churches multiply if they believe it is their primary task to grow (1962:132).

Few members of the school-church are aware that the church ought to grow in any other way than through schools. There is no concept of the Spirit of God at work. The spirit of the school-church is not the Spirit of God but the spirit of the school. The way to become a member is through the school. To many African people, the church is for children while they are in school. Mission schools, whether in Zambia, Malawi, or Rhodesia have not and will not bring great in-gatherings of approachable African tribes.

Of the educational emphasis in India, Pickett has said:
Pinning hope for the growth of the Church in the vil-lages to numerous government grant-in-aid schools (government subsidized mission schools, M. W. R.) is, we consider, to a considerable extent responsible for the present static situation (Pickett, Warnshuis, Singh, and McGavran 1962:90-91).

With reference to Africa, Dougall has written:
We know also that many African boys and girls leave school without any steady attachment and loyalty to the Church. They have simply gone to the Christian school to secure an education (1963:19).

Missions have shut their eyes to weaknesses of the edu-cational approach. The picture has been distorted. African school-church members have a poor concept of evangelism and a low estimate of conversion . . . in some instances so low that it may be no conversion at all.

Absence of Village Evangelism

Through the educational approach to evangelism it was assumed that village evangelism was simply not needed. There was little motivation to enter the villages. They were disease-ridden and filled with polygamous, beer-drinking pagans who were beyond redemption. The average missionary soon concluded that help for the villages was not to be secured through evangelism but rather as children were converted in schools. In any case it was difficult to supervise schools and have time for village evangelism. Numerous villages across Africa, distantly touched by mission schools for half a century, have never been visited by a missionary.

Indigenization is Denied

Of what is the average Zambian Christian most aware, the mission or the Church? This is a relevant question. Tippett, writing of Solomon Islands Christianity, has said in his introduction:

The village Christian . . . is far more aware of the mission than of the Church (1967: xvi).

Certainly this is true of Christians in Central Africa in that distinctive kind of church growth so well known in Rhodesia and Zambia, with the school in advance of the Church. African people have been taught that mission is the important enterprise. From repeated demonstrations they have observed that the Church is a minor part of the multi-pronged emphases of missions. If they are favorably disposed or violently opposed, it is towards missions and not the Church. It is impossible to build indigenous churches through the institutional approach. A hundred years of African mission institutionalism shouts that it cannot be done.

The institutional missionary is part of a structured program where authority and continuity are controlled from the top. By its nature, institutional mission is opposed to indigenization, and the bigger the institution in the variety of its functions, demands of its budget, and extent of its geographical outreach, the more this is so. Missionaries involved in institutionalism are not working for an indigenous church. They are working for their institution, for its preservation, for increasing the number of specialists to meet the particular needs, for expanding the budget to satisfy the appetite of the institution, and---not a minor consideration---for their own reputations which stand or fall at the success or failure of the institution.

All this is done with sincerity of purpose. Missionary societies want to share in the evangelization of Zambia. They have acquired land, buildings, and equipment. They have provided hundreds of schools, many hospitals, and numerous social services. They have provided education for thousands of children. They have employed large numbers of trained workers with good salaries and a guaranteed future that provide for retirement and old age. This multi-pronged missions institutionalism is big business. It brings into the country millions of dollars annually. The government may fear it, but it respects it as well. The business houses cater to it. The African people eagerly accept its many ministries.

At no time can missionaries foresee that it will be possible to give the responsibilities completely over to indigenous African leaders. When institutional missionaries do vaguely talk of indigenous leadership, they are usually thinking of mere replicas of the foreign missionary. The missionary is boss. He pays the salaries, makes the purchases, spends the money, hires and fires, draws the designs, and plans the campaigns. His is the last word. The church is under his direction. The schools are his domain. The hospitals with their smell of disinfectant are his holy ground. Under such circumstances missionaries anticipate that for many years the mission field will be their home, and so they build attractive houses with all the refinements that make for comfortable living.

George R. Upton, as quoted by Hodges, has vividly described the consequence of this approach. It is a picture reproduced in every country served by missions, but in a peculiar and unique sense by missions in Central Africa:

> After fifteen or twenty years of this type of work, he (the missionary, M.W.R.) may wonder why the native church does not show some signs of standing on its own feet. The workers do not manifest any initiative. The people do not show any concern for the salvation of their neighbors, nor manifest a willingness to assume financial responsibility for any phase of the mission work. He realizes that his removal from the oversight of the mission would practically bring the whole project to a standstill, unless another missionary took over. What is the reason for this? Simply the plan he has followed. He has treated the people like irresponsible children. He has led them, thought for them, relieved them of all financial responsibility for years. He has unintentionally robbed them of those practical processes which develop strong characters in any walk of life. . . Actually he has founded a sort of spiritual hospital, over which he must be chief nurse

as long as it remains. His work has become a liability instead of an asset. He has sown his own leadership and domination and provision of every need, and he has reaped servitude and malnutrition of a community of undeveloped spiritual children. How difficult to avoid this result in a mission that runs predominantly to institutional development (1953: 6-7).

Nida has said "the far-sighted missionary is alert to the possibilities of subordinating the mission to the Church," (1954:266), but the truth is that so long as missions remain structured with overseas dominance and with the perpetual costs of educational and medical institutions, they cannot be subordinated to the Church.

Contemporary mission demands brave and fearless personnel. When Christians think of mission and the Church, they must be acutely aware of the Church. Mission must become servant of the Church. Great changes must be made. Fortunately for the Church, government is taking its proper place in education, and by 1970 most schools in Zambia were in control of the Department of Education. The same thing has, or will have happened in every country of Africa.

Institutional missionaries must make an about-face, and emphasis must be given to the Church. By this I mean not only the Church in its universal connotation, but also the local church. The Church will not become indigenous until each local congregation is indigenous. Its authority, its finance, and its continuity---all so essential that indigenization cannot come if one feature is missing---must flow from the local church.

Tippett has said:

It is possible for missionaries and mission stations to concentrate effectively on raising standards, yet overlook the basic encounter of the village congregations with its environment. The stress should not be on raised educational standards per se, but on standards that can be translated into relevant encounter on the part of the local group . . . The success or failure of the Church . . . with this generation will be determined there---at the local congregational level. Mission policy and leadership can stimulate this growth or

obstruct it, can help or hinder the emergence of the
Church---but in the final analysis the local Church has
to emerge itself, and demonstrate its own relevance
within every village situation (1967: xvii).

From the purely educational point of view the missionaries
did a tremendous job in Northern Rhodesia prior to October
24, 1964, when the colonial territory became independent
Zambia. The combined results of their labors, however,
were small in the face of so great a need.

Education in Independent Zambia

The Minister of Education in Zambia, Mr. John Mwana-
katwe, at the opening of the new school hall at Canisius
College, Chikuni, Zambia, said on July 16, 1967:

It is on the foundations so carefully laid by these
pioneers (the early missionaries, M.W.R.) of half a
century ago that the educational system of today has
been built. To the Jesuits of Chikuni, to the White
Fathers in the East and North, to the Paris Evangelical Mission in Barotse Province, to the Methodists,
to the Church of Scotland, to the London Missionary
Society, to the Plymouth Brethren, to the Capuchin
Fathers, the Universities Mission, the African Reformed Church and to a number of other voluntary
agencies, the people of Zambia owe an enormous
debt of gratitude. It is true that Zambia entered upon
its Independence totally inadequately equipped with
educated manpower. We had only one hundred Zambian graduates, only fifteen hundred Zambians with
school certificates, and just over six thousand Zambians with as much as two years of secondary education. It is not, however, the voluntary agencies who
are to be blamed for this unhappy state of affairs. It
is clear from the records and from the minutes of the
Advisory Board in particular, that missionaries were
constantly pressing the government of the day to increase education in the country. Without the persis-
tence and the dedication of the mission workers, the
colonial government would have done even less for

African education than they did. I echo the words of His Excellency the President, who, at his installation as Chancellor of the University of Zambia, thanked God for the men and women of conscience and dedication who labored to lay the foundations of education (Zambia Press Release No. 1387/67).

The Zambian government is determined that the educational picture must change. One of the first things it did when coming into power was to establish the machinery for change. By 1970 there will be universal primary education, government-sponsored and controlled. (Press release No. 1864/66). Missions were informed that the government was prepared to take over all primary schools at once. Many agencies were quick to follow the invitation of the government.

On October 15, 1966, the Minister of Education said:
It is clear that the promotion of universal primary education, which is the government's objective from 1970, will necessitate the opening of a vast number of new primary schools. It seems to me that to continue to maintain a proportionate share in this field is almost certainly beyond the resources of the missions agencies . . . The government appreciates very much the degree of confidence which has led to most mission primary schools being entirely entrusted to it in the last two years. Such schools thus attract one hundred per cent government responsibility in both the transitional and the national development plans (Press release No. 1864/66).

The Zambia Christian Mission turned its schools back to the Department on January 1, 1968.

In his address to the meeting of the Synod of the United Church of Zambia held in Lusaka on January 4, 1967, President Kenneth Kaunda said:
In the past, as of now, we have been grateful for the work that missionaries did in the field of education. This is exemplified by the fact that most, if not all, members of my Central committee and indeed the Cabinet, have gone through missions schools at some stage during the course of their schooling.

Members of the government of Zambia are anxious that principles of Christianity continue to be taught in schools now that they are under the Department of Education. Missions can, if they desire, continue to teach religious instruction in schools formerly in their care.

The Minister of Education said in October, 1966:

Many of us in the government would share with you the conviction that if education is to be effective in the fullest sense, it must be Christian education. I can assure you that it continues to be the intention of the government that religious instruction should be a significant and central part of the training of all pupils in our schools; and if the provision of specific mission schools means that this training is given by more convinced teachers, then we cannot but regard it as a good end (Press Release 1864/66).

Will there be a future for missions in the government scheme of things? The President of Zambia, speaking to the Churches in January, 1967, said:

Genuine missionaries we still need . . . We have very serious sociological problems in Zambia. Here for the first time all sorts of forces have been unleashed, and society lies bare to all of these . . . Can the Church help here, and is it equiped to meet this challenge? . . . It is the inside of our people that needs putting right, the spiritual and moral sides, and this is mainly the responsibility of the Church. What is the Church doing about these things? The nation is not marching. It is double marching, but I fear it is doing so materially. Morally and spiritually we lag behind.

It is cordially acknowledged that under many circumstances and during some periods, the school approach has paid dividends. Where hostility has been encountered, the school approach may have been the only approach. For new missionaries the school approach provided a more easily worked, a more easily operated system of evangelism. Students of schools with six or eight years of Christian instruction knew more about the Bible and were more civilized than illiterate villagers.

Under such circumstances the school approach may have been a good beginning. Many evidences are found that schools anticipated breaking out into widespread Christianization at some suitable time in the future. For example, Deaville Walker says:

For the present, the supreme task is that of thoroughly training---larger and more efficient provision for training teachers, pastors, evangelists, ministers; the training of boys and girls in our schools, and the more careful training of Christians in our churches. Until, in the not distant future, the whole Methodist Church in Western Nigeria, strong and devoted to its Redeemer and Lord, shall be mobilized for its supreme task---the evangelization of the yet unreached multitudes within its own borders (1942:138).

This has been the rationale for mission work which most missionaries would have given. Unfortunately, after sixty years in Zambia, not only the Methodist Church, but the Christian Church and all others have yet to break out. The educational approach may make a good beginning, but it is a bad place to get stuck.

Discerning missionaries in Zambia are persuaded that releasing the educational institutions to the government was an advantageous move, and that lasting good for evangelism and church growth will result. The future is bright with expectation as Christian men, white and black alike, no longer shackled with the burden of educational institutions, anticipate a great harvest of souls for the Lord.

7

The Medical Approach

African herbalists are easy to find. At any marketplace one can examine their wares spread on old newspapers or burlap near the main thoroughfare of the African market-goers.

The African Doctor and His Medicines

Their medicines are varied. In one herbalist's bag I found a tortoise shell, dried snakeskins, ostrich eggshell, a variety of roasted insects, dead scorpions, the teeth, bones, skin and powdered dung of wild animals, human bones, animal fat, dried fish, crocodile skins, and hundreds of roots, berries, seeds, barks, stalks, and leaves of numerous trees and plants indigenous to Africa.

It is difficult to learn why certain remedies are used. The herbalist might explain that he prescribes as he does because his teacher so taught him, and he could give no better reason. Or his medicines "may have some fancied resemblance to the symptoms of the disease" (Parrinder 1962:105).

Missionaries have often dismissed the African's faith in these remedies as pure superstition. Many Africans claim, however, that their herbalists know ancient remedies of which European medicine is ignorant. There may be justification in their claims, for it is true that "primitive peoples discovered quinine, cascara, cocaine, and morphine" (Nida and Smalley 1959:42). Until recently, however, no serious effort has been made to analyze the medicines used. To assume that a small proportion of the herbalist's medicines are of value might be dangerous. A few are effective, but much superstition and hocus-pocus is mingled with them. His medicines and practices and ignorance of sanitation make the herbalist a threat to all he attempts to heal.

Often the herblist is also a "witchdoctor." Not many of his drugs have pharmaceutical values, and many of them are magical. Disease and death are never purely physical with the African. They are also spiritual, and only the witch doctor can diagnose their spiritual cause. The witch doctor is an honored member of society. He is not a witch or an evil man or a perverted priest seeking to bring harm to his neighbors. Parrinder says:

His function is not to harm but to heal, and to release from their pains those who believe themselves to have been bewitched. It is against the evil activities of nocturnal witches that the doctor operates in the public interest (1962:106).

Scientific Medicine Has Not Eliminated African Medicine

Rotberg says that pioneer missionaries introduced medicine as a sideline (1965:90-91). It soon became a major emphasis, and it was anticipated that where modern medicine was offered, the herbalist and witch doctor would soon be out of business. This naive assumption has been proven false. Parrinder says that

witchcraft is still widely feared, and apparently just as much under the influence of modern civilization and Christianity as ever before (1962:133).

Practice of tribal medicine and the popularity of the witch doctor are symptomatic, not so much of physical illness as of social disease. Peoples are on the move and drastic forces are changing their lives. They are meeting new powers through strangers from unknown tribes with frightening forces at their command. New tensions plague them. Strange illnesses lay them low, and the only explanation is witchcraft. The only recourse is the witch doctor for through him the African believes he has protection from misfortunes and all the evils of life.

Missions Hospitals Miss the Root of the Problem

Medical facilities of missions have been welcomed by the peoples of Zambia, and every hospital is overtaxed with thousands of patients. Modern medicines, however, have not put the herbalist and witch doctor out of business. With the African, the missionary doctor who diagnoses the physical cause of illness and prescribes the right medicines has solved only half of the problem:

> The doctor has not eliminated the influence of the witch who brought on the sickness and who, if not exposed, will only continue to make the victim ill (Nida and Smalley 1959:44).

The mission hospital has neither displaced tribal medicine and the witch doctor nor met the "spiritual" need. This fact is significant for the Christian hospital claiming concern for the spiritual welfare of its patients. Advances have been made in combating illness and disease, but it is likely that fear, superstition, and sorcery are as prevalent today as in 1900.

Our surveys of 1967 revealed the widespread prevalence of disease as it still exists among the people. Victims of sleeping sickness were easily distinguishable. Malaria was everywhere in evidence, and we found cases of typhoid, measles, whooping cough, tuberculosis, smallpox, chicken pox, elephantiasis, leprosy, heart disease, and cancer, many of which we could diagnose. Besides all these, we saw evidences of snakebite, crocodile attack, food poisoning, malnutrition, abrasions and broken bones from accidents, and victims of drunken brawls. Each village had its aged, and every married woman of child-bearing age was either pregnant or carrying a newborn child.

The medical approach as a tool of evangelism has been an appealing argument in favor of dispensaries, clinics, and hospitals sponsored by evangelical missions. Strong reasons can be given in their favor, all of which I have used in presenting our Central Africa Mission enterprise.

The Missions Hospital as a Tool of Evangelism

A concern of the Department of Native Affairs in the recent colonial era was for the physical welfare of the African peoples. The Christian Church came late into Central Africa. As I surveyed numerous areas, I was told that a first condition for our entry was our ability to provide educational and--- in specific cases---medical services. In a number of areas in Southern Rhodesia the only way our mission could enter was through an extensive medical program, together with the provision of schools.

Each hospital employs a trained chaplain. He belongs to the predominant tribe and speaks to the patients in their own dialect. All his time is given to prayers, teaching, and witness. He is largely responsible for whatever evangelistic emphasis the hospital program gives. Through the hospital large numbers are reached with the Gospel. With thousands passing through the institution annually, all of them hearing the message of Christ, the hospital provides a valuable and effective ministry. The above is true and is repeated in mission after mission. Supporting churches refer to these factors repeatedly, but more needs to be said.

Many African patients enter the hospital only after every other resort has failed. They have gone to the witch doctor, have taken his medicines, magical and pharmaceutical, have approached the ancestors and made the sacrifices, and these have failed. Now, often beyond recovery, they are brought to the hospital and perhaps for the first time come into contact with the Gospel, and they are too ill to appreciate it. But perhaps a hundred or more in the course of a year do hear the Gospel and are obedient to it. Their baptism comes at their release and they return to their village with little teaching, with no church in which to worship, with some exceptions, and into their ancestor-worshiping family where too frequently they are sucked back into paganism.

Weaknesses of the educational approach have already

been described. I am convinced that the weaknessess of the medical approach are even more pronounced. Few advantages of the school approach apply to the hospital. It seldom becomes a church on the Lord's Day. Religious instruction is not given daily. No effort could be made to teach patients to read or write, and many cannot do so. The contact between the patient and Christian staff seldom lasts longer than the length of his stay at the hospital. In contrast to the thousands who receive treatment, few become Christian. Those who do become believers return to their villages where often there is no church. I know of one or two outstanding exceptions, but too little effort is made to follow the convert or challenge him to disciple and plant a church in his village.

Every mission hospital is understaffed and overworked. A criticism medical personnel level against their own ministry is that time will not permit them to witness as they came to the field to do. The complaint is oft-repeated and is the heartrending cry of men and women troubled in their souls. They came to use their skills to win multitudes to Christ, and they count in tens and twenties all that are won. Their hours, days, and years are taken to minister to the physical needs of the thousands standing in the queues at the hospital entrance, and little time is available to tell of the Great Physician who died for the sins of the world.

I know many of these doctors and nurses who are dedicated, humble, thoroughly qualified Christian men and women. Their healing ministry is desperately needed, and its value cannot be faulted as a ministry of compassion, but as a vehicle of the Gospel it has very limited success.

The Tension between Medicine and Evangelism

The evangelistic effectiveness of a hospital is, of course, dependent upon its staff, and those hospitals I have known have given consistent witness only insofar as they have maintained dedicated Christian personnel. Examples can be given of medical missions which have brought a great ingathering of souls. Grimley points out that one reason for extensive growth in the Lassa church of Nigeria was the

influence of the hospital and out-village dressing stations:
> All the medical doctors (up to 1962) who have served
> at the Lassa hospital have been ordained ministers
> of the Gospel and have done evangelistic touring,
> making church supervision a part of their weekly
> program (1966:152-153).

Dr. Dale Erickson of Chidamoyo Christian Hospital in
Rhodesia has written:
> One of our hospital converts has established three con-
> gregations some forty miles from Chidamoyo. One
> is yet very weak, but the other two are growing and
> getting stronger all the time. The people call him
> Benjamin the Evangelist. He cycles to all three
> churches every Lord's Day. He does the preaching,
> baptizing and teaching. He is not paid for his work
> (Letter to the author dated July 17, 1969).

It is my opinion that a hospital may be regarded as an
evangelistic agency only to the extent that each doctor and
nurse is committed to evangelism, and this means that, like
the doctors of Lassa hospital in Nigeria and Chidamoyo in
Rhodesia, evangelistic touring will be a rigidly planned part
of the program.

Early in the projection of the African Christian Mission,
a requirement was made that each doctor be an ordained
minister. Nevertheless a number of doctors now have no
Bible college or seminary training. They are thoroughly
dedicated men, but emphasis on evangelism as a priority is
weakening.

The same situation applies to the hospital as applies to
the schools. Once approved, with government subsidies,
the hospitals dare not close. Granted they were founded as
tools for evangelization, and that the high ideal was for every
doctor to be an evangelist. Too soon, personnel so qualified
cannot be found. The institution still has to be staffed.
Doctors and nurses must be found, regardless of their spiritual qualification, or the institution will die, and the institution must not die. Gradually the emphasis on the medical
program as a tool to win the lost diminishes to a whisper,
and keeping the hospital alive becomes the primary end in
view. As Roland Allen says:

We are asked to give money . . . to provide institutions of all kinds; and these seem to be often ends in
themselves. The one real end, the salvation of souls,
the Revelation of Christ, is lost under its pile of
machinery (1964:154-155).

Wrong Motives Encouraged

During our surveys in 1967 we tried to ascertain the
health of the people. I was assured that if we would provide
a clinic, the Sala would become Christian in great numbers.
Their boldness at bargaining their membership in our
churches against our providing them with a clinic should
make use aware of our faulty approaches. We have offered
them medical facilities with the tacit understanding that
they would join our churches. There is little difference in
saying, "We will build you a clinic if you will join our
church," and, "We will join your church if you build us a
clinic."

Major Problems Need Assessing

A number of other major problems concerning medical
work need to be noted. The cost of building a hospital on
the field may reach hundreds of thousands of dollars. Construction costs are a small part of the ultimate outlay. A
few years of operational expense will far surpass the original costs, and the expenses never cease. Examination of
the budget of most missions involved in the multi-pronged
missions approach will reveal that medical mission is most
expensive. Dollar for dollar, it will often surpass all other
costs. Its budget will run many times that allotted to
evangelism.

There would be no objection to high costs if the return in
extension of God's Kingdom was commensurate with the
size of the institution, the number of personnel, and the sums
expended. But souls won through the hospital are few in
number when compared to those won through simple, in-
expensive, direct village evangelism.

The invariable answer to the objection about low returns
is always the same, and as Roland Allen says:

The arithmetical sum recurs again and again. Given
so many men, and so much money, the progress of
the church is assured. And this in spite of the fact
that other voices are warning us that the church does
not make progress as she ought to do. Our common
answer to that is an appeal for more men, more
money, better organization (1964 : 157).

Allen's observations are accurate. Medical mission
seldom produces churches. To this allegation comes the
reply --- given more doctors, more nurses, more orderlies,
more staff, more clinics, more hospitals, more equipment,
and more money with which to provide---medical mission
will plant churches; but few churches come. All the while
the program absorbs more of the available resources. Men
and materials needed to reach the multitudes are buried in
a non-productive program of compassion, and dangers arise,
as Pickett says:

> Not only from the absorption by the institutions of the
> resources that are required for building a church,
> but much more from the concept of Christianity there-
> by established in the public mind as a religion pro-
> fessed for the sake of obtaining services from insti-
> tutions (1960:86).

I do not minimize the blessed ministry of healing, but
I feel that physical healing is not for mission the primary
end in view:

> Doing good to needy people is an obligation for Chris-
> tians, but it is certainly not the only obligation. No
> amount of social work takes the place of proclaiming
> Christ as Lord and Savior and persuading men to be-
> come his disciples (Pickett, 1963: 54).

Expanding a complicated system of medical mission with
hospitals and clinics no longer a means to the end---for which
they were originally founded---not only negates the objective
of mission on the field occupied by these institutions, but
drains off resources needed in other fields and lands ripe
unto harvest.

The purpose of mission is to save the souls of peoples
of all cultures, tribes, races, and nations, and to establish
them in churches in every land:

The New Testament Church's approach to its task is a far cry from the belief, held by many modern missionaries, that philanthropy, community building, and good works are the main ends of mission (Hodges 1965:29).

Once the site of the hospital has been determined by the government---potential responsiveness to the Gospel is never a consideration of the government---and the institution built, it becomes a permanent feature of the landscape. It cannot be moved. It is as immobile as the mountain on which it stands. Possibly the institution will be situated among peoples little interested in the Gospel---villages, clans, and tribes receiving all the amenities of a multi-pronged mission approach often show slight concern for the message of Christ. Whether the people are responsive or not, the institution is fixed, and it must be maintained. Personnel are chained to the institution. Their immobility forces them to concentrate on good works and to justify this ministry--- with their financial supporters---as being equal to the saving of souls.

The immobility of the hospital demands that its personnel be content with compassionate healing. There is little time for anything else, but as William Read has noted,

Small harvest is the price missions pay for immobility which ties them to good works (1965:100).

The Low Return in Souls

A few churches have been planted by the Central Africa Mission through the medical program. With a hundred or more baptized annually through the hospital ministries, in a decade well over a thousand can be claimed. Some, of course, find their way to school-churches, and a few have gone to their homes to plant new congregations, but the majority return to the home village and the old way of life.

Thousands can be won in Africa through nothing more than prayerfully conceived, Spirit-guided evangelism designed to plant churches in the village. The African tribes can be won without adding to the complicated machinery so many have installed in their midst. McGavran's observation is true of many contemporary missions of Africa:

> When men can be won, the churches and missions are
> tied up in education, medicine, literacy, or some non-
> productive form of evangelism. They have been plow-
> ing so long they have forgotten to harvest (1962:86).

The Question of Indigenization

If these complicated services are necessary for planting
churches and winning the peoples of Zambia for Christ, the
job is impossible. The combined forces of Roman Catholics
and Protestants and the government with its interest in its
many tribes cannot meet the medical needs of Zambia's
millions. If her knowledge of Christ must come through
medical evangelism, multitudes of her peoples will never
know Him.

We need to ask, regarding both education and medicine,
"Can we preach the Gospel in Africa without these particular
and costly emphases?" The answer is that we can. Others
are doing it. In Zambia we are doing it too.

Read has said:

> While institutions still liberalize communities, the
> extension of the Church no longer depends upon them.
> An epoch is passing, and institutions suddenly find
> themselves in a completely new situation unable to
> realize that a new day calls for a new vitality and
> emphasis (1965:102).

Granted that medical services opened doors in Central
Africa and that hospitals offer a ministry of compassion.
None can fault this ministry, and this is not an argument for
the disposal of these services so desperately needed. They
need, however, to be kept in perspective. So often they are
said to be essential, and they are not essential.

Roland Allen was speaking to this very issue when he
said:

> Lately missionary leaders have been speaking often
> of education and medicine, as if these were not sub-
> ordinate to any higher dominant, as if they were ends
> in themselves, as if the practice of them were es-
> sential, as if they were in themselves the gospel.

We need to be reminded that the gospel has been spread abroad without them, and we need to be reminded that they are not indispensable. If we forget it, we make social progress our gospel and become more concerned about social progress than spiritual regeneration, and then it can scarcely surprise us if non-Christians see in our mission activities rather than the power of the Holy Ghost (1965:99).

Indigenization of the Church is impossible if its future is dependent upon medicine. Young churches cannot, at any foreseeable time, assume responsibility for staffing, financing, or supervision of hospitals. With the annual operational costs surpassing several times the gross earned income of the church membership served by the hospital, to speak of incorporating these services into the indigenous life of the young churches at any time is absurd. Such institutions are dependent on foreign staffing, supervision, and monetary support. To affirm the necessity of operating medical institutions is to deny the young churches their God-given right of self-expression, growth, and spiritual maturity essential to indigeneity.

Medical Missions in Independent Zambia

Missions in Zambia sponsoring medical programs are asking about the future of their hospitals. Already the majority of primary schools are in the hands of the Department of Education, and the government has indicated that in the near future medical services will be taken from the missions as well. This is the pattern of nationalism. I recognize the possibility of exceptions, but to continue stressing the need for additional medical institutions today is to remain stubbornly ignorant of contemporary African history.

What Read says of Brazil is true of Africa:

The future brings federalization closer. Federalization and secularization go hand in hand. The I.P.B. and mission face a rising pride of nation and sense of independence that may eventually topple these organizations (1965:107).

Robinson, speaking of Southern Nigeria, has said:
The government is increasingly taking into its own
hands both education and medicine and thus reducing
the opportunities and influence of the churches through
these social services (Grimley and Robinson 1966:
362).
Other African governments are following a similar
pattern.

IV

The Necessity
of a New Approach

8

The Contemporary Situation

While at the School of World Mission at Fuller Theological Seminary in the spring of 1967, and with the help of Dr. Alan Tippett, I prepared an instrument to be used in village surveys in Zambia.   I returned to Africa in June, 1967. In early July and August, with other missionaries of the Zambia Christian Mission (Christian Church), I surveyed thirty-seven villages in the Sala area of the Mumbwa district of Zambia.

The evangelistic approach among the Sala (and Shona-Sindebele peoples in their midst) had been tied to education, and in four years we built and opened three double-stream schools with 746 pupils in 1967.

Each school has been a church.   From June, 1963, through June, 1967, 1,158 were baptized---965 were teen-age children coming through the schools.   There was, however, little growth in the churches, and I wondered why. I also wondered why, after sixty years of educational emphasis, the Methodist Church had such a small communicant membership.   With the use of my investigative tool, I hoped to find the correct answers to these questions.

I soon discovered that my instrument of investigation was too large for use in the time at our disposal. It therefore had to be revised. (See Appendix A for the original instrument devised and Appendix B for the revised in-

strument we used.) The new instrument consisted of three
areas for investigation: the village, in which I would determine tribal groupings, decision-making patterns, types of
labor, village wealth, evidences of integration, tribal crafts,
health and cleanliness, beer-brewing and drunkenness, diet,
festivals, and migration to the city; the family, in which I
would investigate family relationships, polygamy, and intertribal marriages; and religion, in which I would inquire
about animistic practices and ancestor worship, the number
of Christians in each village, and church affiliation.

I did not endeavor to acquire data relating to each cate-
gory in each of the villages. My sampling, however, does
provide, I believe, an accurate protrayal of the contemporary
situation. Examination of the survey map indicates that all
but one or two of the villages were within a fifteen-mile
radius of Chief Shakumbila's home. This is the heart of
Sala country. Knowledge of these villages provides a reasonable picture of all the villages of the Sala area.

The survey was arranged in advance through contact
with the local headman. However, with the place and time
of meeting determined, arriving at the village we would
have to wait for word to get to the fields and for the family
heads to return. Much of my information concerning village
wealth, innovations, cattle kraals, granaries, crop diversi-
fication and other data, we gathered by observation while
the people were assembling.

Close to the mission schools we were known, and here
we gathered the best information. The impact, large or
small, made upon the villages by the school-churches were
more obvious. Knowledge of that impact was valuable to
my investigation. Away from the schools, we were unknown.
Some villages were reluctant to give the information sought.
This, too, provided data of value as we contemplate taking
the Gospel to the villages. In few of the villages had we done
visitation and preaching. With the institutional development
there was little time for anything else. We had justified
this neglect by employing an African evangelist who was
responsible for this work.

None of the villagers were well-acquainted with the
missionaries, and the missionaries knew less about the

villagers. We surveyed the large village of Munashintule, eleven miles from our mission home. The old pagan headman told us we were the first missionaries ever to walk through his village. His memory took him back to a time before the first Methodists came to the area.

The Village

Villages are not large. The approximate total population for the communities surveyed was under 5,000. The largest village contained 863 people. The smallest was the home of twenty-six persons. The average village contained 135 people. The huts were generally arranged in two rows facing each other with a distance of perhaps fifty feet between them. Often they formed clusters of from four to six each within the overall design of the village. Each cluster belonged to a family unit. To the rear of each cluster were the granaries for grain and platforms for storing all the paraphernalia of an African household.

July is harvest season, and the harvest was good. Many families had constructed enclosures in which was temporarily stored the crop of corn until it was shelled, sacked, and trucked to market. A number of families owned hand-operated shellers, and we saw one tractor-powered machine. The usual method of shelling corn, however, was by hand flail. Cotton also is a cash crop, and it was common to see great piles awaiting to be bailed for market. Groundnuts and velvet beans too are popular as the African farmers begin to see the value of crop rotation, and these products were being prepared for shipment. We could swing the flail or help lift a few bags of corn, or share in tying the bail of of cotton, much to the joy of our hosts, and it made easy the eliminating of tensions.

Many families had pigeon crofts and kept chickens. Goat kraals consisted of tepee-shaped enclosures of poles tightly fitted together in which the animals were confined. Each village had at least one cattle kraal or more, for there are thousands of cattle in the area. These enclosures, perhaps eighty feet in diameter, made of tightly enmeshed branches of thorn trees (though barbed wire is used increasingly) are situated at the edge of the village.

Water supplies came from large dams, rivers, and wells. Twenty-one villages had dug wells. Twelve obtained their water from rivers, sometimes walking over three miles each way to obtain the supply. At least five government-financed bore holes (drilled wells) provided water for several villages.

Few villages have public buildings. There is a court and jail near Chief Shakumbila's home. Jehovah's Witnesses and Seventh Day Adventists have mud-walled, thatched churches. The Methodists have one brick building. None of these are located in villages. However, the Zambia Christian Mission had (in 1967) one brick and four mud-and-thatch churches, each within a village.

Access has improved as a result of the Zambia Christian Mission entering the area. It took more than two hours to travel the last sixteen miles to the home of the Chief in 1962. Now an all-weather road has been built, and little difficulty is experienced in driving, even in the rainy season.

Tribal Groupings

It is a commentary on the ignorance of many missionaries concerning the social structure that we were ignorant of the diversity of tribes within the thrity-seven villages. I was, of course, aware of the Shona-Sindebele, Rhodesian immigrant community which I followed to Northern Rhodesia in 1963, but I was unaware of their number and the size of the Shona community in comparison to the Sindebele. In 151 immigrant families in the thirty-seven villages, only thirteen were Sindebele. I was surprised as well at the number of Tonga in comparison to the Sala and Ila. We enumerated 136 Plateau Tonga families, fifty-seven Ila, and 195 Sala. Besides these, we found eight Lenje, two Senga, ten Lozi, and nine Kaonde families. Note in Figure 3 the distribution of the nine tribes.

Tonga is the language of the schools and of the Chief's court. There are few tribal differences between the Sala-Tonga-Ila. They have been long associated, and their languages are similar. Murdock (1959:364-368) classifies the Sala as a part of the Ila, and the Ila and Tonga he places

NUMBER OF FAMILIES BY TRIBE IN EACH VILLAGE

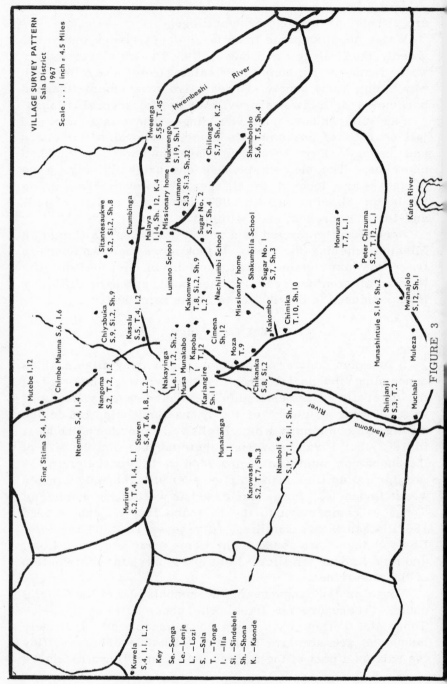

VILLAGE SURVEY PATTERN
Sala District
1967
Scale . . . 1 inch = 4.5 Miles

FIGURE 3

Key
Kuwela S.4, I.1, L.2
Se.–Senga
Le.–Lenje
L.–Lozi
S.–Sala
T.–Tonga
I.–Ila
Si.–Sindebele
Sh.–Shona
K.–Kaonde

Mwembeshi River

Mweenga S.55, T.45
Mukwengo S.19, Sh.1
Malaya I.14, Sh.12, K.4
Lumano S.3, Si.3, Sh.32
Chilonga S.7, Sh.6, K.2
Missionary home
Shambololo S.6, T.5, Sh.4
Sugar No. 2 S.7, Sh.4
Chumbinga
Sitantesaukwe S.2, Si.2, Sh.8
Lumano School
Nachilumbi School
Shakumbila School
Monunza T.7, L.1
Peter Chizuma S.2, T.12, L.1
Kakomwe T.8, Si.2, Sh.9 L.2
Missionary home
Sugar No. 1 S.7, Sh.3
Chiyabuka S.9, Si.2, Sh.9
Kasalu S.5, T.4, I.2
Kakombo
Chimika T.10, Sh.10
Chimbe Mauma S.6, I.6
Mutebe I.12
Nangoma S.2, Si.2, I.2
Cimena Sh.12
Moza T.9
Munashintule S.16, Sh.2
Mwanajolo S.12, Sh.1
Sing Sitima S.4, I.4
Ntembe S.4, I.4
Nakayinga Le.1, T.2, Sh.2
Musa Munakabo
Kapoba
Kariangire T.12
Chikanka S.8, Si.2
Muleza
Muchabi
Shinjanji S.3, T.2
Muriure S.2, T.4, I.4, L.1
Steven S.4, T.6, I.8, L.2
Munakanga L.1
Nangoma River
Karowash S.2, T.7, Sh.3
Namboli S.1, T.1, Si.1, Sh.7
Kafue River

in the same cluster which he calls the Middle Zambezi Bantu.

The Sala-Tonga-Ila are cattle herders and belong to the milking complex. All raise similar crops. The men clear the lands, and the women work the fields. Their villages are small and of the same design. All are similarly structured. All require a bride-price and all practise polygamy. Each household

assumes the form of an independent nuclear or polygynous (polygamous) family rather than an extended family (Murdock 1959:367).

These peoples are fully integrated---17,000 of them in the Sala district and all owing allegiance to Chief Shakumbila.

Decision-Making Patterns

In the area surveyed, the Methodists have majored in education since 1905. They were on the fringes, and until the Zambia Christian Mission opened schools in the heart of the district in 1963, those few children to obtain any education got it through Methodist schools. Chief Shakumbila recounted that as a boy "in skins" he attended the first Methodist school at Nambala. For sixty-five years the Methodists have been working with the school-church approach, yet by village reckoning, only twenty-three of the thirty-seven villages reported any Methodists at all, and then only 121 members. In that figure only adults were counted.

The Zambia Christian Mission, the only other mission involved in schools, fared somewhat better in the reports of the headmen. We found 317 members of the Christian Church in fourteen villages out of thirty-seven, as indicated in Figure 4. One hundred ninety-nine, coming from eight villages, were baptized teen-agers in the schools (Figure 5).

Lumano, Namboli, Sugar Number One, and Kakomwe headmen gladly gave the number of children who had become Christians in their villages. Chikanka, Mukwengo, Kakombo and Chimika, and Sugar Number Two gave us the figures only when we specifically asked. The same was not true of Cimene, Kapoba, Moza, and Kariangire. Ten each from

CHURCH MEMBERSHIP AND TRIBAL GROUPINGS IN THE THIRTY-SEVEN VILLAGES SURVEYED

VILLAGE	A. ZCM	B. Meth.	C. SDA	D. Apos.	E. Other	F. Zambian	G. Rhodesian (Family Groupings)
Chimbe Mauma		8	4	6		12	
Ntembe						8	
Kapoba			30			12	
Nakayinga					6	2	2
Kariangire			40				11
Mutebe		2				12	
Cimena	3	4				3	12
Moza						9	
Munakanga		4				1	
Steven	2	6	12			20	
Lumano	44	10	18			5	35
Chikanka	16	2			2	8	2
Mweenga		16	9		1	100	
Malava			6	4		18	12
Chumbinga			16	6			
Chilonga			10			9	6
Mukwengo							
Mukwengo	20			8		19	1
Shambololo			25		2	11	4
Chiyabuka		2	4		3	9	11
Karowash	2		2	3		9	3
Munashintuli		3	10			16	2
Namboli	60			10		2	8
Kakombo-Chimika	15	3		18	3	10	10
Monunza			7			8	
Peter Chizuma	1	2	9			15	
Sugar No. 1	42					7	3
Sugar No. 2	19	4				7	4
Sitantesaukwe	23	4				2	10
Kakomwe	68	7	10			13	11
Muriure		5	9			11	
Mwanajolo		4	8			12	1
Shinjanji Muleza		1	6			5	
Muchabi		2	4				
Kuwela		8	6			7	1
Sign Sitema		6				8	
Nangoma		10				6	
Kasalu	2	8				11	6
	317	121	187	115	23		

A. Zambia Christian Mission (Christian Churches)
B. Methodist Church
C. Seventh Day Adventists
D. Apostolics
E. Others: 2 Catholics, 16 Watchtower, 5 Zionists.
F. Zambian Tribes (Lenje, Senga, Sala, Tonga, Ila, Kaonde, Lazi.)
G. Rhodesian Tribes (Shona, Sindebele.)

Figure 4

VILLAGES WITH CHRISTIAN CHURCH MEMBERS

VILLAGES	TOTAL REPORTED BY HEADMEN	YOUTH REPORTED BY HEADMEN	BAPTISMAL RECORD
Cimena	3		13
Steven	2		2
Lumano	44	39	48
Chikanka	16	7	20
Mukwenga	20	12	20
Karowash	2		2
Namboli	60	25	60
Kakombo & Chimika	15	6	24
Peter Chizuma	1		1
Sugar No. 1	42	32	42
Sugar No. 2	19	10	21
Sitantesaukwe	23		23
Kakomwe	68	68	68
Kasalu	2		2
Kapoba			99
Moza			8
Kariangire			10
	317	199	373

Figure 5

Cimene and Kariangire, nine from Kapoba, and eight from Moza we knew to be baptized believers, and yet they were not reported at all. When pressed to explain, their simple answer was, "We do not keep such records. You have the records at school"; and this was all they would say. It must be emphasized that this numbering of church members, with the exception of Lumano, Namboli, and Kakomwe, was by pagan men. The information they gave us speaks of the low estimate these pagans had of the Church, whatever the denomination. More is revealed, however, than the low estimate factor. These animistic ancestor worshipers were telling the truth as they saw it. The figures obtained for the Christian Church membership, with the exception of the four villages named above, compared favorably with our own records.

I do not doubt the figures given for the Seventh Day Adventists, the Apostolics, the Methodists and the other denominations (See Figure 4). The only members that were counted were adults, with the exception of the Christian Church, and we only got the numbers of school-Christians when we asked for them.

The Methodists turned their schools back to the government in 1966. Thus, loyalty to the church was no longer an expedient to those attending former Methodist schools. The elders and headmen of the villages had never accepted the fact that these children, without any decision-making authority of their own, were Christian. However, so long as it was expedient to affirm Methodist Church membership, it was affirmed. Now the schools were no longer Methodist. The elders and headmen no longer claimed that which they had never truly accepted themselves---that their children were Christian. At the time of the surveys, the Sala people were not yet aware that Zambia Christian Mission schools would be given over to the government in 1968, and so the figures obtained reasonably compared with our records. It was still expedient in July, 1967, to admit membership in the Christian Church.

It is a problem to know how to save the several hundred youth who became Christian without the approbation of the elders and headmen---the decision-makers. It will take careful teaching and village pastoring to conserve them. The only solution is to establish churches in each of the villages where these youth are found.

Decisions at Tribal Level

When I first met with Chief Shakumbila and his headmen, two decisions were made by them. The first, that our mission be invited to build schools in the area was an easy decision, but it was of major importance to them. They wanted schools. For this they would agree to conditions, and it was of minor importance what the conditions were---so long as they got the schools. That I asked for the privilege of planting a church in each school comunity was to them a small price in return for what they were getting.

It seems odd that I should have sought the decision of the headmen and the chief---going through the proper channels of authority---in gaining permission to build schools, which to me was of secondary importance. I gave little concern to the casual approval of these African leaders for the establishing of churches after the schools, when planting churches was the one valid reason I had for actually coming among them.

I have already pointed out that this required of these animistic headmen a sort of theological decision. Their past experience had taught them that their children would be expected to join the missions church as the price for attending school. They were willing to approve their children becoming church members with the confidence that they would revert to tribal patterns once their schooling was complete.

All this is related to our question concerning the number of Christians in each village. Many of the elders ignored the fact that their children had made a confession of faith and were baptized. It was of no consequence when I asked for the planting of churches as a condition for providing schools. They accepted the condition, and it was of no consequence that their children "joined" the church as insurance for continued schooling. The fact that their children were nominally Christian did not disturb village patterns or structure at all.

The Christian young people had made no effort to lead their parents to Christ or to plead for a church in their village. Admittedly, I had not suggested this, but it could not have been done in any case, springing from the children who are very low in the pecking order in these African villages.

One purpose of our surveys was to suggest a church in each village, but we did not advance the idea through the children. We went where logic argued that we should go— to the persons of authority in each village—though they were pagan animists. A number accepted the suggestion that churches be planted in their villages. This was a real decision. Village churches have, since then, been planted and buildings erected by village leaders.

Decisions at Village Level

One of the queries asked in each village was: "How are village decisions made?" The answer was always the same. The headman, with the elders, was responsible.

Colson says, speaking of the Plateau Tonga, that the authority of the headman is nominal and depends upon his personal qualities. Most residents of the village will have some tenuous tie of relationship with him (1958:36; 1962:214). This is true with the villages among the Sala. We were informed that decisions were made by the headman, with the help of the elders. This pattern was demonstrated in every village we visited.

Decisions at Family Level

According to Colson,
Within the village, the basic unit is the family. This consists of a man, his wife or wives, such of their unmarried children as live with them, and other attached individuals or incomplete families (Colson and Gluckman 1961:121).

Concerning decision-making patterns at family level, we were informed that both the husband and wife share in making decisions. Colson, who is my principal authority concerning the Plateau Tonga, says:

So long as the household contained a married couple, it is theoretically under the authority of the husband. The wife and her children form the house, the "inganda," but the husband is known as the "singanda," "the owner of the house," "the warden of the house," "the person of the house" (1958:105).
But the answers given to our queries likely spoke accurately of any normal family problem requiring a decision.

Opinion Groups

One pertinent example of the power of an opinion group became evident during our surveys, though we made no attempt to find other examples.

Religious instruction on Sunday was required in each of our schools. For two years this class was attended by all school children and a number of adults of the Lumano community. There was, however, an increasing reluctance at Lumano to attend these sessions. A meeting was called and we attended. The difficulty was quick to find. A Jehovah's Witness, with his family and relatives, had canvassed the school community. The result was that all religious instruction was endangered. We dealt with the situation by pointing out the condition approved by the community, including the now-dissident Witness, for opening the school---that all children must take religious instruction on Sundays. The trouble-maker was reprimanded by community leaders and the problem was minimized, but here was an example of a minority opinion group that, by careful propaganda, all but disrupted the teaching of Bible courses accepted by the community as a condition for our providing its school.

Types of Labor

The majority of Sala villagers classified themselves as farmers. A farmer, of course, might be a prosperous Shona tribesman---or a Sala content to eke out an existence from a few garden plants clinging precipitously to the sides of a giant ant heap. However, other types of labor were listed. We learned of men serving with the police, of those trained

as carpenters, of truck drivers, storekeepers, bricklayers,
mechanics, and well diggers.

Village Wealth

Cattle play an important part in the life of the tribes. In
the thirty-seven villages we recorded 3,456 cattle. Shambololo village owned 500 cows that during the dry season were
taken to the Kafue River flats, where each week a different
family was responsible for herding them. This is common
when "failure of surface water in many areas made it essential for cattle to be moved to localities with perennial water"
(Colson 1958:32).

One of the evidences of wealth and advance was the growing number of burned-brick houses. The transition from the
mud-walled, thatch-roofed hut with no windows and a crude
door, to the rectangular, iron-roofed house with glazed windows and hung doors is an European innovation of far-
reaching consequence. We counted 236 brick houses. In
Chilonga village, every residence---eighteen in all---was
made of burned brick, Headman Chilonga's home was roofed
with iron and equipped with bathroom and modern plumbing.

We counted 268 turning plows to be drawn by oxen; but we
also noted fifty-three tractors, many of them new and diesel-
powered, on rubber, and with heavy disc plows and related
equipment. We counted thirteen trucks and two automobiles.
Many villages had hand-powered corn shellers and weighing
scales. Scotch carts we saw by the dozen. Many families
owned the latest prestige symbol---a combination radio-
phonograph, and most villages had at least one family with
a sewing machine.

A day was spent at the Mumbwa agricultural fair. Thousands of Africans were there. We saw samples of corn, peanuts, cotton, millet and velvet beans as fine as any produced
anywhere. We examined the several makes of tractors, plows,
harrows, cultivators, planters, fertilizing machines, grinding
machines and corn shellers---which increasing numbers of
African farmers are now buying. The livestock displays were
similar to those at the typical county fair in America. Here
was a forceful demonstration of the wealth of Zambia.

Village Wealth and Christian Stewardship

What does this wealth say to church stewardship? African Christians, led to want their own church and evangelist, can pay for them themselves. Missions committed to institutional work gave little attention to stewardship teaching. With a budget of overseas gifts and government subsidies amounting to thousands of Rhodesian pounds annually, emphasis on stewardship that might result in receipts into the church treasury of a hundred pounds per year seemed a waste of time or a matter of small consequence. The school-church congregations were made up of children who had little to give in any case. But those contemplating the Christian Way must know that stewardship is a part of that Way.

Evidences of Integration

Everywhere we looked, we saw evidences of innovation and integration. The immigration of the Shona-Sindebele and its forcing of adjustments upon the tribes in the area also brought changes upon themselves. Accommodation had to be made for differences in foods, climate, and terrain and in "the development of economic, social and political arrangements with the indigenous population" (Barnett 1952: 87). The immigrants in this case came as the innovators, bringing radical change.

The Sala and related tribes were ultraconservative. Some of them were still fishers and hunters and food gatherers. They did little farming. Their lands still covered with forests, they were content to leave that way—useful only as pasturelands for their cattle.

The Shona-Sindebele came, and soon fields appeared as the bush was cleared away. Lands were plowed, and soon there were fields of corn, and the corn was harvested and a cash economy introduced. In the following year, the fields had doubled, and tractors made their appearance. Soon trucks were hauling grain to market, and crude roads appeared. Within a year or two liberal-minded Sala were following suit. Chief Shakumbila began clearing land, and local men began doing the same. An economic revolution

began in Sala country that continues to this day. Cash income
meant new machinery, sewing machines, radios, guitars,
bicycles, motorbikes, beds, brick houses, pressure lanterns,
glazed windows, new clothes, new foods, more beer, wider
travel, more wives, and so many things they had never known
before.

The changes continue. Satisfying their recently discovered
needs, as Barnett says, "enriches the soil out of which
others spring. The fulfillment of one need establishes conditions out of which others emerge" (1952:148).

Old values and customs are being swept away. Land
rituals are no longer practised. The shrines are decaying.
A younger generation is pushing aside the old. The significance of all this is that increasing portions of the population
are now receptive to new ideas. The economic revolution is
eroding the tribal religious patterns and they now have less
meaning. Something must take their place. The Gospel could
become the most significant innovation of all.

These people must have something new and stable to cling
to. The Church must fill that need. A house of worship in
each village, provided by the Christians and well care for,
could demonstrate the village's appreciation to God for the
Gospel—a village effort constructed to provide something
worthy of the Good News to be taught and preached there.
This concept needs to be put to them. Providing a house of
worship should be a labor of love. With the old shrines
disappearing, a new place of worship for the only true God
must take their place.

Tribal Crafts

A few miles from our mission home and hidden by heavy
bush are three smelting furnaces where a century ago Sala
artisans smelted iron and shaped it into spears, hoes, and
axes. The furnaces stand within sight of Nachilumbi school.
Few pupils know what the furnaces were for, and few Sala
know the art of smelting. The skill has been lost.

A stroll through one of the villages reveals that many
crafts are disappearing. Seldom will one see the intricately
carved wooden stools. at one time the pride of the elders.

Cast-iron pots have displaced the clay pots of a generation past. In thirty-seven villages we found only two women who knew how to mold and fire clay pots. There is a carelessness in so important a task as thatching. A new cash economy makes it easier to buy a basket at the trading store than to weave one at home.

One senses a feeling of incongruity in noting that boys at school are still taught how to make ox yokes, when the ambition of every young farmer is to buy his own tractor. The sight of women stamping grain in the wooden stamping blocks will soon be a thing of the past, and the grinding stones for making flour are disappearing. The diesel-powered mills are taking their place, and now the woman cycles to the mill with her grain to be ground into meal.

Spears, traps, and snares are giving way to shotguns. The heavy hoe, tool of the African woman with her traditional task of cultivating the gardens, is inefficient in a fifty-acre field of corn. The cultivator is replacing it. With the disappearance of the hoe go many marriage and purification rituals of significance to the animistic ways of the past.

Every village had one or more drums, and we found two "kankobele"—single-stringed instruments—the string struck with a reed while the bow is held in the player's teeth. A few brought their small "African pianos," but we saw not more than five altogether. We found two African marimbas. Several were eager to demonstrate their haunting melody—a sound in danger of disappearing forever. Every village had one or more guitars. This is the instrument replacing the indigenous drums, marimbas, and kankobele—doomed to be relics of the past.

We explained our interest in their instruments, recounting experiences in West Africa where the churches use drums and tamborines and stringed viols. The people were interested. I am convinced that their indigenous music forms and instruments can still be captured and preserved for Christ and His Church.

Health and Cleanliness

There was an obvious parallel between village prosperity

and visible cleanliness. Peter Chizuma's village was clean.
It was one of the wealthiest of all the villages surveyed.
Karowash was also well kept, and its wealth is obvious. In
contrast, villages like Chimbe Mauma, Ntembe, Cimena, and
Moza were in poor repair and often filthy---and poor by
comparison.

Drunkenness

Married women traditionally brew the beer, and there is
much drunkenness. The elders of the Kakombo village said,
"We like to drink a lot." Cimena leaders admitted that there
is "too much" drunkenness. Steven's village is more sophis-
ticated. Its inhabitants drink "Lion Lager" at local clubs,
and this poses a problem of growing magnitude for the
government. Commercial liquors are now available to Africans recently introduced to the new cash economy, and
drunkenness is a national concern.

Diet

The basic food of the Sala is cornmeal. From the meal
"sadza" is made, which is eaten with meat or vegetables,
or with greens and roots gathered in the forests. These
villages are in what Murdock calls "the milking complex,"
but our limited investigation in eight of the thirty-seven
villages revealed only two that used any milk at all (1959:
365). Few villages would kill a cow except on important fes-
tive occasions. Other times beef was eaten only when an
animal died or was killed by a hyena. The eating of wild
game depended on accessibility to hunting areas. Villagers
close to streams added fish to their diet. Only one village
raised pigs.

Through the rains, melons, squash, pumpkins and sweet
potatoes add to the choice of foods of the Sala, and peanuts,
kept in supply through the year, provide essential fats. Thus
far, in spite of the rising cash economy, little change has
come in diet. Their increased income is used to purchase
radios, bicycles, furniture, clothing, cars, trucks, and
tractors.

Festivals

Lumano villagers said that a feast was given by a farmer when he purchased a new truck or new tractor. Chikanka elders told us that when a girl reached puberty a festival was celebrated. Mweenga village added that the feasts were held annually for all girls of the age group reaching puberty during the year. Shambololo elders recounted that a feast with beer and tribal dancing was given at the death of a village resident, at which time a relative would be chosen to inherit his wealth.

Shortly after our village surveys, a feast was given by headman Peter Chizuma. One of our missionaries was there and this is his report:

I arrived at the village at 1.15 (on the motorcycle) having passed an incredible number of people also headed for the same place. The occasion was the "coming out" of Peter Chizuma's daughter. It celebrated the event of the girl's first menstrual period, and signified that she was now of marriageable age. I gathered that in the old days (and sometimes even yet) girls of this area were sometimes confined for as long as four to six months. This was done to teach them the facts of married life, and to keep them out of the sun, so that their skin might become lighter and hence more beautiful. At the end of their time of isolation the girls were given a "coming out" celebration . . . in essence a time to present the young ladies to potential suitors. Peter Chizuma's daughter had been confined only a week because, he told me, "she is a school girl."
There was a great deal of home brew drinking all around. The girl was "brought out" at 2.30. The people clapped and sang. She was dressed in white flower-girl type outfit, and was accompanied by four small girls---all clothed in white also. An adult held an umbrella over her to---I suppose---shield her from the sun. She was led to a chair placed in a shady spot. Her head, hung low from the time she was brought out of her confining hut, was not raised once. She never smiled. In front of the chair a large petrol

drum was placed on end, and on top of this drum a
smiling young man climbed, to raise money for the
girl. He did so energetically. At this time there were
probably 300 people present and, under the enthusiastic urging of the gentleman on the drum, some forty-
one pounds (about $115.00) for the girl were collected.
By 5.00 o'clock the crowd, now over 1,000 strong in
my estimation, was being fed. Four cattle had been
slaughtered and vast quantities of sadza prepared.
Everyone was in a jovial mood, induced, partly at
least, by the drinking of the beer. (Letter written to
the Author by Leroy Randall, September 13, 1967).

These festivals can be won for Christ. A letter from Don
Mechem, missionary in the Sala area, dated February 7,
1968, tells of his village preaching concentrated on four
villages:

Samuel, the church leader at Mamvule, and Mabele,
are planning a Christian feast for Kafololo Village.
They are hoping that through such a feast many people
will be attracted at which time a preaching service
will be held. A call to repent will be given with the
hope many will respond and eventually a church
started in that village.

Such a festival among people in transition from the old
traditions can have tremendous influence in winning the pagan
villages to Christ, especially if it is the climax of a mass
meeting of several hundred tribesmen called together to hear
the Gospel.

Also, if the pattern of taking a special offering of money,
as witnessed by Leroy Randall at the "coming out" party of
Peter Chizuma's daughter, were adopted, it could be a means
of challenging the Sala to finance new chapels in the villages.

Migration to the City

We found few unmarried young men in the villages. Colson
says:

The majority of men have spent some time in employ-
ment, and it is an accepted thing for young men to work
for wages for short periods before settling down to the

reserves . . . Later he goes out again, probably for a longer period . . . Some men, of course, go for good (1958: 66-67).

The Family

Understanding family relationships would be of benefit in planning for village evangelism. We particularly wanted to learn the extent of polygamy. A number of villages were reluctant to answer our queries, but data from fourteen villages gave information that will determine aspects of our future evangelistic approach.

The location of married sons and daughters provided interesting information. In Karowash village "quite a few had left the area. The headman has three sons in the Zambia police force." Many of Munashintuli's married sons and daughters lived in the vicinity. Both Kakombo and Chimika informed us that a number of married children with parents had moved elsewhere by their own choice. Peter Chizuma told us that younger families had moved to work on the railroad. Others had gone to Lusaka.

Colson confirms what we found in our surveys:

Marriage is usually virilocal, but a man's choice of residence is a matter for his personal decision. He may settle with paternal relatives, with maternal relatives, with affines, or with strangers (1962:22). The Tonga themselves know no reason why a man should not live where he will... No rule of residence bound a man or woman to one set of kinsmen rather than another. The Tonga are matrilineal, but tend to be virilocal, since the husband usually takes his wife with him wherever he has settled (1962:180-181).

Marriage Patterns

A number of villages had no intertribal marriages, but seventeen out of eighteen at Chumbinga crossed tribal lines. Namboli reported "many" such unions. We heard of "several" at Peter Chizuma's. Cross-tribal marriages appear to be on the increase. All tribal groups in the area were involved. We were interested in learning where young men found their wives. The answer was always the same. "In nearby Tonga villages." "Where they find them." "In neighboring villages."

There are few bridges for carrying the Gospel better than family web relationships. Our surveys revealed how widely the families were scattered. I believe McGavran's observations regarding the growth of the early church can be duplicated in Zambia:

With every new accession not only did the numbers of persons with one or two Christian relatives increase, but individual Jews began to find that they had large numbers of Christian relatives. A Jew named Joshua might, for example, first hear that his wife's sister's family had become Christian; and then that his own mother's brother's family, including some of Joshua's first cousins, had followed in the Christian way. Then he hears that his own sister and her husband and her husband's parents have accepted Jesus as Messiah. Would not the cumulative effect on Joshua be tremendous? Joshua is typical of the average man in a society where there is a Christward movement afoot. The peoples which make up the nations of Indonesia, China, India, Japan, and Africa keep track of relatives very much more carefully than do individualistic Westerners. Relationships are known more accurately and over greater distances. In such societies movements gather enormous power as relative after relative becomes Christian (1961:21-22).

Marriage patterns are similar. Smith speaks of the "long drawn-out preliminary discussions by members of the two families; the bride's reluctancies, real and simulated; the entry of the bride into her new home---all these things are of great interest." He continues by referring to

certain acts which symbolize the union. At an Ila wedding bride and groom sit face to face with a plate of thick porridge between them; she breaks off a morsel, dips it into relish and gives it to her man; and he then does the same to her. This beautiful ceremony is eloquent in suggestion of the true nature of marriage: eating together means union in the close friend-

ship of equals; the exchange of bread signifies mututal
service.

There are analogous acts among other tribes: here,
an exchange of saliva (a part of themselves) in a cup
of milk; here a mutual anointing; here drinking milk
together; and so on (1946:85).

Audrey Richards describes similar ceremonies among
the Bemba (Colson and Gluckman 1961:182-183), and Colson
recounts marriage rites among the Tonga (1958:336 ff.) which
closely parallel the pattern of marriage described below.

Peter Chizuma gave us the following explanation of a typical marriage arrangement in the Sala-Tonga-Ila area:

When a Tonga young man falls in love with a Tonga
girl and wishes to marry her, he goes first to a friend
who consents to make a first contact with the girl. The
friend goes to talk to the girl. She may express enthusiasm for the proposed match, she may not, or she
may not feel inclined to say anything at all. The friend
reports to the suitor, who gauges the girl's reaction
and determines whether to carry the matter further.
If he is encouraged, he goes next to his father. His
father visits the father of the girl but is told that, before any discussion can be undertaken, something
must be given to "open the girl's father's mouth." The
man is given one or two pounds and the discussion
proceeds. Preliminary agreements may be reached
at this time, but the boy may not marry the girl yet.

Now follows a divided state called "chisassa" in which
the young man and his bride-to-be sleep separately in
a partitioned hut. The young woman is guarded by a
girl. This state continues for an unspecified period.

The father of the girl now lets it be known that before
the girl can be taken out of "chisassa" he must be
given a certain sum, usually between ten shillings and
two pounds. In the old days two hoes were given for
this purpose.

The girl out of chisassa, the father says he should be
given a spear. The spear, and the hunting that can be
done with it, symbolically takes the place of the
daughter.

Finally the father of the girl requests that the bride-price be paid. The payment is made in cattle, usually between five and ten, with one extra to be given to the girl's mother, to repay her for difficulties her daughter caused her, especially when she was small. Often, only half of the cattle are paid initially, and this is accepted practice. When the cattle are given to the girl's father he sets a day on which she will be handed over to her husband-to-be.

When that day arrives three people (two women and one man) are sent from the village of the young man to the village of the girl. They come at dawn and secret themselves in one of the huts of the village . . . the girl must not be allowed to see them or she will run away.

Evening comes and the three people go to the hut of the girl's father. He requests another spear and it is given. The father now calls the young lady. He requests that she give him a cup of water. She does so, he takes some water in his mouth, and spits on the girl. He says, "I give you to... (the name of the husband-to-be). At this point the girl is taken by the afore-mentioned three people, and she puts up a terrific struggle. Her clothing may be badly torn. But she is taken to the village and hut of her husband. In the hut of her husband it is required by Tonga custom that all crying and struggling cease.

Next morning the new husband and wife prepare some porridge (sadza), cooking it very well. They eat it together. At this time the husband may give his wife a new name, often the name of his best friend.

That same morning the people of the village are assembled. They are given porridge to eat, mixed with cattle-fat. The wife is anointed with some of the fat, this being the final demonstration that she is truly married to her man.

If only a part of the bride-price has been paid the father, and the rest of the payment does not come soon enough to satisfy him, he may demand that the girl return home until such a time as the payment is completed.

The sequence of events given is essentially a mixture of the old and the new. Money was, of course, not used in the old Tonga marriage procedures, and today is used as a substitution for objects once given. Many Tonga marriages are similar to the example given here: others vary to a large degree.

The Prevalence of Polygamy

Our data regarding the extent of polygamy came from fifteen villages. Forty-eight of two hundred and ten families were polygamous. Only one village tested had no polygamy to report.

We found that the polygamous family lived in a cluster of dwellings with each wife having a hut for herself and her children which she shared with her husband. He had no dwelling of his own and shared his time and divided his possessions among his wives.

Six men formerly of the Zambia Christian Mission were polygamists. Three had taken second wives following our arrival. The Church had withdrawn fellowship from them. Three others had voluntarily withdrawn for no apparent reason, but we found that they had taken second wives as well.

Animism and Christianity

Few villages offered us information regarding animistic practices. Many denied that such practices continue. Headman Karowash (whom we baptized during our survey) told us that the rain shrines were allowed to decay unless an extended drought occurred. Libations of beer were offered to the mizimu under two trees near the village.

In nineteen villages we found nine rain shrines, four spirit-gates and two hunting shrines. The rain shrines were in a general state of disrepair, but this was the dry season, well before the rains were needed. Come time for the planting season and the rain shrines would be refurbished. The spirit-gates and hunting shrines showed evidence of use. The data given was far from complete. Many people, particularly small children and babies, were wearing charms, and the practice was as prevalent among Christians as among non-Christians.

The headman and elders of one village gave us detailed information concerning the old rituals:

The ancestral spirits are consulted during times of local crisis. Within a given tribe there are many prominent spirits, but the people of a given area or village generally pray only to those they consider "their own" spirits . . . usually there are three or four, and they are the spirits of important people who once inhabited the area. A spirit attains prominence if during its physical life it was a great leader, a wealthy man, an intelligent hunter, or perhaps a good fighter. The prominent spirits of the area are Mwanashingwala, Hakajambihi, Himalumba, and Chizoma. Of these, the most revered is the first mentioned Mwanashingwala.

A local crisis may take the form of a drought, someone's illness, or some disease affecting the livestock. At such a time a spirit medium is called. The medium is usually related by blood to the ancestral spirits to be consulted, and seems to possess a mystical "talent" for dealing with them. Beer is brewed by the women of the village and this beer is used as an integral part of the consultation ritual.

The spirit gates and shrine (if the village still has them) are located on the periphery of the village, or not far from it.

The spirit gate consists simply of a number of poles driven into the ground . . . the number of poles depends on the number of ancestors revered by the village The shrine is a small hut built as a dwelling place of the spirits. Often there are three or four indentations in the floor of the hut, and the people imagine that the spirits sit in these indentations.

The medium takes some of the beer brewed by the women to the spirit gate. He calls and prays to each spirit individually, and they are said to come out of the shrine to listen to him. As he calls for the spirit he ladles beer into the space between two of the poles of the gate said to belong to that particular spirit. . . each spirit has its own space. For a ladle he uses a calabash with a hole in one end. His prayer is simple. After invoking the spirit he says, "We have come to you for . . . ," and he states the reason.

Besides beer, the medium may bring with him other offerings for the ancestral spirits. Sometimes maize (corn) is poured with the libation of beer at the spirit gate. Very often when the medium leaves he will deposit a number of well-made axes inside the shrine hut, one ax for each spirit, and placed at the spot each spirit is thought to occupy. The calabash that was used to pour the beer is also left in the shrine.

The ancestral spirits, after their consultation with the medium, retire to their shrine-home, and discuss the problem brought to their attention. They will make a decision about what should be done.

Both Lumano and Mukwengu had their own rainmakers. Several huts in Chikanka village were abandoned and new ones constructed because a person had died at the old site. There was fear that his "sickness" would affect the abandoned huts. Monunza village insisted that while animistic practices were still popular, all persons in the village went to a neighboring settlement where all the shrines were located. This is common talk. We were convinced it meant they also continued their animistic rituals at Monunza.

In two instances only did we hear that taboos concerning women working with cattle were still remembered. Women at Karowash would not work with oxen, and a few women in Sugar Number One refused to enter the cattle kraals. It is likely that taboos on women coming into contact with cattle is more widespread than we discovered.

Colson has said:

Traditionally girls and women should have no contact with cattle, and were not allowed to approach the cattle kraals. The Tonga maintain that this is only a matter of custom, and that neither women nor cattle can be harmed by the contact; but nevertheless they dislike the expedient of using girls for herding duties (1961: 167).

We believe there was more animism and spirit worship than was revealed, and yet Colson has pointed out that many of the Tonga no longer adhere to the old ways. This is equally true of the Sala:

> Missions have worked in the area since 1905. Many Tonga are Christians, of eight different sects. Others are sceptics who deny the old beliefs without accepting those introduced by the missionaries. Many claim that they have forgotten the "mizimu," and that these no longer affect them in any way. There are whole villages where no one makes offerings to the "mizimu" or considers them in any way. On the other hand, there are many Tonga to whom the "mizimu" are a vital part of life (1961:2).

People at Namboli insisted they did not worship in the old ways any more. They asked that a church be planted in their village. Shortly after the surveys, preaching services began. At the first opportunity offered, forty-five made the confession and were baptized. Thirty-five were adults. By February, 1968, this infant congregation had built its own building with its own resources and labor.

Christians and Pagans

Pagan village headmen ignored any youth who were members of the Methodist Church, with some doing the same with baptized teen-agers of the Christian Church.

Seventeen of the thirty-seven villages had members of the Zambia Christian Mission (Christian Church) according to our records. (See Figure 2.) Thirteen of the seventeen villages compared with our membership figures. Referring to Figure 5, Cimena did not acknowledge the ten baptized teen-agers resident there; nor did Kariangire with ten; Kapoba with nine, and Mosa with eight. By our records seventeen villages should have had 373 communicants. By headman figures, we found 317 --- still a reasonable figure and the one I have used.

Attendance on Sundays confirmed the figures given by the headman. Congregations of school-churches were predominantly teen-age youth. During the school year these young people were faithful. The holidays were a different matter. The number of professing Christians of all denominations in the thirty-seven villages---Christian Church, 317; Adventists, 187; Methodists, 121; Apostolics, 115; Witnesses, 16; Zionists, 5; and Catholics, 2; (Figure 4) was as accurate as as one could hope for. Fourteen villages reported members of the Christian Church, nineteen reported Adventists, twenty-three reported Methodists, nine reported Apostolics, six reported Witnesses, two reported Zionists, and one reported Catholics.

Seven hundred sixty-three communicants of all denominations were found. To determine the total Christian community I multiplied the number of communicants by two* making a total community of 1,526. Figure 6 illustrates what I found.

The strength of the Apostolics and Adventists is noteworthy (Figure 6). Both sects reported only adult baptized believers though both insisted they had many unbaptized children in attendance. Neither group has schools or other institutional work. The Apostolics give emphasis to faith healing. Both groups are indigenous. Only on rare occasions do missionaries visit them and then only to lend encouragement. Their strength and virility have much to say to those institutional missionaries who insist upon continued paternalistic and subsidized mission as the most solid method of evangelism.

Christians in the Whole Sala Area

I assumed that the distribution of Christians in the sample surveyed would be normal for the whole district. True, the Christian Church was strong in the village samples, but the Methodists were strong in the northwest. Using the 5,000 population for the survey area as a base, with 763 Christians,

---

* As I estimated the "Christian" versus the animist population, I resorted to a rule of thumb--- "The Christian community is twice as large as the number of baptized believers." This is an approximation, but when comparing "Christians" with total population it is much more accurate than to compare baptized believers or communicants only.

RELIGIOUS COMMUNITIES BY DENOMINATION
IN THE THIRTY-SEVEN VILLAGES SURVEYED

- - - - -

TOTAL POPULATION 5,000

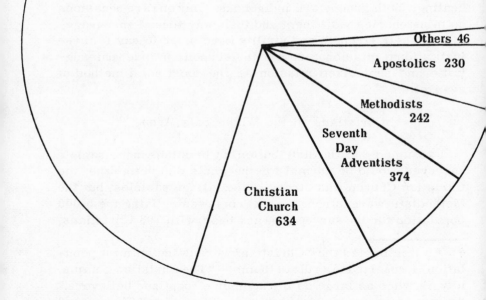

Animists 3,500

Others 46

Apostolics 230

Methodists 242

Seventh Day Adventists 374

Christian Church 634

Figure 6

an average of 153 per thousand was obtained.

With an estimated population of 17,000 for the whole of the Sala, an average of 153 communicants per thousand gave approximately 2,600 Christians for the entire area. Using the same rule of thumb---two times the number of communicants equals the number of Christian community---the total community among the Sala and related tribes is 5,200 people, as graphically illustrated in Figure 7, leaving a total of 11,800 pagan animists, or 70 per cent of the total population.

Christians in Zambia

According to the 1968 *World Christian Handbook* (1968: 97), in Zambia there are 104,000 communicant members in regular churches. The Independent churches claim an approximately 100,000 Christian community, and the Roman Catholic Church reports a community of 550,000.

Applying the rule---two times the number of communicants---would give a Christian community of 208,000 in the regular churches. This figure, added to the Christian community of the Independent and Roman Catholic churches, gives a total community of 858,000 for the whole of Zambia, as indicated in Figure 8. The estimated population of the country in 1970 is 4,000,000.

Comparing Figure 5 with Figure 6 indicates that the number of Christians per thousand for the Sala is somewhat higher than for Zambia as a whole. Approximately 15 per cent of the Sala are baptized believers, as compared to a bit less than 11 per cent for Zambia while about 30 per cent of the Sala may be classified as Christian community as compared to 21 per cent for the country.

These percentages differ radically from those given in the January 1968 issue of the *International Review of Missions* which says, with reference to Zambia, "The Christian population amounts to about 70 per cent of the nation" (Vol. LVII, No. 225, Jan., 1968).

Of highest importance are the two, Figure 5 and 6, indicating that well over 70 per cent of Zambia is pagan. Add to this the fact that the power structure in almost every village is still animistic and that the Christians are small numbers

NON-CHRISTIAN COMMUNITY, AND CHRISTIAN COMMUNITY
AND COMMUNICANTS IN SALA AREA

- - - - -

TOTAL POPULATION 17,000

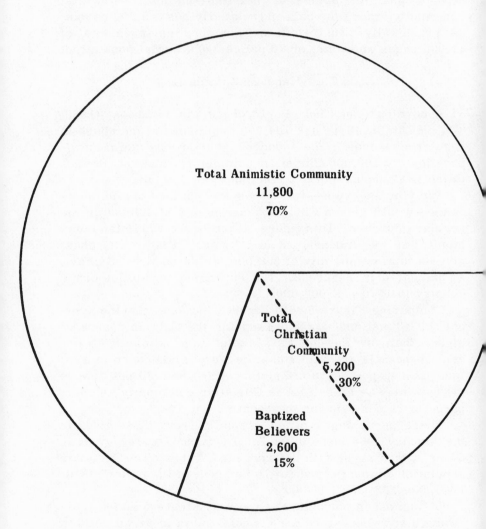

Figure 7

NON-CHRISTIAN COMMUNITY, AND CHRISTIAN COMMUNITY AND COMMUNICANTS IN ZAMBIA

- - - - -

TOTAL POPULATION 4,000,000

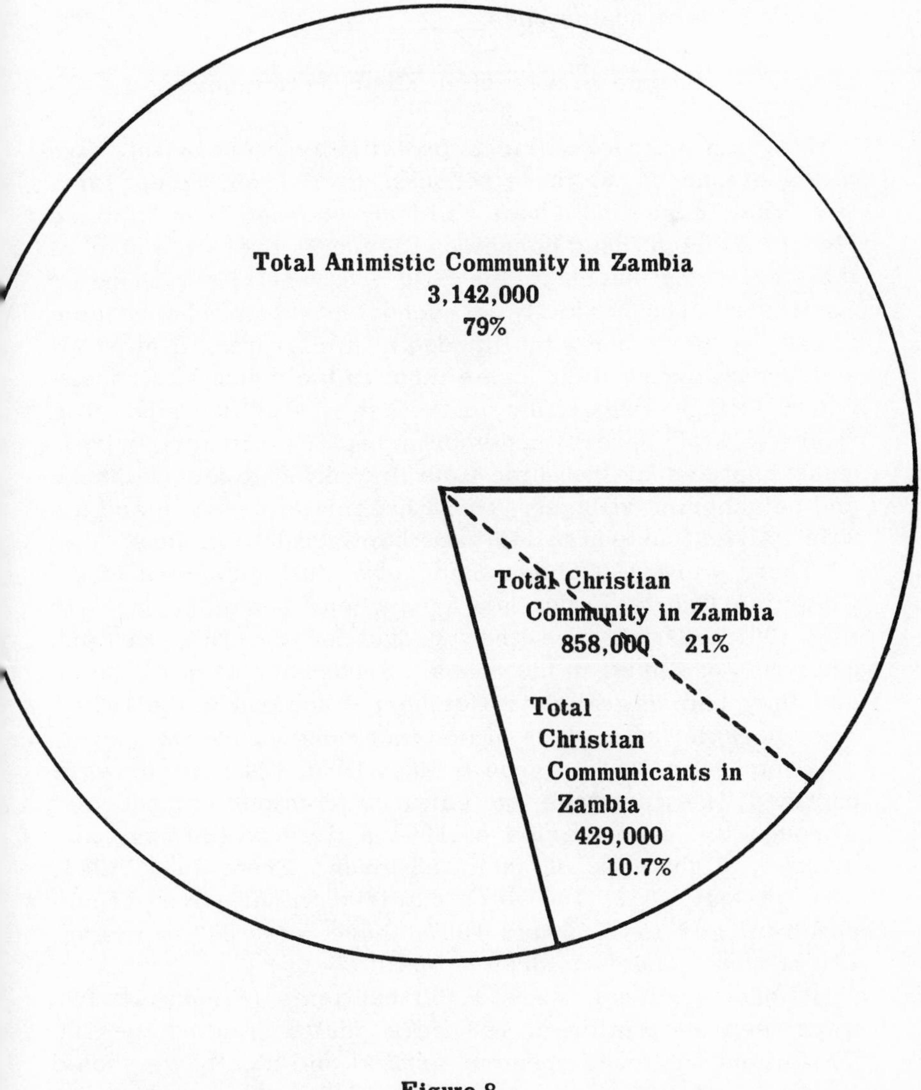

Total Animistic Community in Zambia
3,142,000
79%

Total Christian
Community in Zambia
858,000   21%

Total
Christian
Communicants in
Zambia
429,000
10.7%

Figure 8

of school boys and girls or ex-school youth of various denominations, and one must agree that the Church is not in a
strong position.

The task now is to win the heart of each village, and especially to win the power structure---those responsible for
making village, clan, and tribal decisions. The 70 per cent of
Zambia, still animistic and pagan, are winnable; and God
wants all the winnable ones.

Source of Christian Church Members

The majority of villages investigated were within five
miles of one of our three schools. Until 1966, except for a
few Sala-Tonga-Ila school children who had been baptized
(see lower right hand corner of Figure 9), every member of
the Christian Church in the Sala area was either Shona or
Sindebele. The majority of school children who became
Christian were from the Rhodesia immigrants. Almost all
additions through 1966 came through the schools. Concentrated village evangelism in 1967 suggested that adult Sala
might be won. Several headmen and elders, with their wives,
were baptized at the same time in Mukwengo and Chikanka
and neighboring villages. Tonga headman Karowash and his
wife walked fourteen miles to be baptized late in June.

There were 190 Shona-Sindebele adult members of the
Christian Church in the Sala area when I began our work in
mid-1963. They were the product of the New Zealand
Churches of Christ in the Shabani area of Southern Rhodesia
and they had migrated to Northern Rhodesia in the 1950s.
They became the nucleus of our four congregations.

From June, 1963, through May, 1964, 124 persons were
baptized; 104 were teen-age children from our new schools.
Through the same period of 1964 and 1965, 100 were im-
mersed, eighty-six of them children. From June, 1965,
through May 1966, 104 were baptized, ninety-five of them
children; and in 1966 and 1967, there were 830 baptisms,
680 of them school children.

Altogether there were 1,158 baptisms (Figure 9); 965
were teen-age children; 193 were adults. Adding the 190
Christians we found upon our arrival and ideally we should

have had 1,348 Christians in the Sala area at the time of our village surveys.

Contrasts in Numbers of Children And Adults

The graph of growth (Figure 7) illustrates the contrast between numbers of children and adults baptized over the four-year period. Figure 5 gives the same picture for the villages surveyed. Out of fourteen villages accounting for 317 members of the Christian Church, 199 were young people, and 118 were adults. A further examination of the eight villages from which these children came reveals that thirty-nine of forty-four members at Lumano were teenagers. Seven out of sixteen at Chikanka were young people; twelve out of twenty at Mukwengo; twenty-five out of sixty at Namboli; six out of fifteen at Kakambo and Chimika; thirty-two out of forty-two at Sugar Number One; ten of nineteen at Sugar Number Two; and all sixty-eight at Kakomwe---all of these became Christians through the schools.

It is significant that Lumano village---with thirty-nine out of forty-four members being teen-age young people---is the closest village to Lumano school; that Sugar Number One with thirty-two out of forty-two members being school youngsters, is less than one-quarter mile from Shakumbila school; and that all sixty-eight members at Kakomwe are school children; and Kakomwe is the closest village to Nachilumbi school (Figure 3). In villages close to schools there is apparently a better chance for youth who become Christian to stay Christian.

The Location of the Churches

Survey Map 4 shows the location of each of the four Christian Churches in the Sala area at the time of the surveys (marked C). Late in 1967 a fifth congregation was planted at Namboli village, the result of village evangelism.

The church at Lumano worships in the school as does the church at Nachilumbi. The Shakumbila congregation worships in a burned brick steel-roofed building largely paid for by the mission in 1964.

Only one building—prior to July, 1967—was built by the initiative of the Christian community. Sitantesaukwe is made up entirely of Shona-Sindebele believers, and these people, without consulting the missionaries, provided their own humble sanctuary and worship in it faithfully. In contrast to Lumano, Nachilumbi, and Shakumbila, Sitantesaukwe is a congregation with adult leadership while the school churches are congregations of children with but a handful of older people.

Attendance at the three school-churches has been consistently high through ten months of the school year. At Sitantesaukwe it has been good throughout the year. The contrast between young people and adults was most apparent at services at the schools. Every aspect of the service has been geared to the children. Adults have attended but, in proportion to the children, they are few indeed.

There was a difference in the number of children attending church through the school year and those in attendance during vacation. Were the school-churches inseparably tied to the schools so that it was natural for the communities to believe that vacation from school meant vacation from church as well? Or might it be that here was an example of polytheistic coexistence with the presence of the church accepted as necessary through the school year, but all the while the ancestors are remembered too?

In January, 1969, the Zambia Christian Mission turned its schools back to the Department of Education. Many of the children, with careful pastoral oversight, will remain faithful, but those who attended out of expediency will no longer be there.

There was a greater ingathering of souls from June, 1966, through June, 1967, than at any other time in the short history of the Zambia Christian Mission. Eight hundred and thirty souls were added to the Church in one year. Only 328 were added in the previous three years. Why the significant harvest in 1966 and 1967?

Rapid Growth in 1966 And 1967

In June of 1966, two young missionaries, Don Mechem and

Leroy Randall, moved into the Sala area. Don soon built a modest home near Lumano school. Leroy moved to Sha-kumbila's community, about thirty miles from the Mechems. While both young men were saddled with the oversight of the schools through 1967, they were determined to concen-trate on evangelism, and this took them to the villages. Over 150 people, most of them adults, and many of them Sala-Tonga-Ila tribesmen, made the good confession and were baptized in June, 1967.

I do not regret having used the schools as keys to open the doors of evangelism in the Sala area. We very likely would not have gotten into Zambia without them, but I am thankful for the vision of the young missionaries who refused to be chained to those institutions. There is in Zambia today expectation of great growth as the force of nineteen mission-aries concentrate on soul-winning and planting of churches.

The Future of the Young Christians

What of the young men and women who became Christian from June, 1963, through June, 1967, many of whom have remained faithful? Might they serve as an effective nucleus, in each village, for a church? I believe these young men and women can be saved for the Church and used in the planting of village congregations. They cannot, however, take the initiative alone! They cannot move against the power struc-ture. The solution must come through village evangelism. These youth can be conserved with the blessing of the elders through prayerfully planned evangelism in the villages. If not, the major result of four years' missions endeavor will be lost.

I have referred to my early contacts with the chief and his headmen in obtaining their approval for entering the area and starting the work of the Zambia Christian Mission. Proper procedures were used in gaining permission of the village and tribal leaders to come in. Though, as Colson has pointed out (1962:214-216), the authority of the headman is of little consequence, yet there is a power structure that must be respected. I observed this as early as 1962. Only after much discussion and after they had heard my proposals was the decision made that I could come into their midst. There are lesser power structures within the area which often represent a group of villages. Each of our school communities selected its own committee. Anything I did was carefully channeled through the school committee, for here was the power structure. I would not have gotten far by ignoring that structure. The village power structure is centered in the headman working with the elders. Villages large and small have it, and it would be futile for the missionary to initiate any evangelistic effort outside the power structure. Approval of the leaders must first be obtained.

Dr. Kenneth Kaunda, President of Zambia, has said:

The tribal community was a mutual society. It was organized to satisfy the basic human needs of all its members and, therefore, individualism was discouraged . . . The basic unit of life is not the individual or immediate family (as in industrial societies) but the community. This means that there must be fundamental agreement upon goals and all must act together (Morris and Kaunda 1968:24-25).

What Robinson has said of the Yoruba is true regarding the Sala:

Within these primary social units, individuality is limited. Important decisions, such as changing religious affiliation, are rarely made without the knowledge and consent of the head of the unit. It is sometimes easier for an entire domestic family or larger social unit to embrace a new religion than for an individual to do so alone (Grimley and Robinson 1966: 255).

The Value of the Village Surveys

It was not possible to cover thirty-seven villages in five weeks time. I do not suggest that mine were anthropological studies in depth, though I did apply principles of research that could provide data pertinent to both anthropology and sociology. My purpose was to determine factors that might contribute to the winning of many souls and the planting of many churches. Several conclusions have been reached.

The increasing wealth of the people testifies that the Sala and their neighbors can pay their own way. Their authority patterns say that they can give oversight to autonomous congregations and church programs at either a regional or national level. Evidences of integration everywhere speak of increasing cooperation and nationalism and a diminishing of tribal differences, and suggest a time to come when a strong unified Church among these 17,000 in Zambia can be a reality.

Their tribal crafts still suggest the possibility of churches and forms of worship indigenous to Africa. Their marriage patterns beg for a beautification of Christianity as do their homes and families. The problem of polygamy needs a new approach by the servants of God anxious to lead the African multitudes to the feet of the Master. The prevalence of animism, after sixty years of Christian mission, demands a kind of evangelism that will disciple Africans in their corporate existence---i.e, in their villages, fields, homes, and organized life.

All these and more speak to the contemporary mission in the Sala country and, indeed, in Zambia. The message is exciting, and for the missionary vision, insight, and faith, it tells of multitudes to be won and numerous churches to be planted and nurtured all across the young country of Zambia and much of Africa.

9

A Suggested Strategy
for the Future

It is possible for a mission to divest itself of its institutional handicap and overlook other problems which deny the ingathering of souls its missionaries desire. The Zambia Christian Mission is confronted with this danger.

We Cannot Disciple
Zambia through the Present Churches

A community of several extended family groups of Shona and Sindebele tribesmen had moved in the mid-fifties from Eastern Southern Rhodesia to the Mumbwa district of Northern Rhodesia. There were a thousand or more in this 800-mile migration. Old tribal lands were overpopulated; and these people knew of untouched fertile lands in the Mumbwa area.

Of the 1000, about 150 were Christian, and during the next thirteen years most of the rest have come to consider themselves Christian, though only 400 had become active church members by 1968. Chief Shakumbila of the Sala tribe had offered them residence, and so they came.

In their old tribal homes they had lived in the Dadaya area of the New Zealand Churches of Christ. I knew of this migration from its start. Many of these immigrants were members of the Church of Christ (or Christian Church), and shortly after arrival they selected leaders for the Church, and worship began. By 1955 they were pleading for assistance. In 1963 my wife and I moved in among them.

I recall my first worship service with these brethren, meeting under the traditional "n'daba" tree. They had invited the chief and many Sala elders to worship with us. Hymns were sung in Shona. Announcements and sermons were in Shona. Not one word was spoken in Tonga, the language of the area. Neither the chief nor his elders understood what was going on. It soon became apparent that the Shona-Sindebele Christian community, which by now had become our Christian community, was determined to worship in its own language. A few Shona made it plain they did not want dirty, illiterate, lazy, drunken Sala in their church. Soon I provided new hymnals in Tonga. The Rhodesian immigrants refused to use them. The Tonga Bible was introduced. It seldom was used. The Shona-Sindebele prefer their own tongue.

There has been some growth of the Church, but until June, 1967, it was limited to the Shona-Sindebele community. In 1964 one Sala youth was baptized, but he violated the will of his father to do it. He soon joined the police force and was lost to the Church. Two Sala confessed their faith in 1966. They were in mission employ, and though faithful, they have been absorbed into the Shona-Sindebele Christian community and their witness is lost to their people.

In 1965 the mission employed a Tonga evangelist. Failure to reach the Sala caused growing concern. The Tonga evangelist offered a solution to the problem. Many Tonga had married into the Sala tribe. Language, customs, culture, and ancestral worship patterns were almost identical. He was accepted by the Sala as a Tonga evangelist, but was unsuccessful in reaching them. They saw him as a Tonga evangelist for the Shona-Sindebele church. He was employed by the Mission which had followed the Shona-Sindebele into the area, and they boasted that the mission was theirs. He had gone to Southern Rhodesia for Bible training and had learned the Shona tongue which he used in worship. He was young and unmarried. His council was unheeded. He belonged to the missionaries. They provided his salary, a bicycle, medicines, and clothes. The Tonga-born evangelist for Tonga-

speaking Sala was a failure. The foreign church remained
a foreign church. To reach the Sala the mission built a
church of brick, cement and steel. The Shona-Sindebele
claimed it, and services continued after the old patterns of
of language.

With the Sala, resentment against the foreigners was
growing. Before the advent of the immigrants, there was
plenty of land. Great tracts were covered with forests, and
the Sala were content with their cattle and gardens, and a
few chickens and goats. The forests were left for hunting.
The Rhodesians changed all this. Large areas were cleared.
In a few years the crack of bullwhips and the roar of tractors spoke of crops soon to change the ways and economy of
the indigenous Sala. Now the Sala learned what they had lost.
Good land was gone. Foreigners became rich. No Sala would
belong to a church of people who stole his inheritance.

By mid-1967 it was apparent that methods of evangelism
had to change. The Shona-Sindebele churches were sealed
off from the unreached Sala tribe. Never have the Shona-
Sindebele Christians accepted responsibility for reaching
the Sala with the Gospel. Their responsibilities, they have
declared, are towards their own tribes. By 1968, five congregations of Shona-Sindebele were witnessing among the
few hundred of their two tribes as yet unbaptized. Leaders
were functioning well. Neither churches nor pastors received subsidies. The brethren were learning to give. Two
congregations had mud-walled houses of worship. One wor-
shiped in the building provided by the mission. Others wor-
shiped in schools. But as a means of reaching the Sala, these
churches were of no value.

These Churches Are Sealed Off

These congregations are sealed off from the Sala community. Differences in language and culture, differences in
economy, intense tribal rivalries, loyalty of the Sala to their
own country, growing political consciousness, and swelling
nationalism have been brought to focus on the opposition of
the Sala, not towards Christianity, but towards the church
of the foreigners.

Keith Hamilton discusses this problem as it relates to Equador, Peru, and Bolivia. It is not peculiar to Africa:
There is throughout the highlands a racial or tribal rivalry. This intense local loyalty bears on church growth. What matters is one's own country and one's own people. If the evangelical faith is prospering in a neighboring country, this does not commend it. . . That our people are accepting the biblical faith is the good news which voiced in the basin's own vernacular carries conviction (1962:17).

With the Shona Sindebele, loyalty to tribe and kin, in face of antagonism from the Sala, was what mattered. This loyalty has a bearing on growth of the Church among the Shona-Sindebele. The Church has grown, but it is their church and they jealously guard it. Their church is sealed off from the Sala and deliberately so. They do not want the Sala and have no spiritual concern for them.

That the Church is growing among the Shona-Sindebele does not commend it to the Sala. The Sala say: "They are our rivals. They took our land. They have made us paupers. They would change our customs. They despise our language. They are foreigners. We will not become members of their churches."

I did not see the seriousness of the problem in 1962. It was easy to assume that the Shona-Sindebele, Sala, Tonga, Ila, Lenje, and Bembe would be flocking to church houses soon to be erected by the mission. It did not work that way.

A Choice Must Be Made

Those societies working in fast-growing urban areas such as the Copperbelt, Lusaka, Broken Hill, or Livingstone are meeting similar situations. At this time of rapid transition and change, the problem is continental.

It is the objective of the government to minimize tribal differences with emphasis on the greater importance of national citizenship. This is necessary to unify the nation, but it will take generations to accomplish. A feeling of tribal exclusiveness runs high. To evangelize Zambian tribes, a more tribal approach is needed.

John B. Grimley has recognized this problem:
The advisability of divisions on tribal lines might be
denied on the basis that all divisions of the Church on
racial or tribal lines are sin. However, our question
cannot thus be answered negatively by general insistence upon Christian unity . . . It may be that the
Yoruba people feel superior to the Nupe and vice
versa, but it is of no practical value to insist that both
must worship together simply because the Church is
one in Christ and in it there is neither "barbarian,
Scythian, slave, freeman, but Christ is all in all"
Col.3:11. (1966:172).

Keith Hamilton has come to the same conclusion:
To understand church growth in these Andean countries we must remember that the population is made
up of at least four major kinds of people. . . The
Church does not grow indifferently in all. A mission
which disregards these four kinds of populations and
tries to plant a "Peruvian church" or a "Bolivian
church," or an "Ecuadorian church" into which it
brings all its converts, may not get much church
growth. Aymaras like to join churches where the
preaching, praying, Scripture reading, and singing are
in Aymara. Spanish speaking people like to join Spanish speaking churches. It would be very difficult for
Spanish speaking converts to become happy parts of
a Quechua speaking congregation (1962:30-31).
Tribal antagonisms have to be recognized. Feelings of
superiority cannot be denied, and an attempt to minimize
them will magnify differences. Furthermore it will alien-
ate missionaries. Say the Africans of the missionaries:
"They do not know the traditions of our clan. They do not
know the troubles those foreigners---Africans, mind you,
but of a different tribe---have brought upon us."

We Must Bypass the Shona-Sindebele Churches

Among the Sala and Shona-Sindebele a choice has to be
made. Evangelizing through the sealed-off churches to win
the Sala has failed. We must bypass the Shona-Sindebele

churches. With no intention of ignoring or refusing to work with the Shona-Sindebele Christian community, the missionaries must deliberately bypass it as they proceed to evangelize the Sala and other Zambian tribes.

The language medium must be Tonga, indigenous to the Sala. Churches must be planted in Sala villages, led and supported by Sala Christians. They must build their own buildings, provide their own leadership, and be so filled with the Spirit of God that they will evangelize their own people.*

A close parallel to our situation is found in Northern Ghana. A. C. Krass, assigned to the Evangelical Presbyterian Church of Ghana, recently published a case study in effective evangelism in West Africa. (*Church Growth Bulletin*, Vol. IV, No. 1:1-7). The procedure Krass has

------

*Concluding that we failed to reach the Sala because of affiliation with the Shona-Sindebele churches would be false. It is true that we could not reach the Sala through the Shona-Sindebele churches. They are sealed off, and for that reason I have suggested that they be bypassed, but our failure to reach the Sala was not solely or even largely due to the sealed-offness of the Shona-Sindebele. It was the result, rather, of our school-cum-church approach.

The Shona-Sindebele only arrived in the mid-fifties. The Methodist Church had been working among the Sala since the first decade of this century. They too had concentrated on the school approach and failed to win the Sala for Christ.

The problem is not the tribal situation peculiar to the Sala area, though I have dealt with it here, but the school-church approach common to all of Central Africa.

The educational emphasis does not multiply churches. A new approach that takes Christ to the villages, towns and cities, be they Sala, Tonga, Bemba, Lunda, or Ngoni, must be initiated. The suggestions made here we believe are relevant to most populations in contemporary Zambia.

outlined can be used in many areas in Zambia and throughout the world. Details will differ to meet the peculiarities of varying tribes, culture, language, and setting, but the principles of church growth can be applied to each situation.

In 1964 there was, in Chereponi in northeastern Ghana, a congregation of about forty communicant and noncommunicant members. Slightly more than half were from southern Ghana, working as government servants, teachers, and traders. The balance were young Chokosi who had become Christians while they were in schools forty miles to the south, and some of their wives and acquaintances. Before Krass came, Chereponi had been part of a pastoral district visited by the pastor for a few days each quarter. A native Chokosi evangelist at Chereponi gave oversight to the work.

The dozen or more educated Chokosi in the static Chereponi church are of interest. Their concepts of Christianity were formed as they became Christians in schools. Accepting Christianity was a necessary step to entering into modern life. Because of their education, they could get good jobs.

McGavran says:

These few Chokosi are typical of thousands who come to Christ via the school. Through them the Church gradually gets a toe-hold in the resistent tribe. After fifty or a hundred years maybe five per cent of the total population will be Christian. (Often the percentage is less). . . However, it runs into the difficulty which Mr. Krass relates. The school community creates a kind of church to which illiterate villagers and animists do not flock. . . The school approach actually seals off the adults of many pagan tribes (*Church Growth Bulletin*, Vol. IV, No. 1:7).

Mr. Krass points out that the evangelist to the Chereponi congregation believed his responsibilities to be that of adding members to the Church, teaching in the schools, and irregularly visiting the villages for the purpose of attracting new members to the Chereponi church. There was no thought of planting churches in the villages.

How like the sealed-off Christian Church among the Sala. The Chereponi church had no passion for other than its own

self-satisfied educated membership, and there was no con-
cern for the lost Chokosi---precisely as the sealed-off Shona-
Sindebele churches had no compassion for the 17,000 lost
Sala.

There were about 18,700 people living in the 122 villages
and 1,300 people living in Chereponi town. Contrast between
town and villages was considerable. Traders, government
workers, craftsmen, and teachers representing many tribes
lived in the town and by religion they were either Christian
or Muslim. The villages were 100 per cent agrarian and
Chokosi and animist. Literacy was the rule in town. Illi-
teracy was the rule in the villages.

This sociological analysis explains many factors. The
townspeople, loosely knit, of many tribes, have provided
forty communicant and noncommunicant members for the
Church. The balance of the 1,300 souls in this trader town
are Muslim. Most of the forty church members come from
many tribes. A few more than a dozen are converted,
educated Chokosi youth, sealed off from their own village
people.

Again the parallel between Chereponi town and church in
the Chokosi context and the Shona-Sindebele community and
church in the Sala context is easily drawn. The Shona-Sindebele, made up of two foreign tribes, better educated, more
prosperous, and far less conservative, in which are found
several congregations, and these among 17,000 Sala, have
many points of comparison with the picture drawn by missionary Krass:

> The concentration of evangelistic effort on the town
> and the town congregation was too one-sided and, in
> addition, too likely to be sterile as an approach to the
> village population. It did not seem likely that illiterate
> Chokosi villagers would feel happy in a town congre-
> gation whose members---even the Chokosi members---
> sang European hymns in southern Ghanaian vernacu-
> lars, dressed in foreign style, and worshipped in Eng-
> lish, Ewe, or Twi. The tribesmen need biblical in-
> struction in their own tongues. Nor did it seem likely
> that the town congregations would be happy to worship
> in the Chokosi language or use African type hymns. . .

It therefore seemed best to continue the Chereponi
worship services and church work much as they were.
. . and to run con-currently a vital program of evangelism in the villages aiming at the formation of
Chokosi congregations wholly independent of the town
congregations. (*Church Growth Bulletin* Vol. IV, No.
1:1-2---this last paragraph needs emphasis, M.W.R.)

Mr. Krass's conclusions from this analysis of the Chereponi church are the same as ours as we have viewed the
sealed-off Shona-Sindebele churches. These better-educated,
better-paid, socially conscious, cosmopolitan Chereponi
town dwellers were spiritually impotent as a church. They
had been emasculated by the cultural gap between them and
the 18,700 Chokosi village animists. In the same way, better-
educated, ambitious, harder-working, better-paid, Shona-
Sindebele Christian farmers are sterilized by their advance-
ment. They are cut off from the 17,000 Sala animists.

Mr. Krass "simply bypassed the town congregation and
started a new pattern among the Chokosi." His solution is one
that has worked hundreds of times. Provision was made for
the town congregations, but no longer was a missionary tied
to it.

Missionaries laboring under similar circumstances must
do as missionary Krass in northeastern Ghana. Sealed-off
congregations must be bypassed and churches planted in
every village, clan and tribal group receptive to the Gospel.

We Must Preach so that the Village as a Unit Can Come to Christ

Donald McGavran insists that
the future of the Christian Movement . . . is in the
villages. It is not in the central station. The center
of attention should be in the villages (Pickett, Warnshuis, Singh and McGavran 1962: 82).

True, he was writing about India, but the affirmation is
also true about Zambia today. Yet, with the exception of the
Separatist churches, Seventh Day Adventists and Jehovah's
Witnessses, I know of no attempt to plant village churches
by established missions in Zambia. The missions church was

invariably found meeting in the school or mission station.

With institutional missions the emphasis has not been on the villages or on group conversion, thus establishing churches of adults. Concentration has been given to individual decisions of school children, thus obtaining congregations made up of teachers and their older pupils.

W. R. Hogg has observed in "History's Lessons for Tomorrow's Mission,"

Most preaching sought for individual rather than group conversion. This reflected Western individualism, influences of the Evangelical Awakening, and belief that in a non-Christian land the Church was set against and drawn out from society (1960:160).

The philosophy of the missions-school approach argued for one-by-one conversion, snatching young men and women from village society before they were claimed by paganism and baptizing them before they could become polygamists. There was no need, it was said, for village itineration and preaching.

Years of failure to win for Christ the power structure or a substantial part of the power structure in a single village, and sixty years of failure of the Methodists to win enough people in a village so that the household of God began properly to affect the village life, demanded a review of our methods, for our approach had been the same. The Methodists concentrated on individual conversion of children through schools. We followed the same pattern. These youth were then sent back to the pagan society and again and again were absorbed by it. There was little renunciation of Christ, but there was abundant gradual backsliding. To date in Central Africa, the village unit has been largely ignored.

Grimley had this problem in mind in Nigeria:

I believe the individualistic approach of evangelists and convinced Christians meeting non-Christians one by one, usually causing social dislocations for the new convert, must be shifted to a broader base that will bring whole families, clans, hamlets, and villages into the Church through multi-individual decisions for Christ (referring to the type of decision where each individual in a group makes a decision based upon his

own conviction in fellowship with others of like conviction.) (1966: 156).

The decision confronting missionaries in the program of
evangelism in Zambia is to turn to the village as the place
of action and to anticipate villagers becoming Christian by
multi-individual, mutually interdependent decision in sizable
groups of families. There must be a joyous expectation that
families and clans can become Christian, and they must be so
encouraged.

Pickett says:

One way of Christianization permits and encourages
groups of families to come to salvation without social
dislocation in a constant and ever-widening stream.
Whereas another way of Christianization permits and
encourages individuals of many peoples having been
torn from their societies, to come to salvation in
an intermittent and gradually diminishing trickle.
(Pickett, Warnshuis, Singh and McGavran 1962: 64).

Like the overwhelming majority of Western missionaries
from individualistic cultural backgrounds, I feared that
"group movements produced an inferior, if not a purely nominal brand of Christianity," but in view of our failure, along
with denominational missions, to plant numerous village
churches in our respective areas of witness, I am forced to
believe that, in tribal society at least, the method of one-by-
one conversion against the social stream is faulty.

Careful study of group conversions or people movements
as they are recounted in the New Testament, in history, and
in contemporary missions suggests that soundly Christian
people movements would happen repeatedly in Central Africa
were they not stifled by heavy-handed institutionalism.

With reference to Nigeria, Grimley has observed that
"the tribesmen of the Central Belt want to become Christian
in group fashion, of this there is much evidence" (Grimley
and Robinson 1966: 126).

The same is true in Zambia. Response of village elders
made during our surveys was always the same. Their desire
for a church in their own village was enthusiastically affirmed. "We would like it, Umfundisi," they declared. Sala
villages wanted to become Christian as village units.

A Need for Understanding People Movements

So little is known about people movements. McGavran has declared:

At least two-thirds of all converts in Asia, Africa, and Oceania have come to Christian faith through people movements. In many provinces, nine-tenths of all those who first moved out of non-Christian faith to Christianity came in people movements. Most Christians in Asia and Africa today are descendents of people movement converts. But for people movements, the Churches in these continents would be very different and much weaker than they are. People movement growth has accounted for considerable ingathering in Latin America too. A people movement results from the joint decision of a number of individuals---perhaps five and perhaps five hundred---all of same people, which enables them to become Christians without social dislocation, by remaining in full contact with their non-Christian relatives, thus enabling other groups of that people, across the years, after suitable instruction, to come to similar decisions, and form Christian churches made up exclusively of members of that people (1969: 298)

Robert Glover tells of the work of the American Baptist Missionary Union (now the American Baptist Foreign Mission Society) in the Telugu country of India:

The Lone Star Mission of Ongole, after twenty-eight years of seed-sowing, had reaped a meager harvest of only thirty souls. Three times the mission had been on the verge of closing; but the divine restraint was felt. With the arrival of Dr. and Mrs. John E. Clough in 1865 the mission took on new life; and shortly afterwards revival broke out with the conversion of Yerranguntla Periah, an outcast Madiga. In a single day, July, 1878, Dr. Clough baptized 2,222 outcast believers. By the end of the year, 9,606 persons had been received into the Church. Since that time more than a million outcast Malas and Madigas have been won to Christ in this area (1960: 85-86).

Mrs. Howard Taylor, recounting J. O. Fraser's missionary ministry in Southwest China, refers to his success in
1916 in Turtle Village, high in the mountains.

> Here were twenty-four families ready to declare
> themselves Christians. Thirteen of these destroyed
> their demonolatry in one day. . . When only Mottled
> Hill and adjacent villages had been visited, Fraser
> could write of forty-nine families out of fifty-nine,
> which had broken down their demon altars and turned
> Christian . . . fully 600 people in 129 families were
> won to Christ (1964: 196, 198).

The missionaries of Zambia may anticipate similar people
movements. No other pattern will bring the tribes and nation to faith and obedience. Extended families, minor lineages
and villages, or parts of them, must be expected to move into
the Church together. The missionaries must plan and pray
for such group decisions to take place. Emphasis needs to be
laid, as the Gospel is proclaimed to the villagers, that this is
the normal way they should plan to come (Sunda, 1963: 21-22).

A Suggested Strategy

Adult populations of Zambia have not been won by the
educational approach. A plan must be devised that will reach
adults and plant sound churches in the villages.

One lesson learned in our surveys was that the village
people of the Sala district form part of a complex social structure. They are not "Zambians" in the way that a Londoner is
an Englishman. Most are Sala, or Shona, or Sindebele by
tribe. Most villages contain two or more tribal groups. However, each person was a member of a specific tribe, a specific
clan, a specific extended family, and a specific nuclear family.
There was never difficulty ascertaining the exact families of
Sala, Tonga, Barotse, Shona, or Sindebele. None answered
vaguely, "We are Africans," or "We are Zambians."

Until 1967 I had ignored this social structure. Among
missionaries the tendency has been to minimize the tribe,
clan, language, and social levels. When I disregarded these
factors and simply proclaimed Christ "universally," I failed
to use the accepted structure of communication between

individuals, families, villages and tribes. Converts from "school boys and girls" were thrown together from many villages and several clans and tribes. The Church grew slowly around the schools and not at all in the villages.

In many villages the Christian Church had a few members, one in this, two in that, and four in a third, but in others we found not one professing Christian of any faith. To follow these Christians far removed from the school had been a task seldom accomplished. Many villages deep in the forest had never been visited by a missionary before our survey. I met members of our church I had not seen for years. It was too far for them to walk from their village to the church I had built for them in 1965. There had to be a better way of presenting the Gospel to the Sala and other tribes of Zambia.

How were other missions endeavoring to meet this problem? A plan used in Nigeria in recent years suggest ways of reaching the tribes of Zambia. The report is found in Grimley and Robinson's study of Church growth in Central and Southern Nigeria.

The plan had been introduced in 1962 by Eugene Rubingh and Ralph Baker of the Christian Reform Church Mission among the Tiv tribe around Sevav. The Tiv people live in structured groups. They are Nigerians, but not merely Nigerians. In addition each person is a member of a particular family, clan, or tribe. •

In thirteen years at Sevav there had not been one baptism. The Christian community was thinly spread across the countryside, one Christian in this village, none in the next, and one or two in the next. To form these brethren into effective churches was nearly impossible.

The missionaries concluded there must be a better way and devised the following plan:

> In the social structure of the Tiv the smallest unit or segment is called the "ipaven u ken iyou." This normally consists of from nine to twelve extended family compounds. The segment head lives in the central compound. Mr. Rubingh determined as a pilot project to evangelize one segment and to obtain catechumens and eventually baptize believers who were all members of the same segment.

This plan was explained to the leaders of the local church and a team of men enlisted who would give one day a week for fourteen weeks to work in the chosen segment. Mr. Baker prepared a syllabus of fourteen lessons that explained the way of salvation.

The team on the first of the fourteen days went to the segment and there divided so that in each compound one man taught the assigned lesson, and told the assigned story.

At the close of the fourteen weeks, a three-day conference was held in the compound of the clan head. Decisions for Christ were called for.

Those who responded were organized into a catechumen class and began regular weekly worship. They continued working for the enlistment of other catechumens. While not an organized church, they carried out many functions of a church congregation.

Definite plans for another visit were made previous to the team's leaving.

Mr. Rubingh pointed out that one advantage of this approach is that the Gospel is proclaimed within the cultural setting of the complete family. People declare for Christ within their tribal relationships and not as lone and separate individuals (1966:217-219).

The Sevav plan needs some revision to fit the Sala of Zambia, but the scheme is sound.

The Plan as It Affects the Villages

In the 1967 surveys among the Sala the other missionaries and I offered the idea of a church of their own in their own villages. Here was a new concept the Sala people had never heard of. In more than sixty years no missionary had suggested a church for the village, with its own indigenous leadership, self-supported, self-governed, and self-propagated. Animists and Christians alike approved.

I suggested that nine African evangelists be chosen---the missionary making the tenth---to evangelize ten selected villages over thirteen weeks. The object would be to plant a church in each village.

Such a plan must be very carefully prepared. The men enlisted must be Tonga-speaking Sala. Understanding of the object to be attained is essential. The change from the mission-centered school approach to the village preaching approach must be understood. The evangelists are invited to share because they want to---they must not be paid. The importance of prayer must be established through hours and days of preparatory prayer.

Thirteen each of lessons, sermons, and Bible stories must be prepared, studied, rehearsed, discussed, and firmly planted in the minds of each evangelist. Many hearers will be animists with little knowledge of God or Jesus Christ or the way to Eternal Life. The plan of redemption from creation to Christ and His Second Coming must be revealed. The work, the healing ministry, the teaching of Christ, and the will of God must be preached. Bible lessons must be taught. Winsome stories must be told. Sermons on "thou shalt not" should be notable for their absence. Pagan practices will not be eliminated by ridicule and condemnation but as the Sala embrace the all-powerful Christ as Lord of their lives.

Care must be exercised in the choice of villages. Key villages must be chosen where the elders are eager for services to be held each week for the three-month period. This must be understood before the series begin. A place of meeting near the headman's kraal must be selected. Each evangelist must be at his appointed place at the accepted time. Each will preach his given sermon, teach his planned lesson, and tell his pre-determined Bible story. Each of the ten villages will hear on the appointed day the same sermon, lesson, and story of the three-months series, and each from the mouth of its own evangelist.

The village must be addressed as a unit. Mr. Krass, in describing the plan of evangelism among the Chokosi villagers of northeastern Ghana, said:

We would always speak to villagers as a whole. We never made an approach merely to individuals. We never referred to "those who might accept our teachings." We never, in fact, raised the question of acceptance or rejection. We simply said, in effect, "This

is the Gospel. This is how God acted on your behalf. This is how God is speaking to the people of
Famisa. This is what God wants for the people of
Famisa (or any other village in which we might be
speaking) to do." Prior to our coming, the village
had always acted as a village and we assumed it
would act as a unit with respect to our preaching
(*Church Growth Bulletin* Vol. IV, No. 1: 2).

There are advantages to this kind of approach. The Gospel is preached within the cultural context of the family.
Most of the villages among the Sala are composed of one or
two extended family units.

Few people outside Western individualistic society decide
for Christ as separate persons. Decisions are made within
their family or clan relationship. Such is the pattern among
the Sala, and when a group decision has been made within
the village

a nucleus is formed in which each believer acts as a
stabilizing influence upon every other, supplying
Christian support in times of persecution and increasing Christian enthusiasm in winning others and
building... churches (Grimley and Robinson 1966:219).

This is a startling assumption for missionaries to make.
It runs counter to Western society in Eurica where decisions
are made individually, often against one's family. Among
Africans, it is betrayal to act in any other way.

This approach will work among Sala villages. Robinson,
with his knowledge of the tribal patterns of southern Nigeria
writes:

It is normal for residents of the multitudinous villages
and hamlets of southern Nigeria to make important
decisions together, at the same time, after talking
matters over, and keeping the same leaders as they
had before. These multi-individual and mutually
interdependent decisions fit society in southern Nigeria. They are often loosely called "group conversions." The advantages and methods of group conversion should be taught and programs of evangelism
aimed at winning persons in their natural groups
rather than winning individuals and isolating them

from their families and social circles (Grimley and Robinson 1966: 372).

The response we enjoyed in the Sala village surveys in 1967 leads me to believe we may anticipate great obedience to the Gospel (Romans 16: 26) if this evangelistic thrust is made.

Biblical and Contemporary Examples Should Be Given

Encouragement should be kept before the villages. Becoming disciples of Christ by groups is African. It is Sala. It is common among tribesmen all over the world. It is Biblical. The missionaries expect this kind of movement. Africans have known too long that missionaries insist on individual decisions against the group.

From the Book of Acts come examples of multitudes---thousands---turning to the Lord; of whole villages accepting the Christian Way----and that must be recounted again and again.

New Churches to Build Own Houses of Worship

The Sala reaction to our suggestion that they build their own church houses astounded us. We should not have been surprised had many contended that building churches was the responsibility of the missionaries, but the Sala accepted the idea of their own church in their own village. In a number of cases the older men of the power structure were so enthusiastic they set about immediately selecting committees and determining sites. They would not wait for the evangelist. The building would be ready when he got there.

Buildings would not be elaborate---no burned brick or steel girders or glazed windows or steel roofs! Their churches would be constructed with mud walls and thatched roofs. Floors would be plastered with cow dung, and windows would be openings in the wall. Out of such materials they build their own houses. God's house requires no more. Only one thing did we stress. God would not be pleased if His house were not constructed equally as well or better than their own.

Too often the missionary judges the Church, not by its spiritual stones but by its brick, cement, steel, glass, furniture, churchly architecture, and dimensions. Larger stations are marked by cruciform church buildings with steeples, parapets, gables, towers, columns, arches, domes, naves, chancels, baptistries, fonts, candelabra, and all the furniture, symbolic and functional, of a medieval cathedral. Such structures excite supporting churches back home but have little meaning to the African Christian. They are another of the institutions paid for by overseas money and requiring perpetual oversight by foreign missionaries. African Christians will seldom preserve them.

It is not easy for missionaries to insist that rural churches build and pay for their own church houses. (Urban needs will be discussed later.) Efforts of the young church usually appear to missionaries, in light of their resources, as nothing. The missionaries are therfore tempted to provide the buildings for the congregations. To yield to the temptation will stunt the new church and stop other congregations from attempting to build.

Hodges recounts:

Some of our congregations in Central America have struggled for ten years to build their chapel. They have begun in a private home, moved into a thatch-roofed hut of their own, and finally after years of sacrifice and labor, have completed their frame or adobe building. Their little chapel means infinitely more to them than if it had been provided by the mission. . . A bamboo house with a straw roof and mud walls built with native money and full of people is better than a beautiful brick and cement structure built with foreign funds that has but a half dozen in the congregation (1953: 72-73).

Of the Church in Tabasco, Mexico, McGavran has noted,

Almost all church buildings were pole and thatch structures at first. Many such "temples" exist today. This is a Church of the common people who build churches they can afford (1963: 90).

The present church-building pattern in Zambia is missions buildings. One can travel many miles through heavily populated areas with hundreds of villages and seldom see a church. Established missions did not encourage school congregations to erect houses of worship. Youthful Christians could worship in schools, and the mission had neither time nor money to erect duplicating churches.

The school congregation is only a "Sunday church." With classes throughout the week and with missionary and school staff involved in school activity, there is neither time nor place for congregational meetings except on Sunday.

A growing church demands daily worship, and daily worship involves a place of worship essential for each church planted in the villages.

McGavran says:

This may be simply a sacred spot under a tree, fenced to keep out the cattle, goats, and pigs, or it may be a village home. Soon it should become a chapel built by the people, probably in a style of a village house, understood to be theirs, used daily, and honored as a place of worship (Pickett, Warnshuis, Singh and McGavran 1962: 112).

From the beginning of evangelistic efforts and as village churches begin to multiply, principles of self-support must be stated repeatedly. Subsidies will dangerously hinder church growth. Certainly their own houses of worship, paid by their gifts and built by their hands, can serve as an object lesson as to the value of supporting their own church.

I had noticed in West Africa that Ghanaian Christians use indigenous instruments in worship and that chapels were sometimes decorated by their own artists. Many Africans paint well, and their wood carving is known over the world. We suggested their art forms, instruments, and music voicing the message of Christ, be used in their worship. The suggestion was accepted enthusiastically. Missions encouraging African art forms are few in number, though churches in other lands have used indigenous art to an advantage.

Alan Tippett has written of chapels he saw in Sulufou Village in Tai Lagoon, Malaita:

In all cases local artists had either painted or inlaid the decorative work of the sanctuary, altar, lectern,

and baptismal font. . . It represents the dedication of
the best artistic talent of the island to the glory of
God (1967: 168).

Edwin Smith, stressing the significance of indigenous art
forms, quoted from Tambaram, 1938:

We strongly affirm that the Gospel should be expressed
and interpreted in indigenous forms, and that in
methods of worship, institutions, architecture, etc.,
the spiritual heritage of the nation and country should
be taken into use (1946: 31).

From an Indian context, Pickett has emphasized the same
thing:

The native Ooriya dancers, the Ooriya drums, and
cymbals and Ooriya village tunes to which are set
various local compositions have been encouraged. . .
The Christian religion appears before the people in
Indian costume . . . village musical instruments are
kept, and skill in their use is inculcated (Pickett,
Warnshuis, Singh and McGavran 1962: 23-24).

Urging the use of indigenous African art as I do, one
factor must be stressed:

It should no longer be possible for men and women to
to go into the field totally ignorant of the social structure, of the religion, the customs of the people; ignorant of the way in which native institutions may be
used for building up the Church (Smith 1946: 32).

If this policy had been adopted by missionaries over the
past sixty years in Africa, many blunders would not have
been made. Missionaries have often done more harm than
good because they did not understand the black man's culture and way of life.

Teaching Leadership to Begin at Once
at Local Church Level

Few things in a movement where large segments of the
population are turning to Christ are more important than
training local church leadership. By "the Church" I mean
those local village groups who have recently professed
faith in Christ. The temptation to be resisted by the mis-

sionary is that of choosing leaders himself. There are bright young men, educated in mission schools, who speak fluent English, are well-behaved and well-dressed, who flatter the missionary's "superior" judgment, and who must be avoided like the plague. Ministerial training schools are filled with these young men who often become the source of trouble when passed on to congregations that neither ask for nor want them.

Churches to Choose Own Leaders

Young churches must choose their own leaders. No people movement could happen without strong indigenous leaders to break the path for others to follow. The new congregation knows these trailblazers. They are the natural leaders for the new flock. To bypass those leaders would kill the movement. This indigenous leadership is a potent factor. The Church must be theirs. These chosen stalwarts must have a large part in the new Church, and it must so obviously be the Church of the Lord Jesus that they know the Church is theirs. Some will object that leadership out of such an environment may be illiterate or poorly educated. The risk is genuine among the Sala. Still the rule must be followed. The new church must choose leaders best suited by its judgment.

When the Sala decide for Christ they may do so quickly. Large groups may come at once. Such an ingathering demands immediate training of locally chosen leaders. A number may be illiterate. They should be taught the worship service by heart, along with hymns and lessons from Scripture. Africans have ability to memorize that must be harnessed.

They must likewise be led to practise stewardship. Such men must be committed to building a great solid Church leading all the village to the feet of Christ. It is important that the leaders be indigenous, unpaid, and accustomed to tribal life, but these will not arise by themselves. On the contrary, the people movement to Christ will succeed only if the missionaries---or church and minister---do a very thorough job of training.

Classes must be conducted by the missionary and his trainees at the local church. Leaders of the new churches must be trained at the place most convenient for them. I strongly believe that training institutes must be set up at the local church level. Leaders chosen will be older men with families who cannot leave home for extended periods of study.

The missionary must keep his program pliable enough to meet local circumstances. The best time for extended classes among the Sala is during the dry season while the community is at ease.

Courses should be kept short. These men are babes in Christ, and there is a danger in overtaxing their spiritual capacity. Their knowledge should keep pace with their spiritual growth but should not surpass it. Among Aymara Indians of the Andes highlands, Keith Hamilton found that

two to three day church institutes and two to four week Bible institutes have proven fruitful. If there is a four or five day "fiesta break" for the children of this world, then use it thankfully for the children of light. If there is a two-month school vacation or a long quiet period between harvest and "spring plowing," use it by all means (1962: 131-132).

After the study course, students should be encouraged to begin preaching, telling neighboring villages all they know about Jesus and how He saved them. There are advantages to this. Their faith is new and knowledge gained in study needs such anchoring in their minds as only exercise of witness can give. Also, the joy of witness will create desire for further learning.

The strategy calls for a simple, decentralized teaching plan to meet specific needs of young churches. A college program is not proposed. All who come will be taught, regardless of age or educational qualification. Hodges says:

There is real advantage in having a decentralized training program. The school can then be carried to the districts and it is not necessary to depend entirely upon students coming to the central location. The nearer we can keep our training program to the source of workers, i.e., the local churches, the more

effective it will be. Perhaps there is no better method
of strengthening the churches of a district than to
take a short course of Bible studies to one of the
central churches of the area. (1953: 57).

Though this program is designed to meet the needs for
leadership immediately new churches are planted, yet the
training of lay leadership is not a short-term need. Demand
for teaching indigenous local church leadership must be
anticipated and continuing instruction provided. A part of
each slack season must be set aside for this essential work.

Training Must Keep Pace with Leadership Growth

A number of these men will soon develop into natural
church leaders. The best of them will seek further study.
Provision must be made so that, as their abilities increase,
the courses of study may be expanded. Within a few years
a school—still not a college—but perhaps with a sixth or
seventh grade educational base, must be established. This
school should be situated near the tribal cluster of churches.
Among the Sala it should be in the Sala area. The term of
study will have to be lengthened, but it will still convene
between the harvest and the first rains. All the while these
men are busy witnessing, preaching, winning souls, and
planting churches among their tribe, working where they are,
supporting themselves, and living with their families. There
must be no unsettlement for these natural, chosen, local
church leaders. Their services are valid only with the people
who have chosen them.

Among these, a few with exceptional ability will rise to
the top. They are the best preachers and workers. They are
exceptional students. Their abilities will be recognized by
their brethren who will encourage them to assume increasing
responsibilities.

A Similar Strategy for the Cities

The strategy used in reaching the villages can, with modi-
fication, be used in reaching the urban centers. The cities of
Zambia are sharing exploding population increase. Rural

Africans are rushing to the cities from every area and every tribe. Their origins have great bearing where they find their homes in the city and, if they have a church affiliation, on where they worship. Immigrants arriving for the first time find first their own tribe.

Tribal unity still finds expression in the cities. A plateau Tonga moving to Lusaka will find others of his own tribe and settle with them. A Tonga tribal entity all living in the same confined area will result. Sala, Barotse, Ila, and Bemba will follow the same pattern, and in each area the language and customs will be that of the tribe resident in that area. So recently have these people moved that ties with their people "back home" are still strong, and these ties will remain for a generation or more. All this must be remembered as plans are laid for city evangelism, and the wards of the city must be defined.

Back in the Sala area, when the intensified evangelistic effort begins, it will be with the help of evangelists who are Sala by tribe and tongue. The same principle must follow in the city. In an urban community with several major language groups it will be wise for the missionary to find his evangelists, a Tonga for the Tonga, a Bemba for Bemba, a Sala for Sala, and a Marotse for Barotse.

These men too, must be adequately prepared. They must understand the object in view and be eager to give themselves to the work. They must be Spirit-filled men. This is their program and they and their people must know that the anticipated church is their church.

Again, thirteen sermons, lessons, and Bible stories will be prepared and implanted in the minds of these co-laborers, and for thirteen weeks at a designated time and place within each tribal ward each evangelist will teach and preach to his own people. No decision will be asked for during the three months, but the people will be told repeatedly that a time of decision will come, and they are urged to anticipate it.

It is expected that many will come when the opportunity is given. These must be molded into congregations with leadership chosen out of each group by the group itself. Training of these leaders should follow a pattern similar to that among the villages.

A House of Worship of Their Own

At first it will be possible for these small churches to worship in a home, but this will only be temporary. A church of their own is necessary. The municipality will insist upon it. In a township with three or four tribal congregations, it is suggested that one adequate building be constructed to meet the needs of all three or four, each congregation meeting at its own designated times.

The building in the city dare not be as simply constructed as one among the rural Sala. Rigid building codes require strict adherence, and construction costs are high and beyond the reach of young churches. The mission must assist the young city churches with their buildings. I suggest that monies offered the new congregations in the form of long-term loans without interest be repaid, a few pounds per year, not back to the mission, but into a growing fund belonging to the churches. These monies in the future are to be used and controlled by the African Christians to build churches for other urban congregations.

A Self-Help Financial Program

The Church of Christ Mission in South Africa has adopted a plan for helping congregations provide for their own houses of worship. Each circuit is asked to give each year in proportion to its membership. These monies are placed in a revolving building fund that now amounts to several thousand dollars annually, enough to build one or more new church houses each year. Such a plan has much to commend it. From the first, new congregations must be taught the merits of Christian stewardship, and with the rising economy of Zambia the churches could soon become self-supporting.

No Subsidies

As churches are established ministers will be needed. Within a decade a score of congregations will be large enough to need the services of part-time or full-time shepherds. But who will pay these men?

One problem with which the Central Africa Mission in Rhodesia has been troubled is the question of ministers' salaries. With the mission involved in schools and paying salaries of teachers, howbeit government subsidized, ministers insist on being paid comparable salaries as well. "The teachers are paid," they contend. "We too must be." Though the mission is now solving the problem, in the past it has been paying.

No subsidy for either rural or urban churches must be the rule in Zambia.

Hodges has quoted William Shillingsburn in *The Pilot*, who says:

> No money for native preachers and native churches is not a handicap nor hindrance; it is a challenge to missionary ability, and a policy that if adapted generally and more rigidly, would save many a heartache and produce a stronger, more humble church in the foreign field (1953: 74).

Hodges adds his own observations:

> The pastor needs to feel that his responsibility is to his congregation rather than to the mission. Quite naturally the mission paid worker is responsible to the mission, if it is paying his salary. As long as he has the approval of the missionary, he has nothing to fear. The pastor who is not supported by the mission, but chosen and maintained by the congregation feels his responsibility to his flock. The congregation will also feel a closer tie with its pastor (1953: 74).

Grimley of Nigeria says that a dynamic influence in the Languda response was the fact that the mission did not pay its evangelists!

> The mission when it arrived did not pay the young men who were evangelists. In 1936 there were nine such evangelists, in 1946 eighteen, and in 1961 thirty. An unpaid lay leadership that looked after the congregations and preached the Word to all was an important part of the church growth picture (Grimley and Robinson 1966: 137).

The corollary to no subsidized salaries is the important emphasis on the churches paying their own pastors.

Hodges has written:

Missionaries who make appeals asking for money to
support native workers, to erect church buildings,
etc., should carefully weigh the long range conse-
quences and be sure that their procedure will truly
strengthen the church, not weaken it. The future of
the Church should not be sacrificed for the sake of
temporary advantage. Missionaries who plead for
funds, asking for foreign help to do for the native
church that which it should rightfully do for itself,
should examine their position to see if they are on
Scriptural ground. Sometimes we get the impression
that the missionary believes that the work of the Holy
Spirit depends on the amount of money available (1953:
67-68).

New churches must be taught to support themselves.
Giving as a habit will not automatically establish itself. It
must be prayerfully taught as God's provision for His Church.
Great expectation for rapid growth must be prayerfully entertained, but as the ingathering comes it must be taught the
blessings of self-support.

The Church must be given direction in anticipation of
great growth. Such preparation, when the ingathering begins,
will encourage continued expansion. Numerous missions
have lost their opportunity when rapid growth began because
they were not prepared for it.

Roy Shearer has said regarding Korea:

Great and early growth determined the policies of
Pyongang Station missionaries, and these methods
were such as to favor continued rapid growth. For
instance "self support" is more readily achieved in
a greatly growing Church; it becomes an easier and
indeed, the only feasable method to follow. Self-support can be defined as the encouragement of a young
church to support its own organization wherever possible. . . Fortunately, self-support principles were
followed by these northern missionaries, and these
principles naturally suited the situation (1966: 121).

Read has observed of the Congregacio in Brazil, "This
Church is not dependent on funds from overseas" (1965:36).

Here is a principle to which Zambia missionaries must
cling. In rural areas and cities growth will come. Prayerfully adhered to, the self-support principle will help perpe-
tuate that growth.

The Need for a College and Seminary

There is place, at the proper time, for a ministerial
college and ultimately a seminary. It is unnecessary, however, to create a costly institution to provide the essentials
for such a school. By the time the churches in Zambia need
a college they should be ready partially to underwrite the
cost. It should be planned with the Zambian brethren so that
the churches can share in the enterprise. The ultimate need
must be kept before the churches. They must know that it is
within their capability to help provide it.

A pitfall faced by missionaries is an insistence upon
schools patterned after American colleges and seminaries.
Campuses are built. Theological books with problems alien
to anything encountered by the African pastor are taught
chapter by chapter. Patterns of residence are duplicated.
Standards for entry are lifted to the level maintained overseas, and the required number of years in school have full
approval of the supporting societies, churches, and missionaries. Dr. Ralph Winter has observed that

probably at no point is the carry-over of U. S. methods
causing a greater bottleneck to church growth than in
areas of leadership development for the local congregation. (*Church Growth Bulletin* Vol. IV, No. 2: 5).

When needs in Zambia require a ministerial college or
seminary, it must be designed to meet the needs of the field.
Hodges has written:

At least some of the difficulty arises from the fact
that missionaries are given to patterning their Bible
training program after the Bible institute or seminary
in the homeland, instead of adapting it to needs of the
field. Sometimes, too, natural love of institution cause
the missionary to permit the institution to become an
end in itself. He is actually striving to make the Bible
school a great institution instead of merely using it as

a tool for attaining a greater end: the development of
the Native Church. If our present methods are not
helping us to reach our goal of a strong indigenous
Church, then those methods should be revised or
discarded (1953: 55-56).

What Hodges has said of a Latin American problem can
be a Zambian problem too. It must be avoided.

Winter was also writing out of experience in Latin
America:

We must soberly consider the possibility that where-
ever the Church is growing rapidly, or wants to,
among vast multitudes that do not happen to be college
people, that the best U. S. standards are not best at
all but only bottlenecks to progress. A very different (albeit transitional) kind of education must be
employed. Ideally, we must maintain the "parity of
the clergy" in the bonds of a single program with
different levels of training. (Church Growth Bulletin,
Vol. IV, No. 2: 6).

I concur with Winter. Leadership training for churches
in Zambia must grow to keep pace with growing leaders.
It must keep ahead of them but not too far ahead. Insisting
on a ministerial college and seminary from the beginning
is to start from the wrong end.

Zambian Christian women must also receive training. In
a matrilineal social structure this is particularly essential.
A worker of the French Reformed Church "who has considerable experience of youth and social work during the past
twenty years has summed up the pioneering spirit of the
African women she met in the following words":

Nothing stops them, neither the weight of tradition nor
their elders' lack of understanding, nor the need of
constantly inventing a new style of life to suit unprecedented situations. They are rarely helped by the
men, who are themselves too occupied with their own
evolution. They are on the march with bewildering
speed like all Africa. Their obedience, or their dis-
obedience, concerns not only Africa, but the whole
Church. (Cit. in Mia Brandel-Syrier's Black Woman in
Search of God, 1962: 11).

Christian Women Need Training

African Christian women have too often been neglected or forgotten. The demands on the missionaries of schools, hospitals, theological programs, and other responsibilities have denied Christian women the attention and place they must have in the Church.

Over southern Africa, Thursday afternoon is the traditional time for the women's prayer meeting and Bible study. Here is the opportunity for the wife of the missionary to share in a ministry second to none in the development and growth of the Church in Zambia

A New Approach to the Problem of Polygamy

The greatest problem facing the missionary in Africa is polygamy. No question receives more consideration. Many customs were abhorrent to the missionary, but none have motivated so consistent opposition as the practice of keeping many wives. The murderer, adulterer, thief, slanderer, liar, and sluggard were forgivable, but the continuing sin of polygamous men was sufficient to bar them from salvation.

Barrett has written,

Polygamists with their families . . . could not be fully received into the Church. (1968:117).

McGavran has said,

Polygamists could not become Christians, In order to be baptized, men had to give up all but one wife. (Church Growth Bulletin, Vol. V, No. 4: 1).

Rotberg says that the early missionaries

denied Church membership and baptism to polygamists and their wives, and eventually persuaded some men to cast aside all their wives but one. (1965:128).

Reaction to the problem varied greatly. Most agreed that Christians must be monogamous, but there were differing opinions about the status of wives previously married by tribal custom.

According to Welbourn,

For some missions, this was no marriage at all. On becoming Christian, a man might leave them all

and marry a new Christian woman. For some he
might keep the first; for others he might choose which
he would keep. (1965: 117).

Nida has observed,

It has not been uncommon for several wives of a man
to become Christians and to be admitted into the
Church, but for the husband, on deciding to become
a Christian, to find that he is barred unless he turns
out all but one wife. (1954: 130).

Some missionaries, however, took exception to this rigid
stand. A medical evangelist in Northern Rhodesia could find
nothing in the New Testament

that would move him to deny the sacraments to an
African solely because he had married several women. "Are we ever justified," he asked, "in laying down
laws which are not in the Word of God?" (Rotberg 1965:
129).

John William Colenso, the 19th century Bishop of Natal,
also wondered

if . . . to force an honest polygamist to divorce his
wives is to attack his feelings of justice and duty with
reference to his wives. The question as to which wife
is to be kept offers endless difficulties. What is to
become of the dismissed women and their children?
(Rotberg 1965: 129).

Lesslie Newbigen in his book about *Honest Religion for
Secular Man,*   says this:

In the history of Missions in Africa it has been more
or less taken for granted that the abandonment of polygamy is always and at all times an essential mark of
conversion. There are some, of whom I am one, who
believe this is both wrong on theological grounds and
disastrous in missionary practice. (*Church Growth
Bulletin* Vol. III, No. 1: 10)

The early missionaries attributed the plurality of wives
to a man's lust. Kenyatta says, "The missionary associated
polygamy with sexual excess and insisted that all those who
want salvation of their souls must agree to adopt monogamy"
(1932: 261). The sexual factor, however, was not a primary
cause for polygamy.

Polygamy had many functions. Luzbetak lists eleven: 1. Prestige derived from having several wives; 2. Prestige from having a large potential offspring; 3. Prestige from being able to fulfill social and religious obligations; 4. It enabled the supplying of a large labor force for the family; 5. It reduced the work load for women; 6. It was a means of providing a defence for the family; 7. It provided social security for women; 8. It provided companionship for women where separation of the sexes was enforced; 9. It provided a means of sexual adjustment where taboos demanded lengthy abstinence; 10. It was a means of fostering intertribal and interfamilial relationships; and 11. It satisfied personal reasons such as lust and revenge (1963: 247).

The above functions have not lost their significance, and monogamy cannot fulfill them. In time, through the continuing action of acculturation, polygamy may cease, but it is now a pertinent problem to the Church. The missionary assault for over a hundred years hardly affected it. Barrett says:

> In fact, the consequence all over the continent has been a strong reaction even inside the missions churches favoring polygamy as the natural form of the African family. Missions in most areas therefore appear to have made a fundamental mistake on this issue by attempting to force African society to abandon polygamy too rapidly, instead of allowing the indigenous Christian conscience to evolve its own solution (1968: 117-118).

So far, missionaries have harshly equated polygamy with sex, lust, bestiality, fornication, and perpetuated adultery of a base, pagan society. The real issues have seldom been faced. The African extended family, with the grandfather and his wives and their children, and their husbands and wives and children, has many attributes worthy of the Church's blessing. No person loses his privileges. None have extreme burdens to carry. The aged, orphans and widows are cared for. There is a sharing of work and the assurance of protection. Here are commendable social values which ought to be won for Christ. The Church has held numerous views regarding polygamy, though almost unanimously, its rejection has been the proof of genuine conversion.

Tippett lists six different attitudes of missions towards the acceptance of polygamists, in the various areas of the world:

1. Baptize the women and children but not the men; 2. Baptize none at all if they have anything to do with polygamy; 3. Baptize all on a testimony of faith---polygamists or not; 4. Let the husband retain the first wife and divorce the rest; 5. Let him divorce all but the preferred one; 6. For the first generation baptize on a profession of faith, but demand monogamy thereafter (*Church Growth Bulletin* Vol. V, No. 4:62 63).

To list these attitudes is to accentuate the inconsistency of missions and the seriousness of the problem. Attitudes that create injustices are not Christian.

I have already emphasized that in Zambia people should be encouraged to come to Christ as village groups. To accomplish this the headmen and elders must be converted, but many are polygamists. The question of baptizing them is consequently urgent and demands much study and prayer. I am not suggesting justification of polygamy as a way of life, but the principle is a Biblical one that we must meet men with the Gospel where they are. In Africa missionaries are called to work with people molded by circumstances established by the tenets of their culture before they were exposed to Christianity.

The problem must be resolved by the Word of God. The decisive issue is:

What says the Word of God about requiring believing polygamists to put away legally married wives before permitting them to be baptized? (McGavran, *Church Growth Bulletin* Vol. V. No. 4: 66).

This is not an academic question. The salvation of millions potentially winnable is the crucial issue. Many Independent Churches in Africa have been liberal towards tribal marriage patterns and have baptized polygamists. It is extremely significant to the African Bible student that God has marvelously used men who were polygamists. He understands that the Old Testament accepted polygamy. He also knows that the Ten Commandments forbade adultery. He

reads of David's many wives, but God did not judge him for
his wives, but because he committed adultery with Bathsheba,
the wife of another man. He also notes that the New Testament does not even speak of polygamy; not a chapter, or a
verse, or a word "condemns polygamy or prohibits the baptism of the polygamist" (McGavran, *Church Growth Bulletin*,
Vol. V. No. 4: 67).

If the New Testament refers to polygamy, it is by inference only. Among the qualifications of elders and deacons
in I Timothy 3:2 and 3:12 and in Titus 1:6 is the restraint
that elders and deacons must be— "the husband of one wife."
Apparently there were men in the Church with several wives
sufficiently qualified otherwise that, but for Paul's judgment, might have been chosen for those offices.

If this is true, the inference is that there were in the
early Church men with a plurality of wives—believing, baptized polygamists out of a non-Christian culture. Social
custom of the times justify this conclusion. Both Jewish and
Greek culture approved the practice of polygamy. It seems
obvious, with no Scripture or historical notation to the contrary, that numerous polygamous households were won to
Christ out of Judaism or paganism without disrupting the
family on the one hand or the Church on the other.

Numerous problems are involved in introducing monogamy to polygamous societies. This does not justify polygamy. It is not desirable. Polygamy violates New Testament ethical principles, but it is not openly condemned.
Though the problem was present with the Apostles and their
contemporaries, we have no clue as to how they met it.
There is no indication that any polygamist was denied baptism because of his marriage state nor that he was required
to put away all his wives but one as a condition of his salvation. Such passages as Mark 10:2-9, Ephesians 5:33, I Corin-
thians 7:1-11, and I Thessalonians 4:3-8 excepted, which do
lay down principles of Christian monogamy, polygamy as a
problem confronting New Testament evangelists is not mentioned. Monogamy is the Christian norm, but numerous polygamous pagan households in Zambia have neither known
the monogamous ideal nor the faith that motivates it. When
they hear and believe, and desire to accept the Faith, it is

denied them because of polygamous circumstances now beyond their ability to change.

A Suggested Plan for Meeting the Problem

Simply upon the confession of their faith, men, women, and children of polygamous households should be baptized. The difficult condition that insisted on a polygamous husband breaking up his home and driving away all his wives but one, with their children, to be accepted as a believer, must be rejected. It has not worked. On the confession of their faith only, polygamous households should be encouraged to become obedient to the Gospel.

Only one condition is necessary for this radical proposal. After careful Biblical teaching about marriage and the home, they must be persuaded to renounce polygamy. This does not mean that a polygamist embracing Christianity must cast away his wives, but it does mean that he must not marry others.

Such a change in missions policy will necessitate careful teaching in the Church. This new approach does not alter the position of the Church regarding monogamy. No Christian may enter into a polygamous relationship.

A few missions across Africa have, in recent years, taken this approach. So far, no widespread factual study of its results has been made. In my opinion it will work far better than the rigid opposition of the past.

New approaches are needed, not only with reference to polygamy, but with regard to many new problems, new challenges, and new evangelistic opportunities in New Zambia. Bold faith and a resolve to reevaluate and, if need be, reject unfruitful methods of the past is needed. Determination to learn what others have successfully done and a willingness to apply their methods is necessary. A firm resolve constantly to examine and measure one's labors against the supreme task of winning the multitudes is essential. And a fearless will to formulate and put into practice new methods is required.

Conclusion

Growth of the Church in Zambia has been slow. After eighty years only 10.7 per cent of the population is Christian if one combines the communicant membership of Roman Catholic, Independent, and Regular Churches. If one limits the communicant membership to the regular Protestant Churches, less than 2.5 per cent of Zambia's 4,000,000 people are professing believers. This is not good mission, and changes must be made if large numbers of the population of Zambia are to be won to the Lord.

So far, little has been done to improve upon the past. This book is written, believing that improvements can be made but only as radical changes are swiftly inaugurated.

The proposals made in this volume are yet to be carried to fruition. They have been used successfully, however, in bringing other clans and tribes of Africa back to God, and I am convinced they can do the same for Zambia.

A Need for Continuing Research

A thorough study from a church growth point of view needs to be done for all of Zambia. Whole tribal areas, village by village, need to be surveyed. Tribal groupings, decision-making patterns, animism and ancestor worship, the impact of Christianity on the villages and neighborhoods, the number of Christians per village, the relationship between schools and the Church, and other important factors need investigation and analysis to ascertain the strength and weaknesses of the past and the changes to be made in the future. It is imperative that the missions of Zambia discover how the Church grows in each clan and tribe.

Further research is needed concerning the place and contribution of educational, medical, and other institutions in direct relationship to their soul-winning value. Thorough investigation of what happens to the thousands of school-church converts after they have finished with school is yet to be done. It is imperative that in-depth studies be made, and very soon, of this unanswered question.

Few have questioned until recently the lasting worth of the institutional approach in Zambia---or in southern Africa. Institutionally oriented missionaries have, in all honesty, claimed satisfying results in steady ingathering of souls to the church year after year through mission schools, but bold affirmations of solid and lasting growth through the institutions cannot be proven.

Zambia missionaries need an awareness of what their co-workers are doing in other parts of Africa and over the world. Methods that are bringing great growth in Liberia, Ghana, Kenya, Nigeria, and Tanzania, in Africa; or Brazil, Chile, and Argentina in South America; or Indonesia and the Philippines in the South Pacific, need to be carefully studied and adapted, if possible, to the evangelistic needs of Zambia.

Contemporary Missionaries Must be Geared for Action

The criterian of good mission must no longer be determined by the thousands in schools, or the numbers of patients in the hospitals, though these valued services are of tremendous import to the uplift, health, and economy of the country. The criterian of mission is church growth---the number of men, women, and young people led through confession of faith and baptism to the Lord and into numerous spiritually sound churches strategically planted in village, town, and city throughout the whole country.

Missionary forces and monies must be concentrated on those peoples among whom there is great response. It is sinful to continue pouring resources and personnel into areas of limited, slow, strongly resisted growth when in the same land there are multitudes receptive to the Gospel.

I concur with Roy Shearer who has written:

Nothing wins men to Christ like good church growth. Yet this principle has been denied in the practice of our Churches and missions. Not only have we failed to realize that church growth can be achieved by concentration on responsive areas, but we also have deceived ourselves into conducting auxiliary activities in nonresponsive areas. These activities, while good in themselves, do not produce church growth. No one questions the validity of educational and medical work for serving human needs, but if church growth is our object and there are responsive populations where we can act, we are mistaken in using these Christian services in nonresponsive areas hoping to "soften up" the people so that they eventually will become Christians. We are mistaken in using these expensive institutions as indirect evangelistic tools in nonresponsive areas where nearby are populations which would respond to direct evangelism if we would send many workers there (1966: 221).

Effective evangelism means the conversion of many responsive people in extended family, clan, and tribal groups. It means that villages will decide as villages to renounce their fetishes, idols, and shrines and accept instead Jesus Christ as Lord of their lives. It means that numerous churches in multiplied tribal situations will be planted among receptive populations, churches that have instilled within them the ability to support, govern, and multiply themselves.

Towards these ends the Gospel must be powerfully communicated, and for this purpose new proposals designed to speed evangelization are offered with the fervent prayer that the receptive peoples in the clans and tribes of Zambia, and in the nations of Africa might become a living part of the Church of the Lord Jesus Christ.

APPENDIX A

ORIGINAL INSTRUMENT OF INVESTIGATION

A. Name of the Village
  1. The number of families in the village?
  2. The number of souls in the village?
  3. The number of married men? married women? single men?
     single women? boys of school age? girls of school age? and
     children under school age?

B. Family Relationships
  1. Number of generations in the village? Number of polygamous
     households? Number of monogamous households?
  2. Location of husband's father, grandfather, etc.?
  3. Location of married sons and daughters, brothers, sisters,
     maternal uncles and aunts, and paternal uncles and aunts?

C. Decision-making Patterns
  1. How are village decisions made?
  2. Family decisions?
  3. Church, commercial, and political decisions?
  4. Opinion groups?

D. Tribal Groupings in the Village
  1. Sala, Tonga, Ila, Shona, Sindebele, Bemba, others?

E. Village Wealth
  1. Number of huts? Brick houses?
  2. Water sources? River? Pools? Wells, dug or drilled?
  3. Cash crops? Volume of harvest?
  4. Number of Cattle? Oxen?
  5. Tractors? Plows? Automobiles? Trucks? Other machinery?
  6. Radios? Sewing Machines? Furniture? Beds?

F. Education
  1. Number of men who can read and write? Women?
  2. Number of children in school? Primary? Secondary? Technical?

G. Christianity in the Village
  1. Number of Christians? Church affiliation? Number of Christians
     won through schools?
  2. How did they become Christians? Through family relationships?
     Friendships? Business relationships? Preaching?

3. Strength of independent church movement.
4. Number of adult Christians? Number of children Christians?
5. Number of Bibles and other religious literature.

H. Evidences of animism?
    1. Rain shrines? Spirit gates? Witchcraft? Sorcery? Offerings to the "mizimu"? Rituals? Festivals? Dancing? Special days?

I. Evidences of integration?

J. Tribal crafts
    1. Indigenous musical instruments? Tools? Weapons? Thatching?

K. Types of labor
    1. Farmers? Carpenters? Builders? Truck drivers? Well diggers? Policemen? Herbalists? Mechanics? etc.

L. Health in the Village
    1. Village cleanliness? Diseases apparent? Beer brewing? Drunkenness?

M. Marriage Patterns? Bride-price?
    1. Where do the men get their wives?
    2. The go-between?
    3. Cross-tribal marriages?

N. Foods used by the Villagers
    1. Grains? Vegetables? Wild game? Domestic animals? Milk? Fish? Commercial food?

O. Amount of Migration to the City?

APPENDIX B

MODIFIED INSTRUMENT OF INVESTIGATION

A. Name of the Village
   1. Tribal groupings in the village?
   2. Decision-making patterns in the village?
   3. Types of labor?
   4. Village wealth? (Data gained by observation.)
   5. Evidences of integration? (Data gathered by observation.)
   6. Tribal crafts? (By observation and query.)
   7. Health and cleanliness? (By observation and query.)
   8. Beer brewing and drunkenness?
   9. Diet of the people in the village?
   10. Migration to the city?

B. The family.
   1. Number of families in each village? Number of souls?
   2. Marriage patterns? Polygamous households? Bride-price?
   3. Where do men get their wives? Go-betweens?
   4. Intertribal marriages?
   5. Family decision-making patterns?

C. Religion
   1. Evidences of animism? Shrines? Rituals?
   2. Number of Christians in the village? How did they become Christians?
   3. Church affiliation? Independent church movements? Number of Bibles?

D. Education
   1. Men and women who can read and write?

BIBLIOGRAPHY

BOOKS

Allen, Roland   London, World Dominion Press.
  1949   THE SPONTANEOUS EXPANSION OF THE CHURCH.
Allen, Roland   London, World Dominion Press.
  1960   MISSIONARY METHODS: ST. PAUL'S OR OURS?
Allen, Roland   Grand Rapids, Eerdmans.
  1962   THE MINISTRY OF THE SPIRIT.
Allen, Roland   London, World Dominion Press.
  1964   MISSIONARY PRINCIPLES.
Anderson, Gerald   New York, McGraw-Hill.
  1965   THE THEOLOGY OF CHRISTIAN MISSION.
Anderson, Gerald, editor   New York, Abingdon.
  1967   CHRISTIAN MISSION IN THEOLOGICAL PERSPECTIVE.
Anderson, Morshead   London, Universities Mission
  1909   HISTORY OF THE UNIVERSITIES MISSION TO CENTRAL AFRICA
Barnett, H. G.   New York, McGraw-Hill.
  1952   INNOVATION: THE BASIS OF CULTURAL CHANGE.
Barrett, David R.   London, Oxford University Press.
  1968   SCHISM AND RENEWAL IN AFRICA.
Bascom, W. & Herskovits, M.   Chicago, University of Chicago Press.
  1959   CONTINUITY AND CHANGE IN AFRICAN CULTURES.
Bavinck, J.   Philadelphia, Presbyterian & Reformed Co
  1964   AN INTRODUCTION TO THE SCIENCE OF MISSIONS.
Benedict, Ruth   Boston, Houghton Mifflin Company.
  1959   PATTERNS OF CULTURE.
Brandel-Syrier, Mia   London, Lutterworth Press.
  1962   BLACK WOMAN IN SEARCH OF GOD.
Brelsford, W.   Lusaka, Government Printer.
  1957   THE TRIBES OF NORTHERN RHODESIA.
Brelsford, W., editor   London, Cassell and Company.
  1960   HANDBOOK OF THE FEDERATION OF RHODESIA & NYASALAND.
Bullock, C.   Cape Town, South Africa, Juta.
  1927   THE MASHONA.
Chadwick, Owen   London, Hodder and Stoughton.
  1959   MACKENZIE'S GRAVE.
Churchill, Rhona   London, Hodder and Stoughton.
  1962   WHITE MAN'S GOD.
Clegg, Edward   London, Oxford University Press.
  1960   RACE AND POLITICS.
Clements, Frank   London, Methuen and Company,
  1959   KARIBA.

Clinton, Desmond   London, Longmans, Green and Company.
  1937   THE SOUTH AFRICAN MELTING POT.
Clinton, Iris   Bulawayo, Stuart Manning.
  1959   THESE VESSELS.
Clutton-Brock, G.   London, Hodder and Stoughton.
  1959   DAWN IN NYASALAND.
Colson, E.   Manchester, Manchester University Press.
  1959   MARRIAGE AND THE FAMILY AMONG THE PLATEAU TONGA
Colson, E.   Manchester, Manchester University Press.
  1960   SOCIAL ORGANIZATION OF THE GWEMBA TONGA.
Colson, E.   Manchester, Manchester University Press.
  1962   THE PLATEAU TONGA OF NORTHERN RHODESIA.
Colson, E. & Gluckman, M.   Manchester, Manchester University Press.
  1961   SEVEN TRIBES OF BRITISH CENTRAL AFRICA.
Cook, Harold   Chicago, Moody Press.
  1954   AN INTRODUCTION TO THE STUDY OF CHRISTIAN MISSIONS.
Cook, Harold   Chicago, Moody Press.
  1959   MISSIONARY LIFE AND WORK.
Cook, Harold   Chicago, Moody Press.
  1967   HIGHLIGHTS OF CHRISTIAN MISSIONS.
Davis, Raymond   Grand Rapids, Zondervan.
  1966   FIRE ON THE MOUNTAINS.
Dodge, Ralph   Westwood, N.J., Revell.
  1964   THE UNPOPULAR MISSIONARY.
Doke, Clement   London, Harrap.
  1931   THE LAMBAS OF NORTHERN RHODESIA.
Dougall, J. W. C.   Edinburgh, Saint Andrew's Press
  1963   CHRISTIANS IN THE AFRICAN REVOLUTION.
Fage, J.   Cambridge, University Press.
  1965   AN INTRODUCTION TO THE HISTORY OF WEST AFRICA.
Fallers, Lloyd   Chicago, University of Chicago.
  1965   BANTU BUREAUCRACY.
Foskett, R., editor   Edinburgh, University Press.
  1964   THE ZAMBEZI DOCTORS.
Franck, Thomas   New York, Fordham University.
  1960   RACE AND NATIONALISM.
Fraser, Donald   New York, Dutton and Company.
  1914   WINNING A PRIMITIVE PEOPLE.
Frazer, James   New York, McMillan.
  1963   THE GOLDEN BOUGH.
Gann, L.   Manchester, Manchester University Press.
  1958   THE BIRTH OF A PLURAL SOCIETY.
Gelfand, M.   Cape Town, Juta.
  1956   MEDICINE AND MAGIC OF THE MOUNTAIN.
Gelfand, M.   Cape Town, Juta.
  1959   SHONA RITUAL.
Gelfand, M.   Cape Town, Juta.
  1962   SHONA RELIGION.
Gibbs, Peter   London, Arthur Baker.
  1961   AVALANCHE IN CENTRAL AFRICA.
Glover, R. H. & Kane, J. H.   New York, Harper and Row.
  1960   THE PROGRESS OF WORLD-WIDE MISSIONS.
Gluckman, Max   Manchester, Manchester University Press.
  1955   THE JUDICIAL PROCESS AMONG THE BAROTSE OF NORTHERN
            RHODESIA.

Grassi, M.   Maryknoll, Maryknoll Publications.
1965   A WORLD TO WIN.
Gray, Richard   London, Oxford University Press.
1960   THE TWO NATIONS, ASPECTS OF THE DEVELOPMENT OF RA
          RELATIONS, IN THE RHODESIAS AND NYASALAND.
Griffiths, James   London, Epworth Press.
1958   LIVINGSTONE'S AFRICA.
Grimley, J. B., & Robinson, G. E.   Grand Rapids, Eerdmans.
1966   CHURCH GROWTH IN CENTRAL AND SOUTHERN NIGERIA.
Groves, C.   London, Lutterworth Press.
1964   THE PLANTING OF CHRISTIANITY IN AFRICA. (4 Volumes)
Gulliver, Philip   Boston, Boston University Press.
1963   SOCIAL CONTROL IN AN AFRICAN SOCIETY.
Hahn, C.   Cape Town, Cape Times.
1928   THE OVAMBO IN THE NATIVE TRIBES OF SOUTHWEST AFRIC
Hall, Richard   New York, Praeger.
1965   ZAMBIA.
Hamilton, Keith   Lucknow, Lucknow Publishing House.
1963   CHURCH GROWTH IN THE HIGH ANDES.
Hatch, John   New York, Praeger.
1960   AFRICA TODAY—AND TOMORROW.
Haw, Richard   Bulawayo, Stuart Manning.
1960   NO OTHER HOME.
Herskovits, Melville   New York, Alfred A. Knopf.
1962   THE HUMAN FACTOR IN CHANGING AFRICA.
Hodges, Melvin   Springfield, Mo., Gospel Publishing House.
1953   THE INDIGENOUS CHURCH.
Hogg, W.   New York, Friendship House.
1960   ONE WORLD ONE MISSION.
Hughes, John   New York, Longmans, Green and Compaı
1961   THE NEW FACE OF AFRICA SOUTH OF THE SAHARA.
Hughes, Thomas   London, Macmillan.
1893   DAVID LIVINGSTONE.
Hunter, Guy   London, Oxford University Press.
1963   THE NEW SOCIETIES OF TROPICAL AFRICA.
Jacobs, Melville   Homewood, Dorsey Press.
1964   PATTERN IN CULTURAL ANTHROPOLOGY.
Jahn, Janheinz   New York, Grove Press.
1961   MUNTU.
Jones, Neville   Glasgow, University Press.
1953   RHODESIAN GENESIS.
Karefa-Smart, John and Rena   New York, Friendship House.
1959   THE HALTING KINGDOM.
Keesing, Felix   New York, Holt, Rinehart, and Winston.
1965   CULTURAL ANTHROPOLOGY.
Kenyatta, Jomo   New York, Vintage Books.
1932   FACING MOUNT KENYA.
King, Paul   Cape Town, Citadel.
1939   MISSIONS IN SOUTHERN RHODESIA.
Kingsnorth, G.   Cambridge. University Press.
1965   AFRICA SOUTH OF THE SAHARA.
Kraemer, Hendrick   London, Edinburgh House Press.
1947   THE CHRISTIAN MESSAGE IN A NON-CHRISTIAN WORLD.
Kraemer, Hendrick   Philadelphia, Westminster Press.
1960   WORLD CULTURES AND WORLD RELIGIONS.

Kroeber, A.   New York, Harcourt, Brace, and World, Inc.
   1948   ANTHROPOLOGY.
Lanternari, Vittorio   New York, Mentor Books.
   1965   THE RELIGIONS OF THE OPPRESSED.
Lessa, W. & Vogt, E.   New York, Mentor Books.
   1965   READER IN COMPARATIVE RELIGION.
Lessing, Pieter   London, Michael Joseph.
   1962   AFRICA'S RED HARVEST.
Lienhardt, Godfrey   London, Oxford University Press.
   1964   SOCIAL ANTHROPOLOGY.
Lindsell, Harold   Westwood, N.J., Revell.
   1955   MISSIONARY PRINCIPLES AND PRACTICE.
Lindsell, Harold, editor   Waco, Word Books.
   1966   THE CHURCH'S WORLDWIDE MISSION.
Livingstone, David & Charles   New York, Harper and Brothers.
   1866   EXPEDITION TO THE ZAMBEZI.
Lowie, Robert   New York, Grosset and Dunlap.
   1962   PRIMITIVE RELIGION.
Luzbetak, Louis   Techny, Divine Word Publications.
   1963   THE CHURCH AND CULTURES.
Mackintosh, C.   Livingstone, Rhodes-Livingstone Institute.
   1950   SOME PIONEER MISSIONS IN NORTHERN RHODESIA
             AND NYASALAND.
Mair, Lucy   Baltimore, Penguin.
   1964   PRIMITIVE GOVERNMENT.
Malinowski, Bronislaw   Garden City, Doubleday Anchor.
   1954   MAGIC, SCIENCE, AND RELIGION.
Malinowski, Bronislaw   New York, Dutton Paperback.
   1961a   ARGONAUTS OF THE WESTERN PACIFIC.
Malinowski, Bronislaw   New Haven, Yale University Press.
   1961b   THE DYNAMICS OF CULTURE CHANGE.
Marquard, Leo   London, Oxford University Press.
   1966   THE PEOPLES AND POLICIES OF SOUTH AFRICA.
Marris, Peter   Chicago, Northwestern University Press.
   1962   FAMILY AND SOCIAL CHANGE IN AN AFRICAN SOCIETY.
Marsh, Z. & Kingsnorth, G. W. Cambridge, University Press.
   1966   AN INTRODUCTION TO THE HISTORY OF EAST AFRICA.
Matthews, Basil   New York, Friendship House.
   1960   FORWARD THROUGH THE AGES.
McGavran, Donald   London, World Dominion Press.
   1961   THE BRIDGES OF GOD.
McGavran, Guy, Hodges, & Nida Lucknow, Lucknow Publishing House.
   1962   CHURCH GROWTH IN JAMAICA.
McGavran, Donald   Grand Rapids, Eerdmans.
   1963   CHURCH GROWTH IN MEXICO.
McGavran, Donald, editor   New York, Harper and Row.
   1965   CHURCH GROWTH AND CHRISTIAN MISSION.
McGavran, Donald   Grand Rapids, Eerdmans.
   1969   UNDERSTANDING CHURCH GROWTH.
McNeile, Michael   Cape Town, Cape Times.
   1957   THIS AFRICA OF OURS.
Millin, Sarah Gertrude   London, Chatto and Windus.
   1933   CECIL RHODES.
Mitchell, J.   Manchester, Manchester University Press.
   1956   THE YAO VILLAGE.

Moreira, Eduardo   London, World Dominion Press.
  1936   PORTUGUESE EAST AFRICA.
Morris, Colin   London, Longmans, Green and Company.
  1961   THE HOUR AFTER MIDNIGHT.
Morris, C., & Kaunda, Kenneth   Lusaka, United Society for Christian Literature.
  1960   BLACK GOVERNMENT.
Morris, C. & Kaunda, Kenneth   Nashville, Abingdon Press.
  1968   A HUMANIST IN AFRICA.
Murdock, George   New York, McGraw-Hill.
  1959   AFRICA, ITS PEOPLES, AND THEIR CULTURE HISTORY.
Neill, Stephen   London, Oxford University Press.
  1961   CHRISTIAN FAITH AND OTHER FAITHS.
Neill, Stephen   Baltimore, Penguin.
  1964   A HISTORY OF CHRISTIAN MISSIONS.
Neill, Stephen   New York, McGraw-Hill.
  1966   COLONIALISM AND CHRISTIAN MISSIONS.   •
Newbigin, Lesslie   New York, Friendship House.
  1965   THE HOUSEHOLD OF GOD.
Newbigin, Lesslie   London, S.C.M. Press.
  1966   HONEST RELIGION FOR SECULAR MAN.
Nida, Eugene   New York, Harper and Row.
  1954   CUSTOMS AND CULTURES.
Nida, Eugene   New York, Harper and Row.
  1960   MESSAGE AND MISSION.
Nida, E. & Smalley, W.   New York, Friendship House.
  1959   INTRODUCING ANIMISM.
Niebuhr, R. & Williams, D., eds. New York, Harper and Row.
  1956   THE MINISTRY IN HISTORICAL PERSPECTIVES.
Northcott, Cecil   London, Lutterworth Press.
  1957   LIVINGSTONE IN AFRICA.
Ottenberg, Simon and Phoebe   New York, Random House.
  1964   CULTURES AND SOCIETIES OF AFRICA.
Oliver, Roland   Cape Town, Longman Green and Company.
  1952   THE MISSIONARY FACTOR IN EAST AFRICA.
Packer, J.   Chicago, Inter-Varsity Press.
  1965   EVANGELISM AND THE SOVEREIGNTY OF GOD.
Parrinder, E.   London, S, P. C. K,
  1962   AFRICAN TRADITIONAL RELIGION.
Pickett, J. Wascom   Lucknow, Lucknow Publishing House.
  1960   CHRIST'S WAY TO INDIA'S HEART.
Pickett, J. Wascom   New York, Abingdon Press.
  1963   THE DYNAMICS OF CHURCH GROWTH.
Pickett, J., Warnshuis, A., Singh, G., and McGavran, D.
                                    Lucknow, Lucknow Publishing House.
  1962   CHURCH GROWTH AND GROUP CONVERSION.
Pienaar, S. & Sampson, A.   London, Oxford University Press.
  1960   SOUTH AFRICA.
Powdermaker, Hortense   New York, Harper and Row.
  1962   COPPERTOWN: CHANGING AFRICA.
Price, Willard   London, Heinemann.
  1961   INCREDIBLE AFRICA.
Radcliffe-Brown, A.   London, Cohen and West.
  1945   STRUCTURE AND FUNCTION IN PRIMITIVE SOCIETY.

Radcliffe-Brown, A. & Forde, D.   London, Oxford University Press.
1950   AFRICAN SYSTEMS OF KINSHIP AND MARRIAGE.
Ram-Desai   Denver, Allan Swallow.
1962   CHRISTIANITY IN AFRICA AS SEEN BY AFRICANS.
Randall, Max Ward   Joliet, Mission Services.
1960   LIGHT FOR THE DARK COUNTRY.
Randall, Max Ward   Joliet, Mission Services.
1965   WE WOULD DO IT AGAIN.
Rayner, William   London, Faber and Faber.
1962   THE TRIBE AND ITS SUCCESSORS.
Read, Margaret   New Haven, Yale University Press.
1960   CHILDREN OF THEIR FATHERS.
Read, William   Grand Rapids, Eerdmans.
1965   NEW PATTERNS OF CHURCH GROWTH IN BRAZIL.
Redfield, Robert   Chicago, University of Chicago Press.
1965   THE LITTLE COMMUNITY PEASANT SOCIETY AND CULTURE.
Retief, M. W.   Lovedale, The Lovedale Press.
1958   WILLIAM MURRAY OF NYASALAND.
Richards, Audrey   London, Oxford University Press.
1939   LAND, LABOUR, AND DIET IN NORTHERN RHODESIA.
Roberts, John   Augusta, S.C., Allen and Company.
1875   THE LIFE AND EXPLORATION OF DAVID LIVINGSTONE.
Rosenthal, Eric, compiler   London, Frederick Warne and Co.
1964   ENCYCLOPAEDIA OF SOUTHERN AFRICA.
Ross, Emory   New York, Friendship House.
1952   AFRICAN HERITAGE.
Rotberg, Robert   Princeton, Princeton University Press.
1965   CHRISTIAN MISSIONARIES AND THE CREATION OF NORTHERN
          RHODESIA, 1880-1924.
Savage, Murray   Gisborne, Te Rau Press.
1949   ACHIEVEMENT.
Schapera, I.   London, Chatto and Windus.
1945   APPRENTICESHIP AT KURUMAN.
Schapera, I.   London, Chatto and Windus.
1960   LIVINGSTONE'S PRIVATE JOURNALS.
Schapera, I.   London, Chatto and Windus.
1961   LIVINGSTONE'S MISSIONARY CORRESPONDENCE.
Schapera, I.   London, Chatto and Windus.
1963a   DAVID LIVINGSTONE'S FAMILY LETTERS. (2 Volumes)
Schapera, I.   London, Chatto and Windus.
1963b   LIVINGSTONE'S AFRICAN JOURNAL. (2 Volumes)
Scudder, Thayer   Manchester, Manchester University Press.
1962   THE ECOLOGY OF THE GWEMBA TONGA.
Shearer, Roy   Grand Rapids, Eerdmans.
1966   WILDFIRE, CHURCH GROWTH IN KOREA.
Shepperson, George   Edinburgh, University Press.
1965   DAVID LIVINGSTONE AND THE ROVUMA.
Shepperson, G. & Price, T.   Edinburgh, University Press.
1958   INDEPENDENT AFRICAN.
Smith, Edwin   London, World Dominion Press
1928   THE WAY OF THE WHITE FIELDS IN RHODESIA.
Smith, Edwin   London, United Society for Christian Literature.
1946   KNOWING THE AFRICAN.
Smith, Edwin, editor   London, Edinburgh House Press.
1950   AFRICAN IDEAS OF GOD.

Smith, E. & Dales, A.   London, Macmillan.
    1920   THE ILA-SPEAKING PEOPLES OF NORTHERN RHODESIA. (2 Vols.)
Spiro, Herbert   Ithaca, Cornell University Press.
    1963   FIVE AFRICAN STATES.
Sunda, James   Lucknow, Lucknow Publishing House.
    1963   CHURCH GROWTH IN WEST NEW GUINEA.
Sundkler, B. G. M.   London, Oxford University Press.
    1962   BANTU PROPHETS IN SOUTH AFRICA.
Sundkler, B. G. M.   London, S.C.M. Press.
    1962   THE CHRISTIAN MINISTRY IN AFRICA.
Tanser, G.   Cape Town, Juta.
          A HISTORY OF NYASALAND.
Taylor, Mrs. Howard   Chicago, Moody Press.
    1964   BEHIND THE RANGES.
Taylor, J. V.   London, S.C.M. Press.
    1958   PROCESSES OF GROWTH IN AN AFRICAN CHURCH.
Taylor, J. V., & Lehmann, D.   London, S.C.M. Press.
    1961   CHRISTIANS OF THE COPPERBELT.
Tippett, A. R.   New York, Friendship House.
    1967   SOLOMON ISLANDS CHRISTIANITY.
Tippett, A. R.   Grand Rapids, Eerdmans.
    1970   CHURCH GROWTH AND THE WORD OF GOD.
Tucker, John   London, World Dominion Press.
    1956   ANGOLA, THE LAND OF THE BLACKSMITH PRINCE.
Turner, V.   Manchester, Manchester University Press.
    1957   SCHISM AND CONTINUITY IN AN AFRICAN SOCIETY: A STUDY OF
             NDEMBU VILLAGE LIFE.
Visser 't Hooft, W.   Philadelphia, Westminster Press.
    1963   NO OTHER NAME.
Walker, Deaville   London, Colgate Press.
    1942   A HUNDRED YEARS IN NIGERIA.
Walker, E.   London, Longmans, Green and Company.
    1957   A HISTORY OF SOUTHERN AFRICA.
Wallis, J., editor   London, Chatto and Windus.
    1945   THE MATABELE MISSION.
Weber, Max   London, Collier-Macmillan.
    1964   SOCIAL AND ECONOMIC ORGANIZATION.
Welbourne, F.   London, Oxford University Press.
    1961   EAST AFRICAN REBELS.
Welbourne, F.   London, Oxford University Press.
    1965   EAST AFRICAN CHRISTIAN.
White, C.   Manchester, Manchester University Press.
    1960   AN OUTLINE OF LUVALE SOCIAL AND POLITICAL ORGANIZATION.
Wilson, Monica   London, Oxford University Press.
    1951   GOOD COMPANY: A STUDY OF NYAKYUSA AGE-VILLAGES.
Wilson, Monica   London, Oxford University Press.
    1957   RITUALS OF KINSHIP AMONG THE NYAKYUSA.
Wilson, Monica   Cape Town, University of Cape Town.
    1958   THE PEOPLES OF THE NYASA-TANGANYIKA CORRIDOR.
Wilson, Monica   London, Oxford University Press.
    1959   COMMUNAL RITUALS OF THE NYAKYUSA.
Wolfe, Alvin   Chicago, Northwestern University Press.
    1961   IN THE NGOMBE TRADITION.
World Student Christian Federation   Geneva, Switzerland.
    1960   HISTORY'S LESSONS FOR TOMORROW'S MISSION.

PUBLIC DOCUMENTS

Zambia.   ZAMBIA TODAY.   Lusaka, Government Printers. 1964.
Zambia.   COPY OF ADDRESS GIVEN BY PRESIDENT KAUNDA before the
           Synod of the United Church of Zambia, Lusaka, January 4, 1967.
Zambia.   ZAMBIA PRESS RELEASE. No. 1387/67.
Zambia.   ZAMBIA PRESS RELEASE. No. 1864/66.

ARTICLES AND PERIODICALS

Barnes, J.   "The Fort Jameson Ngoni" in Colson, Elizabeth, and Gluckman,
              Max (editors) SEVEN TRIBES OF BRITISH CENTRAL AFRICA.
              London: Oxford University Press, (1961).
Barnes, J.   "Marriage in a Changing Society," Oxford University Press,
              Cape Town, Rhodes-Livingstone Papers, 20. (1951).
CHURCH GROWTH BULLETIN, Vol. III, No. 1. Donald A. McGavran, ed.,
              265 Lytton Ave., Palo Alto, California.
CHURCH GROWTH BULLETIN, Vol. IV, No. 1. Donald A. McGavran, ed.,
              265 Lytton Ave., Palo Alto, California.
CHURCH GROWTH BULLETIN, Vol. IV, No. 2. Donald A. McGavran, ed.,
              265 Lytton Ave., Palo Alto, California.
CHURCH GROWTH BULLETIN, Vol. V, No. 4. Donald A. McGavran, ed.,
              265 Lytton Ave., Palo Alto, California.
Cunnison, Ian.   "History of the Luapula," Oxford University Press, Cape Town,
              Rhodes-Livingstone Papers, 21. (1951)
Cunnison, Ian.   "History and Genealogies in a Conquest State,"
              AMERICAN ANTHROPOLOGIST. (1956). 59: 109-139.
Gibson, Gordon, "Double Descent and Its Correlates Among the Herero of
              Ngamiland," AMERICAN ANTHROPOLOGIST. (1956). 59: 109-139.
Gluckman, Max.   "The Lozi of Barotseland in North-Western Rhodesia," in
              Colson, Elizabeth, & Gluckman, Max (editors), SEVEN TRIBES OF
              BRITISH CENTRAL AFRICA. London: Oxford University Press (1961)
Gluckman, Max, Mitchell, J., and Barnes, J. "The Village Headman in British
              Central Africa," AFRICA, 19-89-106, (1949).
Hambly, W.   "The Ovimbundu of Angola," FIELD MUSUEM OF NATURAL
              HISTORY, ANTHROPOLOGICAL SERIES. (1934), 21: 2.
Hopgood, C.   "The Future of Bantu Languages in Northern Rhodesia," RHODES-
              LIVINGSTONE JOURNAL, II (December, 1944).
INTERNATIONAL REVIEW OF MISSIONS, Vol. LII, No. 206: 168. (1963).
INTERNATIONAL REVIEW OF MISSIONS, Vol. LVII, No. 225: 46.
Jaspar, M.   "The Ila-Tonga Peoples of North-Western Rhodesia," ETHNO-
              GRAPHIC SURVEY OF AFRICA, WEST CENTRAL AFRICA, 4 (1953).
Johnson, C., AGRICULTURE FOR AFRICANS IN THE MAIZE BELT OF
              NORTHERN RHODESIA. Lusaka, Government Printer, (1945).
Krass, A.   "A Case Study in Effective Evangelism in West Africa," in the
              CHURCH GROWTH BULLETIN. (1967), IV: 1-4.
Macmillan, Harold. "The Winds of Change," THE CAPE ARGUS, Cape Town.
              (February 4, 1960).
McCulloch, Merran. "The Southern Lunda and Related Peoples," ETHNOGRAPHIC
              SURVEY OF AFRICA, WEST CENTRAL AFRICA, 2, (1952).
Mitchell, J.   "The Yao of Southern Nyasaland," in Colson, Elizabeth, and
              Gluckman, Max (editors), SEVEN TRIBES OF BRITISH CENTRAL
              AFRICA. London: Oxford University Press, (1961).
Mitchell, J., and Barnes, J. "The Lamba Village: Report of a Social Survey,"
              COMMUNICATIONS FROM THE AFRICAN STUDIES, 24, (1950).

Morreau, J. "Survey of Social Conditions in the Native Church," PROC. GEN. MISSIONARY CONFERENCE, NORTHERN RHODESIA. (1927).

Pierson, Arthur, editor, "Tidings of Awakenings and Revival Come from the French Missions on the Zambezi," THE MISSIONARY REVIEW OF THE WORLD, 720, (1896).

Pierson, Arthur, editor, "M. Coillard who is Returning from the Zambezi Broken Down in Health," THE MISSIONARY REVIEW OF THE WORLD, 720, (1896).

Pierson, Arthur, editor, "Baptism of an African Crown Prince," THE MISSIONARY REVIEW OF THE WORLD, 135-136, (1900).

Pierson, Arthur, editor, "Calamity on the Zambezi," THE MISSIONARY REVIEW OF THE WORLD, 973, (1900).

Pierson, Arthur, editor, "A Sunday Service at the Zambezi," THE MISSIONARY REVIEW OF THE WORLD, 957, (1902).

Pretorius, Pauline. "An Attempt at Christian Initiation in Nyasaland," INTERNATIONAL REVIEW OF MISSIONS, XXXIX, 155:284-291, (1950).

Randall, Max Ward, "A View and a Review of One Year in South Africa," SOUTH AFRICAN TORCH, (November, 1951).

Richards, Audrey. "Some Types of Family Structure Amongst the Central Bantu," in Radcliffe-Brown, A., and Forde, Daryll, editors, AFRICAN SYSTEMS OF KINSHIP AND MARRIAGE, London: Oxford University Press. (1950).

Stannous, N. "The Wayao of Nyasaland," HARVARD AFRICAN STUDIES, 3, Cambridge, Harvard University. (1922).

Tew, Mary. "The Peoples of the Lake Nyasa Region," ETHNOGRAPHIC SURVEY OF AFRICA, EAST CENTRAL AFRICA, 1, (1950).

Turner, V. "The Lozi Peoples of North-Western Rhodesia," ETHNOGRAPHIC SURVEY OF AFRICA, WEST CENTRAL AFRICA. 3, (1952).

Whitely, Wilfred, Stefaniszyn, B., and Slaski, J. "Bemba and Related Peoples of Northern Rhodesia," "With Contributions on the Aambo," and "The Peoples of the Lower Luapula Valley," ETHNOGRAPHIC SURVEY OF AFRICA EAST CENTRAL AFRICA. 2. (1951).

Wilson, Godfrey. "The Nyakyusa of Southwestern Tanganyika," in Colson, Elizabeth, and Gluckman, Max (editors), SEVEN TRIBES OF BRITISH CENTRAL AFRICA. London: Oxford University Press, (1961).

Winter, Ralph. "Cultural Overhang and the Training of Pastors," CHURCH GROWTH BULLETIN, Vol. IV, 2: 6, (1967).

Winter, Ralph. "Agonizing Reappraisal at the Quiche Bible Institute," CHURCH GROWTH BULLETIN, Vol. IV, 4: 8-10, (1968).

OTHER SOURCES

Chizuma, Peter. In an interview with Leroy Randall, reported in a letter to the Author, September 13, 1967.

Erickson, Dale. Letter to the Author, July 17, 1969.

Mechem, Don. Letter to the Author, February 7, 1968.

Randall, Leroy. Letter to the Author, September 13, 1967.

WORLD CHRISTIAN HANDBOOK. London, World Dominion Press. (1949-1952-1957-1962).

WORLD CHRISTIAN HANDBOOK. London, Lutterworth Press. (1968).

ACKNOWLEDGMENTS

The author acknowledges with gratitude the permission
to quote from the following publishers and authors:
THE UNPOPULAR MISSIONARY, by Ralph Dodge, copyright
1964, by the Fleming H. Revell Company, Old Tappan, N. J.
CHRISTIAN MISSIONARIES AND THE CREATION OF
NORTHERN RHODESIA, 1880-1924, by Robert I. Rotberg,
copyright 1965 by Princeton University Press, Princeton.
CHRISTIANS IN THE AFRICAN REVOLUTION, by J.W.C.
Dougall, published by St. Andrew Press, Edinburgh, 1963.
ZAMBIA, by Richard Hall, 1965, published by Praeger
Publishing House, 111 Fourth Avenue, New York, New York.
KNOWING THE AFRICAN, by Edwin W. Smith, 1946;
BLACK WOMAN IN SEARCH OF GOD, by Mia Brandel-
Syrier, 1962; BLACK GOVERNMENT, by Colin Morris and
Kenneth Kaunda, 1960; THE WORLD CHRISTIAN HAND-
BOOK, edited by Coxhill and Grubb; LIVINGSTONE IN
AFRICA, by Cecil Northcott, 1957; THE PLANTING OF
CHRISTIANITY IN AFRICA, 1964; permission granted by
the Lutterworth Press, 4 Bouverie Street, London, E.C.4.
READER IN COMPARATIVE RELIGION, by Lessa and
Vogt, 1965; THE PROGRESS OF WORLD-WIDE MISSIONS,
by Glover and Kane, 1960; CHURCH GROWTH AND CHRIS-
TIAN MISSION, by Donald A. McGavran, 1965; CUSTOMS
AND CULTURES, by Eugene Nida, 1954; COPPERTOWN:
CHANGING AFRICA, by Hortense Powdermaker, 1962;
permission granted by Harper and Row, publishers, New York.
RACE AND NATIONALISM, by Thomas Franck, published
in 1960 by Fordham University. AN INTRODUCTION TO
THE SCIENCE OF MISSIONS, by J. Bavinck, 1964, copy-
right by the Presbyterian and Reformed Company. THE
CHURCH'S WORLD-WIDE MISSION, by Harold Lindsell,
copyright by Word Books of Waco, Texas, 1966. INTER-
NATIONAL REVIEW OF MISSIONS, Volume VII, No. 225.
THE INDIGENOUS CHURCH, by Melvin Hodges, 1953, the
Gospel Publishing House, Springfield, Missouri. AFRICAN
TRADITIONAL RELIGION, by E. G. Parrinder, 1962, the
S.P.C.K. THE CHURCH IN CULTURES, by Louis Luzbetak,
1963, copyright Divine Word Publications, Techny, Illinois.

CHRISTIAN MINISTRY IN AFRICA, by B. G. M. Sundkler, 1962; CHRISTIANS OF THE COPPERBELT, by Taylor and Lehmann, 1961; PROCESSES OF GROWTH IN AN AFRICAN CHURCH, by J. V. Taylor, 1958; permission granted by the S.C.M. Press of London. FORWARD THROUGH THE AGES, by Basil Matthews, 1960; and INTRODUCING ANIMISM, by Eugene Nida and William Smalley, used by permission of Friendship Press, New York. LIVINGSTONE'S MISSIONARY CORRESPONDENCE, by I. Shapera, 1961, published by Chatto and Windus of London, used by kind permission. AFRICA: ITS PEOPLES AND THEIR CULTURE HISTORY, by George Murdock, 1959; INNOVATION: THE BASIS OF CULTURE CHANGE, by H. G. Barnett, 1952; used by permission of the McGraw-Hill Book Company, New York, N.Y. MISSIONARY PRINCIPLES, by Roland Allen, 1964; NEW PATTERNS FOR CHURCH GROWTH IN BRAZIL, by W.R. Read, 1965; WILDFIRE: CHURCH GROWTH IN KOREA, by R. E. Shearer, 1966; CHURCH GROWTH IN MEXICO, 1963; and UNDERSTANDING CHURCH GROWTH, 1970, by D. A. McGavran; CHURCH GROWTH IN CENTRAL AND SOUTHERN NIGERIA, by Grimley and Robinson, 1966; used by permission of the W. B. Eerdmans Company, Grand Rapids. NO OTHER NAME, by W. A. Visser t'Hooft, 1964, published in the U.S.A. by the Westminster Press, copyright in 1963 by the S.C.M. Press of London, used by permission. BEHIND THE RANGES, by Mrs. Howard Taylor, 1964, by permission of Moody Press, Moody Bible Institute, Chicago. FIVE AFRICAN STATES: RESPONSES TO DIVERSITY, by Gwendolen M. Carter, editor, reprinted from "The Rhodesias and Nyasaland," by Herbert J. Spiro, copyright by Cornell University in 1963, used by permission of Cornell University Press. A HUMANIST IN AFRICA, by Kenneth Kaunda and Colin Morris, copyright by Kenneth D. Kaunda and Colin M. Morris 1966, used by permission, Abingdon Press, Nashville. HISTORY'S LESSONS FOR TOMORROW'S MISSION, 1960, published by the World Student Christian Federation, Geneva. THE HOUR AFTER MIDNIGHT, by Colin Morris, 1961, used by permission of Longmans, Green and Company.

William Carey Library
PUBLICATIONS

Africa

PEOPLES OF SOUTHWEST ETHIOPIA, by A. R. Tippett,Ph.D.
A recent, penetrating evaluation by a professional anthropologist of the cultural complexities faced by Peace Corps workers and missionaries in a rapidly changing intersection of African states.
1970: 320 pp, $3.95. ISBN 0-87808-103-8

PROFILE FOR VICTORY: NEW PROPOSALS FOR MISSIONS IN ZAMBIA, by Max Ward Randall.
"In a remarkably objective manner the author has analyzed contemporary political, social educational and religious trends, which demand a reexamination of traditional missionary methods and the creation of daring new strategies...his conclusions constitute a challenge for the future of Christian missions, not only in Zambia, but around the world."
1970: 224 pp, Cloth, $3.95. ISBN 0-87808-403-7

THE CHURCH OF THE UNITED BRETHREN OF CHRIST IN SIERRA LEONE, by Emmett D. Cox, Executive Secretary, United Brethren in Christ Board of Missions.
A readable account of the relevant historical, demographic and anthropological data as they relate to the development of the United Brethren in Christ Church in the Mende and Creole communities. Includes a reformation of objectives.
1970: 184 pp, $2.95. ISBN 0-87808-301-4

APPROACHING THE NUER OF AFRICA THROUGH THE OLD TESTAMENT, by Ernest A. McFall.
The author examines in detail the similarities between the Nuer and the Hebrews of the Old Testament and suggests a novel Christian approach that does not make initial use of the New Testament.
1970: 104 pp, 8 1/2 x 11, $1.95.
ISBN 0-87808-310-3

Asia

TAIWAN: MAINLINE VERSUS INDEPENDENT CHURCH GROWTH, A STUDY IN CONTRASTS, by Allen J. Swanson.

A provocative comparison between the older, historical Protestant churches in Taiwan and the new indigenous Chinese churches; suggests staggering implications for missions everywhere that intend to promote the development of truly indigenous expressions of Christianity.

1970: 216 pp, $2.95. ISBN 0-87808-404-5

NEW PATTERNS FOR DISCIPLING HINDUS: THE NEXT STEP IN ANDHRA PRADESH, INDIA, by B.V. Subbamma.

Proposes the development of a Christian movement that is as well adapted culturally to the Hindu tradition as the present movement is to the Harijan tradition. Nothing could be more crucial for the future of 400 million Hindus in India today.

1970: 212 pp, $3.45. ISBN 0-87808-306-5

GOD'S MIRACLES: INDONESIAN CHURCH GROWTH, by Ebbie C. Smith, Th.D.

The fascinating details of the penetration of Christianity into the Indonesian archipelago make for intensely interesting reading, as the anthropological context and the growth of the Christian movement are highlighted.

1970: 224 pp, $3.45. ISBN 0-87808-302-2

NOTES ON CHRISTIAN OUTREACH IN A PHILIPPINE COMMUNITY, by Marvin K. Mayers, Ph.D.

The fresh observations of an anthropologist coming from the outside provide a valuable, however preliminary, check list of social and historical factors in the context of missionary endeavors in a Tagalog province.

1970: 71 pp, 8 1/2 x 11, $1.45. ISBN 0-87808-104-6

Latin America

THE PROTESTANT MOVEMENT IN BOLIVIA, by C. Peter Wagner.

An excitingly-told account of the gradual build-up and present vitality of Protestantism. A cogent analysis of the various subcultures and the organizations working most effectively, including a striking evaluation of Bolivia's momentous Evangelism-in-Depth year and the possibilities of Evangelism-in-Depth for other parts of the world.

1970: 264 pp, $3.95. ISBN 0-87808-402-9

LA SERPIENTE Y LA PALOMA, by Manuel Gaxiola.
   The impressive success story of the Apostolic
Church of Mexico, (an indigenous denomination
that never had the help of any foreign missionary),
told by a professional scholar now the director
of research for that church. (Spanish)
   1970: 200 pp, $2.95. ISBN 0-87808-802-4

THE EMERGENCE OF A MEXICAN CHURCH: THE ASSOCIATE
REFORMED PRESBYTERIAN CHURCH OF MEXICO, by James
Erskine Mitchell.
   Tells the ninety-year story of the Associate
Reformed Presbyterian Mission in Mexico, the trials
and hardships as well as the bright side of the
work. Eminently practical and helpful regarding
the changing relationship of mission and church in
the next decade.
   1970: 184 pp, $2.95. ISBN 0-87808-303-0

FRIENDS IN CENTRAL AMERICA, by Paul C. Enyart.
   This book describes the results of faithful and
effective labors of the California Friends Yearly
Meeting, giving an analysis of the growth of one of
the most virile, national evangelical churches in
Central America, comparing its growth to other evangelical churches in Guatemala, Honduras, and El
Salvador.
   1970: 224 pp, $3.45. ISBN 0-87808-405-9

Europe

THE CHALLENGE FOR EVANGELICAL MISSIONS TO EUROPE:
A SCANDINAVIAN CASE STUDY, by Hilkka Malaska.
   Graphically presents the state of Christianity
in Scandinavia with an evaluation of the pros and
cons and possible contributions that existing or
additional Evangelical missions can make in Europe
today.
   1970: 192 pp, $2.95. ISBN 0-87808-308-1

THE PROTESTANT MOVEMENT IN ITALY: ITS PROGRESS,
PROBLEMS, AND PROSPECTS, by Roger Hedlund.
   A carefully wrought summary of preliminary
data; perceptively develops issues faced by Evangelical Protestants in all Roman Catholic areas of
Europe. Excellent graphs.
   1970: 266 pp, $3.95. ISBN 0-87808-307-3

U.S.A.

THE YOUNG LIFE CAMPAIGN AND THE CHURCH, by Warren Simandle.

If 70 per cent of young people drop out of the church between the ages of 12 and 20, is there room for a nationwide Christian organization working on high school campuses? After a quarter of a century, what is the record of Young Life and how has its work with teens affected the church? *"A careful analysis based on a statistical survey; full of insight and challenging proposals for both Young Life and the church."*
1970: 216 pp, $3.45. ISBN 0-87808-304-9

THE RELIGIOUS DIMENSION IN SPANISH LOS ANGELES: A PROTESTANT CASE STUDY, by Clifton L. Holland.

A through analysis of the origin, development and present extent of this vital, often unnoticed element in Southern California.
1970: 304 pp, $3.95. ISBN 0-87808-309-X

General

THEOLOGICAL EDUCATION BY EXTENSION, edited by Ralph D. Winter, Ph.D.

A husky handbook on a new approach to the education of pastoral leadership for the church. Gives both theory and practice and the exciting historical development in Latin America of the *"Largest non-governmental voluntary educational development project in the world today."* Ted Ward, Prof. of Education, Michigan State University.
1969: 648 pp, Library Buckram $7.95, Kivar $4.95. ISBN 0-87808-101-1

THE CHURCH GROWTH BULLETIN, VOL. I-V, edited by Donald A. McGavran, Ph.D.

The first five years of issues of a now-famous bulletin which probes past foibles and present opportunities facing the 100,000 Protestant and Catholic missionaries in the world today. No periodical edited for this audience has a larger readership.
1969: 408 pp, Library Buckram $6.95, Kivar $4.45. ISBN 0-87808-701-X

CHURCH GROWTH THROUGH EVANGELISM-IN-DEPTH, by
Malcolm R. Bradshaw.
*"Examines the history of Evangelism-in-Depth
and other total mobilization approaches to evangelism. Also presents concisely the 'Church
Growth' approach to mission and proposes a
wedding between the two...a great blessing to the
church at work in the world."* WORLD VISION
MAGAZINE.
1969: 152 pp, $2.45. ISBN 0-87808-401-0

THE TWENTY FIVE UNBELIEVABLE YEARS, 1945-1969, by
Ralph D. Winter, Ph.D.
A terse, exciting analysis of the most significant transition in human history in this millenium
and its impact upon the Christian movement. *"Packed
with insight and otherwise unobtainable statistical
data...a brilliant piece of work."* C. Peter Wagner.
1970: 120 pp, $1.95. ISBN 0-87808-102-X

EL SEMINARIO DE EXTENSION: UN MANUAL, by James H.
Emery, F. Ross Kinsler, Louise J. Walker, Ralph D.
Winter.
Gives the reasons for the extension approach to
the training of ministers, as well as the concrete,
practical details of establishing and operating
such a program. A Spanish translation of the third
section of *THEOLOGICAL EDUCATION BY EXTENSION*.
1969: 256 pp, $3.45. ISBN 0-87808-801-6

ABOUT THE WILLIAM CAREY LIBRARY

William Carey is widely considered the "Father of Modern Missions" partly because many people think he was the first Protestant missionary. Even though there was a trickle of others before him, he deserves very special honor for many valiant accomplishments in his heroic career, but most particularly because of three things he did before he ever left England, things no one else in history before him had combined together:

1) he had an authentic, personal, evangelical passion to serve God and acknowledged this as obligating him to fulfill God's interests in the redemption of all men on the face of the earth.

2) he actually proposed a structure for the accomplishment of that aim - he did indeed, more than anyone else, set off the movement among Protestants for the creation of "voluntary societies" for foreign missions, and

3) he added to all of this a strategic literary and research achievement: shaky those statistics may have been, but he put together the very best possible estimate of the number of unreached peoples in every part of the globe, and summarized previous, relatively ineffective attempts to reach them. His burning conclusion was that existing efforts were not proportional to the opportunities and the scope of Christian obligation in Mission.

Today, a little over 150 years later, the situation is not wholly different. In the past five years, for example, experienced missionaries from all corners of the earth (53 countries) have brought to the Fuller School of World Mission and Institute of Church Growth well over 800 years of missionary experience. Twenty-six scholarly books have resulted from the research of faculty and students. The best statistics available have at times been shaky -though far superior to Carey's - but vision has been clear and the mandate is as urgent as ever. The printing press is still the right arm of Christians active in the Christian world mission.

The William Carey Library is a new publishing house dedicated to books related to this mission. There are many publishers, both secular and religious, that occasionally publish books of this kind. We believe there is no other devoted exclusively to the production and distribution of books for career missionaries and their home churches.

Rev. Max Ward Randall, D.D., served for sixteen years as a missionary under the Central Africa Mission Churches of Christ, working in the countries of South Africa, Rhodesia, Zambia, and Ghana. He has been called the organizing genius behind the remarkable growth of the mission and of the Churches of Christ in that section of Africa.

After receiving a B.D. and M.A. from the Cincinnati Bible Seminary, Rev. Randall earned an M.A. in Missions from the School of World Mission and Institute of Church Growth at Fuller Theological Seminary. <u>Profile</u> <u>for</u> <u>Victory</u> is an edited version of his thesis, which has already had a profound influence on the work of his mission in Africa. Twelve new congregations have been planted in the last year alone, and in a recent letter he states that "we are confident if the present conditions bear out that by the end of 1972 we will have brought to Christ a large percentage of the Sala Tribe."

Dr. Randall currently is Professor of Missions at Lincoln Christian College and Seminary and is a popular national and international conference speaker for his brotherhood.

MISSIONS IN ZAMBIA
LEGEND
INITIALS OF MISSIONS

RC: Roman Catholic Missions
SAB: South Afr. Bapt. Mission
CMML: Christian Missions in Many Lands
(Plymouth Brethren)
SDA: Seventh Day Adventists
BC: Brethren in Christ

ZCM: Zambia Christian Missi
A: Anglican Church (Universi
Mission to Central Africa)
SAGM: South African General
(African Evangelical M
CC: Church of Christ Mission
SA: Salvation Army

P: Paris Evangelical
LMS: London Missionary Society
CS: Church of Scotland Mission
M: Methodist Mission
DRC: Dutch Reformed Church Mission